Comparative Governance

Decision-making is at the heart of governing and governance and is a more challenging task compared to just a few decades ago as a result of increasing social complexity and globalization. In this book, B. Guy Peters and Jon Pierre propose a new framework for the comparative analysis of governance, arguing that government remains a central actor in governance. By articulating the functionalist dimension of governance, they show how goal setting, resource mobilization, decision-making, implementation, and feedback can be performed by a combination of different types of actors. Even so, effective governance requires a leading role for government. The framework is also applied to a taxonomy of governance arrangements and national styles of governing. *Comparative Governance* advances our knowledge about governance failure and how forms of governance may change. It also significantly strengthens the theory of governance, showing how governance can be studied conceptually as well as empirically.

B. GUY PETERS earned his PhD at Michigan State University and has four honorary doctorates from European universities. He is the author or editor of over seventy books in comparative politics, public administration, and public policy. He was the founding coeditor of *Governance* and *The European Political Science Review* and is the founding president of the International Public Policy Association.

JON PIERRE (PhD, University of Lund, 1986) is the author or editor of more than thirty books and numerous journal articles. He is a former coeditor of *Governance* and associate editor of *European Political Science Review* and *Urban Affairs Review*. His research focuses on public administration, governance, and urban politics.

Comparative Governance

Rediscovering the Functional Dimension of Governing

B. GUY PETERS
University of Pittsburgh

JON PIERRE
University of Gothenburg

CAMBRIDGE
UNIVERSITY PRESS

CAMBRIDGE
UNIVERSITY PRESS

University Printing House, Cambridge CB2 8BS, United Kingdom

One Liberty Plaza, 20th Floor, New York, NY 10006, USA

477 Williamstown Road, Port Melbourne, VIC 3207, Australia

4843/24, 2nd Floor, Ansari Road, Daryaganj, Delhi – 110002, India

79 Anson Road, #06–04/06, Singapore 079906

Cambridge University Press is part of the University of Cambridge.

It furthers the University's mission by disseminating knowledge in the pursuit of education, learning, and research at the highest international levels of excellence.

www.cambridge.org
Information on this title: www.cambridge.org/9781107163799

First published 2016

Printed in the United States of America by Sheridan Books, Inc.

A catalogue record for this publication is available from the British Library.

ISBN 978-1-107-16379-9 Hardback
ISBN 978-1-316-61541-6 Paperback

Contents

Preface

Governance has become one of the most commonly utilized terms in political science, and to some extent also in the other social sciences. Although the term "governance" is now commonly used, this concept is often misunderstood and is used in a variety of different, and sometimes even contradictory, ways. This book is intended to advance the study of governance and to enhance the utility of the concept in understanding politics, in general, and comparative politics, more specifically. In order to make those contributions, we are emphasizing three central features in this book.

The first, and perhaps most basic, contribution of this book is that governance is conceptualized as a powerful foundation for studying comparative politics. That emphasis is indicated in the title of the book and permeates the discussions in each chapter. While there are numerous interesting aspects of politics in all our countries, all these can be understood in terms of the basic need to govern. Elections and other aspects of individual-level behavior are interesting and perhaps even amusing at times, but they are relevant only because they contribute to governance. By having a clear conception of what constitutes governing, that comparison becomes more meaningful and more directed toward the fundamental characteristics of politics and government.

The second major contribution of this book on governance is to develop a functionalist model of governing. Functionalism has not been a popular approach to the social sciences for several decades, but still has an important place in analysis. Just as functionalist approaches served as a foundation for understanding political development, so too is it an appropriate means of elaborating governance. We have chosen to develop the functionalist model presented here for several reasons. The most important reason is to be able to overcome some of the academic squabbling about the relative roles of the state and social actors in governing. If we begin with an agnostic position and use a set of functions to elaborate governance, we can answer questions in a more empirical manner. Further, the functionalist approach allows us to identify more readily the interaction among social actors and the state, emphasizing the manner in which these potential sources of governance interact. Finally, the functionalist approach to governance helps to identify processes as well as actors involved in governance.

The identification of fundamental processes of governing brings us to the third major contribution of this book. This is the linkage of governance and the study of public policy. As we developed the functionalist approach, we recognized that it resembles the process models in public policy, such as those developed by Charles O. Jones and William Dunn. But the linkage of governance is much more fundamental. Some decades ago, Harold Lasswell argued that politics is most fundamentally about "Who Gets What?" That very basic question is as true as it is about policy studies. And indeed public policies represent the final product of governance processes. The actions taken through the functions of the process cumulate in the policies taken by governments and their allies in the private sector.

In summary, we believe that this book develops an important conceptualization of governance. It develops a set of fundamental functions required for governing and demonstrates how these can be used to compare political systems. It also demonstrates the close connection between public policy analysis and governance. And ultimately it demonstrates that governance must be central to understanding the world of politics and governance.

We are very much indebted to David Levi-Faur and Paul 't Hart for detailed comments on an earlier version of the text. Yasemin Irepoglu Carreras has offered valuable assistance with the reference list. We also want to thank the two reviewers for their many constructive suggestions.

Like Moliére's M. Jourdain, speaking prose before he knew it, many scholars have spoken of governance without knowing it. We dedicate this book to them and to Monika and Sheryn for sometimes knowing about governance without talking about it.

1 | *The Governance Problem*

Governance is about governing, and governing is predominantly about making decisions. This might appear to be a truism, but we assert that much of the governance literature, in general, and the development of governance theory, in particular, have lost perspective on what constitutes the core issue of democratic governance – governing. Equally important, governing frequently means making and enforcing unpopular decisions which require a solid institutional framework and a regulated process. Again, decision-making is at the heart of governing and governance. It is generally acknowledged that governing contemporary society is a more challenging task compared to just a few decades ago as a result of increasing social complexity and globalization. Governments around the world address this complexity by engaging societal partners in the process of governing, but this strategy has entailed complex contingencies related to the organization and management of collaborative forms of governance.

Most academic observers of governance have interpreted these developments as proof of a "shift" in the locus of political power from government to networks and other forms of exchange between state and society. In an effort to produce new analytical models to study the collaborative dimension of governance, most political scientists seem to ignore the fundamental circumstance that the state remains very much at the center of governance. Understanding contemporary governance, we insist, is a matter of understanding the transformation, not elimination, of the state (Bell and Hindmoor, 2009; Pierre and Peters, 2000; Sørensen, 2004). In fact, this book will argue that what is required of governance theory is not further distancing from the state, and with the distancing emphasizing the society-centric approach to governance, but rather the opposite – to probe deeper into the state apparatus to understand how a set of new, or exacerbated, contingencies have changed the preconditions for governing.

It appears to us as if most observers of governance became so intrigued by the emerging role of non-state governance partners that they became oblivious of the continuing role of the state in governance and also of the governance role played by conventional participants in governance, like political parties. The analytical perspective on governance, we suggest, should depart from the institutional capabilities of the state; no other actor in society can challenge the formal political mandate of the state (see Bell and Hindmoor, 2009). Recent transformations in governance should prompt scholars of governance to dissect the process of governing into its core functions and to assess this transformation in empirical detail.

The purpose of this book, then, is to outline a theory of governance that contributes to our understanding of the changing societal role of the state and societal partners in governance. We know a great deal about the emergence of new modes of governance, but we know very little about how they impact the key governing roles of the state or the democratic underpinnings of government (Héritier and Rhodes, 2011; Koppenjan, 2008). Again, we believe this shortcoming to be the result of an almost exclusive attention to societal partners and state–society exchanges in governance with only scant attention to the state itself.

Our point of departure is that governance can be analytically structured into a limited number of critical roles or functions. By defining these functions, we can raise empirical questions about the degree to which the state and other actors in society can deliver those roles and the consequences of public or private control of those functions. This leads us to the belief that comparison across time and space is essential to theorizing governance. As this book will demonstrate, combining the three approaches of functionalism, governance theory and comparative politics allows us to outline an analytical model of governance which represents a significant step toward a more comprehensive theory of governance. These three pillars and how they gel into an analytical model of governance are the leitmotifs of the book.

Defining Governance

Given the enormous proliferation of governance research, it is no surprise that there is today any number of definitions of governance available in the literature, such as "the traditions and institutions by which authority in a country is exercised for the common good" (Kaufmann,

2005:82); "the processes and institutions, both formal and informal, that guide and restrain the collective activities of a group" (Keohane and Nye, 2000:12); "the tools, strategies and relationships used by governments to help govern" (Bell and Hindmoor, 2009:2); "the reflexive self-organisation of independent actors involved in complex relations of reciprocal interdependence, with such selforganisation being based on continuing dialogue and resource-sharing to develop mutually beneficial joint projects and to manage the contradictions and dilemmas inevitably involved in such situations" (Jessop, 2002: see also Rhodes, 1996:652–3); or "the sum of the many ways individuals and institutions, public and private, manage their common affairs ... a continuing process through which conflicting or diverse interests may be accommodated and cooperative action may be taken" (Commission on Global Governance, 1995:2). Against this backdrop, the definition advanced by the present authors some time ago now, that governance could be defined as "the pursuit of collective interests" (Peters, 2001; Pierre and Peters, 2000), might appear conceptually and intellectually poor, although we see little reason to offer a significantly different definition of the concept at this time. Ours may lack the eloquence of some of the other definitions, but since it was intended to offer a generic, baseline definition, we believe it still works.

These definitions have several themes in common; they all emphasize that governance is a process bringing together a multitude of actors of different types toward some collective goal. A broader sweep through this burgeoning literature suggests that there are three different general meanings of governance. One such meaning is quite simply governance as an empirical phenomenon, typically referring to joint public–private forms of collaboration, such as networks, partnerships and other forms of hybrid organizations. This meaning of governance also refers to more abstract phenomena such as what March and Olsen (1989, 1995) call "shared meanings," i.e. values, norms, and objectives that transcend jurisdictional and institutional borders. To some extent, all these aspects of governance reject the traditional notion in liberal democratic theory about a clear empirical and normative distinction between state and society and between governors and governed. Also, the emphasis on shared values and a prerequisite for coordination reduce the applicability of governance at the global level where there are fewer shared values and, partly as a result, power plays a crucial role.

Another meaning of governance, related to the previous point, is that of a normative model of governing. Hybrid organizations epitomize the idea of "new governance" which gained political momentum in the 1980s and 1990s, sustained by the fundamental idea that the state could (and should) govern more efficiently by coordinating the actions of a variety of societal actors rather than organizing, funding, and delivering services and regulations itself. Thus, this meaning of governance depicts a specific normative model of state–society relationships and collaboration – the implicit rejection of cleavages based on economic or political values – which is accorded a strong value in itself (see Hall, 1986; Migdal, 2001).

The normative meaning of governance also includes "good governance." Initially promoted by the World Bank, "good governance" emerged as an objective of foreign aid and aimed at promoting democratic government, fighting corruption and quality of public administration (Doornbos, 2001, 2004). Closely related to these objectives were also neoliberal goals, such as the elimination of trade barriers, deregulation and opening up for competition in public service delivery (Leftwich, 1994). Thus, the "good governance" program was highly prescriptive not just in terms of government performance but also in terms of government policy and regulations. We will return to this discussion in subsequent chapters.

The third meaning of governance is that of a theory of steering and coordination. This is the most generic aspect of governance which would be relevant to private corporations (corporate governance), universities (university governance), and so on which, when applied to systems of democratic government, is referred to either as democratic governance (March and Olsen, 1995) or simply "governance." The Bielefeld project (Kaufmann, Majone, and Ostrom, 1988) was one of the earliest manifestations of this perspective on governing, and it also linked guidance and control to evaluation.

Theories of governance are still emerging and generally lack the conceptual sophistication of full-fledged theories in the social sciences. Gerry Stoker makes the important point that "the contribution of the governance perspective to theory is not at the level of causal analysis. Nor does it offer a new normative theory. Its value is as an organizing framework" identifying "what is worthy of study" (Stoker, 1998:18). In addition, governance theory explores the rationale for autonomous actors to submit to collective regimes (Ostrom,

1990; Rhodes, 1997) and how such collaboration impacts those actors. Most political scientists involved in governance research take an interest in the extent to which political power can be transferred to private actors and the hybridization of public organizations. Again, governance as an organizing framework does not stipulate causation but merely helps identify what Stoker (1998) calls "objects worthy of study."

The remainder of this book will explore these issues in much greater detail. From governance theory and a functionalist approach, it is not very far to bring in comparative analysis as a component of our model. The full potential of the functionalist perspective is best realized through systematic comparison of how critical governance roles are performed in different systems of government. Thus the book rests on the integration and synergy of three analytical pillars – functionalism, governance theory and comparative politics.

Several other concepts that are used to describe the structures and actions involved in steering the economy and society will appear in this book and may cause some confusion with the analysis of governance. Both government and governing have the same etymological root as governance but have somewhat different meanings. By government we will be talking about the formal structures of the public sector and the set of actors exercising state power, and hence would be associated with a state-centric conception of governance. That said, however, governments also interact with, and mobilize, actors in society to perform governance tasks. Additionally, by government we do not mean the "government of the day" but rather the formal apparatus of the state including bureaucracy and the courts.

We will be treating governing more as a verb, meaning the actions and practices of attempting to provide or coordinate governance. The concept governing thus implies some purposive action on the part of actors, be they agents of the state, of society, or both. Like governance, therefore, this concept does not imply that any specific actor or set of actors is involved or at the helm. It merely suggests that there are attempts by public or private actors to provide collective organization and action and some steering to the society. Nor does this concept imply that the actors are successful in steering, only that there are attempts at steering. To say that this steering has actually occurred will require the addition of some adverb such as "successfully."

Governance and State–Society Interaction

Although the rapidly growing popularity of governance, both as a model of governing and as a framework for analysis, in the 1980s and early 1990s was to a significant extent explained by the novelty of the concept, the pursuit of good and effective governance is as old as government itself. All systems of democratic government are embedded in society; all are dependent on resources from economic actors and individuals; all have emerged to promote some societal values and norms; and all are dependent on some degree of consent from society (Migdal, 2001). Certainly, these aspects of democratic government display huge variations across time and space, but creating effective links between state and society has been a perennial issue in institutional design.

The overarching objectives of that pursuit have varied over time. The consolidation of the nation-state entailed a need to ensure that state policies were effectively implemented across the territory. Conversely, during the emergence of democracy, citizen engagement, political control of the executive branch of government and electoral accountability became the main concerns. Later, during the development of welfare-state regimes in many western countries, democratic objectives were supplemented by goals related to material standards and social justice. And in the era of "public management," finally, customer choice and market-inspired arrangements of service provision have emerged as attractive alternatives to state-driven models of collective goods and services. Throughout these changes and developments, designing effective and sustainable governance institutions and processes – the web of exchanges between citizens and the state – has been a continuing concern.

Governance, as already mentioned, is basically about the definition and pursuit of collective interests. In constitutional theory as well as in liberal-democratic theory – not to mention the array of introductory textbooks in political science – collective interests are *ex definitione* defined and pursued by the state. The governance approach converts these stipulations to empirical questions. What makes the functionalist approach so attractive in governance research is that it defines core functions of governing generically, i.e. it makes no prejudgments about the degree to which government institutions fulfill those functions or, for that matter, whether governance is democratic.

Additionally, we find that the functionalist approach is also relevant to the discussion on governance failure and failed states (see Rotberg, 2003). It appears as if parts of the failure of states could be described as incapacity to fulfill core governing functions. That does, however, not mean that the functions per se are not occurring; even in the most severe cases of state failure, some form of order is enforced by groups like street gangs and even forms of public service may be provided by civil society or loose coalitions of societal actors (Haldén, 2011). Indeed, in cases like Gaza, the distinction between civil society actors and government may be extremely murky or non-existent.

Governance should be conceived of as an interactive process wherein the citizenry and the political elite exchange preferences on how to facilitate concerted action and its objectives. Organizing governance – the design of the processes and institutions that make up the democratic system of a state, a region or a city – is influenced by several, potentially conflicting objectives like efficiency and effectiveness (institutional autonomy, policy capacity and integrity of elective office), on the one hand, and democracy (transparency, citizen engagement, and accountability), on the other. In some cases, though, democracy may be more or less absent.

If governance thus is an interactive process, it is also a very dynamic phenomenon. The forms of governance that were believed to be efficient a hundred years ago – we need only think of de Tocqueville's romanticizing accounts of local democracy in the United States – are not geared to solve the governance problems of the 21st century. Similarly, the specific forms of governance we can see in states with extensive welfare-state sectors differ from those of small public sector, neoliberal states. The ways in which a state seeks to organize its exchange with its external environment depends to a large extent on what it wants to do and what its citizens expect it to do. And once in place, the institutions of governance tend to reinforce that particular form of governance they are created to facilitate (March and Olsen 1989, 1995).

It is clear already from these introductory observations on governance that we are dealing with a phenomenon which sits at the very center of democratic government. Yet, interestingly, governance has not been widely debated or studied until the past ten to fifteen years. Much of the recent interest in issues related to governance can be dated to the late 1980s and early 1990s in the wake of severe cutbacks in public expenditures in most western countries (Stoker, 1998). The limited capabilities of the allegedly "hollow state" (Rhodes,

1994; but see Holliday, 2000; Milward and Provan, 2000) to govern society, and, indeed, the governability of the globalizing society, were factors which propelled an interest in processes of coordination among both political and societal actors. We will return to these issues later in this chapter in greater detail.

Today, governance has become a very popular term in political science and public administration although it remains unclear whether governance is more than a convenient term to employ in place of a good deal of the conventional language of political analysis (see, for instance, Frederickson, 2007). Like so many terms that have become popular, "governance" has been applied in any number of ways and risks becoming meaningless through "stretching" and overuse. We will not try to review the host of literature that exists today on governance. Instead, we will devote the remainder of this introductory chapter to demonstrate that governance-related problems and issues have had a strong impact on governments in the advanced democracies long before "governance" had entered the political science vernacular.

We identify two broad clusters of such issues about managing and steering society. One is "demand politics," that is, the articulation of societal expectations on government and public service. The other set of issues is "supply politics," i.e. the capacity of government to address these expectations and to solve societal problems against the backdrop of increasing costs for public service and ensuing increasing taxes. Again, we see governance as an interactive process structured by political institutions and intermediary structures such as the political parties. "Demand politics" and "supply politics" echo the arguments advanced during the 1970s and 1980s about the "ungovernability" of society and the "overloaded" government (Birch, 1984). Indeed, these problems were considered to be so serious during the 1970s that observers spoke of a "crisis of democracy" (Crozier, Huntington, and Watanuki, 1975). Essentially, we argue, these problems and crises were governance issues more than anything else.

The Origins of the Governance Debate

Since governance refers to different types of concerted processes or actions across the public–private border in society, and most of what governments do in some way or other presupposes such transgressing exchanges, understanding how governance changes requires an analysis of the interactions between state and society. These interactions become institutionalized and are given meaning by collective expectations on the state. The level of political encroachment on society is, at any given time and in any given national setting, reflective of such a logic of appropriateness (Maier, 1987; March and Olsen, 1989) or idealized vision of what we want the state to do. Interestingly, numerous studies have shown that citizens often tend to evaluate their own personal exchanges with political institutions in a positive way – and their positive evaluation of the public sector is positively correlated with the frequency of such exchanges – at the same time as they tend to have fairly negative views about government more broadly (Kumlin, 2004).

It appears as if society's image of the state's performance in some respect (be it in terms of democratic responsiveness or public services) matters more than some objective measure when it comes to assessing the nature of the interactions constituting governance. Governments with a very generous service production, for instance the Scandinavian welfare states, are often criticized for not being generous enough. At the same time, governments in other countries with much lower levels of service provisions, like the United States, may be criticized for too much and too generous public spending and that taxes ought to be cut.

Interestingly, however, we do not see governance occur very frequently in the scholarly literature until the late 1980s and early 1990s. Instead, the debate on the advantages and disadvantages of different models of governance has been conducted in a different political and institutional language, shaped by what has been seen as the defining problem during different time periods. For example, at one point in the debate the issue was the capacity of the welfare state to sustain itself in the face of economic and political challenges. At others, the question was how to promote democratization and effective governance in less-developed systems.

One of the main reasons why we today concern ourselves with governance issues is because of growing problems related to governability, government overload and social complexity. The 1970s and 1980s showed that society's material demands on the public sector tended to be insatiable as increasing levels of service only raised expectations for even more extensive services. At the same time, there was growing opposition to further tax increases. The 1990s and early 2000s saw governments cutting back and inviting societal partners into service delivery and other forms of collaborative governance. Thus, governance issues remained high on the political agenda although the specific nature of those issues has changed over time.

Demand Politics. The first more significant debate on governance problems occurred during the 1970s and was centered around two aspects of state–society relationships – overload and ungovernability. Both of these problems refer to a "misfit" between the structure and capabilities of the state, on the one hand, and the configuration and inherent dynamics of society, on the other. "Overload" (Crozier, Huntington, and Watanuki, 1975) was an umbrella concept for the problems associated with the ever-increasing expectations on government from citizens, organized interests and the business community. To some extent, overload was a revolution of rising expectations; in most western countries, the 1960s and early 1970s had seen a steady increase in public services. Somewhat paradoxically, perhaps, the rising level of public services probably helped trigger expectations and demands for even more services.

The ungovernability argument emerged from different academic strands. Neo-Marxist scholars saw the state, particularly the welfare state, as subordinate to the capitalist economy, and the main role of the state was to ensure social reproduction (see, for instance, Gough, 1979; Offe, 1984). In terms of governance, subordination set firm and tight boundaries on the scope of state action and governing was perceived as a process conducted within the confines defined by the capitalist economy.

Another factor contributing to ungovernability was increasing social complexity. As Jan Kooiman (1993:4) argued in the early 1990s: "No single actor, public or private, has all the knowledge and information required to solve complex, dynamic, and diversified problems; no actor has sufficient overview to make the application of needed instruments effective; no single actor has sufficient action potential to dominate unilaterally in a particular governing model." Thus, for Kooiman the most efficient strategy for the state to manage growing social complexity is to form alliances with strategic societal partners.

Thus, ungovernability has a number of different explanations. As we will argue later, ungovernability and overload are both relative rather than absolute measures. States could address these problems by strengthening their policy capacity but have for the most part chosen not to follow that path. Indeed, much of public management reform that has been implemented over the past couple of decades has in fact decreased the policy capacity of the state (see Painter and Pierre, 2005).

Another aspect of this development was that political solutions to most societal problems had become the standard mode of addressing these problems. In the United States as well as in Western Europe, the 1960s and 1970s saw a continuous expansion of the scope of the political in society (Maier, 1987). Regulations, subsidies and other policy instruments were employed to address almost all societal problems. Over time, political solutions became the institutionalized strategy of addressing societal problems. Against that background, it is little surprise that citizens increasingly looked to the state to solve a growing number of their problems. Thus to some extent, overload is both the result of the success and the failure of the state.

If overload is a quality of the state, ungovernability is a quality of society. It refers to the inability of government to steer society because of the increasing complexity of society and the limited effectiveness of traditional policy instruments to shape social behavior and markets in the desired directions. That having been said, ungovernability also says something about the state, particularly about the inclination to employ coercive policy instruments. To some extent, societies which – to some part or in some sectors – can be described as ungovernable may on closer inspection turn out to be ungovernable with the policy instruments traditionally used by politicians.

Ungovernability may also be a reflection of goal conflicts among the political elite. Many accounts of economic policy or industrial policy tend to portray policy as reactive rather than proactive and with rather limited influence on the economy or industry. Such a state of affairs is frequently explained by a reluctance among the political leadership to increase their control over private capital or the industry; tightening the political control over private industry would to some extent make society more "governable" but would probably entail massive costs in terms of companies relocating to other and more friendly countries.

The debates – and, indeed, the research findings sustaining those debates – concerning overloaded government and societal ungovernability emerged at a particularly complex and critical governance situation in many western democracies. Corporatism, a traditional governance model in many west European countries, was probably at its peak at this time, in terms of institutionalized roles for organized interests in policy-making and implementation (Schmitter, 1974).

At the same time, much of the successful economic development during the postwar period seemingly came to a halt with the collapse of Bretton Woods, soaring oil prices and galloping budget deficits and inflation in many countries. Overloaded government and ungovernability were to some degree seen as the joint outcome of a developed corporatism and a stagnating economy.[1]

Interestingly, the ungovernability debate preceded globalization by a couple of decades, yet there have been precious few references recently to the ungovernability debate. It might have been expected that globalization would revitalize the debate on ungovernability, but we have not seen that happening to a very large extent. Instead, globalization has triggered a debate primarily on the resilience of domestic institutions and the significance (and range) of domestic policy in the face of globalization (Camilleri and Falk, 1992; Helleiner and Pickel, 2004; Hirst and Thompson, 1999; Swank, 2002; Weiss, 1998). Thus, the degree to which society was governable became a secondary issue when the external environment of the state was redefined to incorporate transnational and global political and economic forces.

That said, much of the current debate on the problems of creating and sustaining governance in an increasingly complex society echoes the debate on ungovernability in the 1970s and 1980s. In retrospect, it seems clear that we should think of both "government overload" and "ungovernability" as typical governance problems, or perhaps even partial governance failures (cf. Jessop, 2000). Overload illustrates not just the inability of government to respond properly to citizens' expectations but also the limited ability of government to shape those demands and to contain ever-increasing expectations on government. Governance, to reiterate a point made earlier, must be conceived of as an interactive process, and an important element of that interaction is informed and responsive political leadership. In that perspective, overload represents a failure on the part of government.

In a similar vein, ungovernability too represents a governance failure on the part of government. To put it bluntly, no one can blame society for being too complex to govern; rather, it is the continuous task of government to adapt to that growing complexity as well as coping with

---

[1] To be sure, some saw a direct causal link between these two developments (Olson, 1984). Others, like Peter Katzenstein, argued that corporatism in fact contributed to change by compensating targeted social groups (Katzenstein, 1984).

contingencies in the exchange between the state and global arenas and actors. Thus, ungovernability is to some extent a manifestation of the decreasing policy capacity of the state (Painter and Pierre, 2005); had the state made sufficient investments in sustaining and developing its policy capacity, even a highly complex society would have been governable.

Ungovernability also has potential normative underpinnings. The argument that society is too complex to be governed could be a convoluted normative stance that the state should not try to coerce social and economic actors to conform to its preferences and objectives. Instead, the state should assume basic regulatory roles but refrain from attempting to steer and intervene in markets and social arenas as such efforts are largely doomed to fail. As Linda Weiss (1998) argues, globalization as a normatively charged concept has played a similar role; since globalization, according to some political actors, is an empirical fact, states have little choice but to dismantle the public sector, deregulate and reduce public expenditures in order to be competitive in a globalized economy. As is the case with ungovernability, globalization has first to be empirically demonstrated before governments analyze the ramifications of those developments.

Supply Politics. The two types of "misfit" between the state and the surrounding society – overload and ungovernability – evolved as we have seen for a number of different reasons. Overload highlights a governance situation which could be described in several different ways. One interpretation would be that the political leadership had failed in explaining to the citizenry the limits of what government can do. Was overload a problem that could have been resolved by increasing public services? Probably not; if the theory discussed earlier about overload as a revolution of rising expectations is correct, further increases in public expenditure and service would only have raised the level of demands even more.

A different interpretation of overload suggests that the institutional system of governance – i.e. government – was not designed to cope with ever-increasing levels of demands and expectations. These institutions became overloaded because, in Easton's terminology (Easton, 1965b), the gate-keeping functions of government failed. However, the debate on overloaded government in the 1970s argued that overload had both a material dimension and a democratic (or, again in Easton's terminology, a "support") dimension. Here, the pedagogical element of political leadership becomes even clearer; any system of governance collapses if too many constituencies raise too many demands – material or immaterial – on the political institutions.

This brief discussion on overload and ungovernability highlights the problems in institutionalizing governance. Samuel Huntington, for example, argued that effective political development in transitional societies involved creating institutional capacities at least as quickly as the increasing levels of demand, and the same logic would apply to more developed countries (Huntington, 1968). As demands increased for the more developed democratic societies, the institutional capacity had difficulty in keeping pace and hence there were claims of overload.

Our approach here is a functionalist model which stipulates a set of core conditions of governance. We furthermore argue that functions which are at the heart of democratic governance, for instance functions which include the exercise of public authority, the enforcement of public law or the management of democratic institutions, should normatively speaking be reserved for democratically accountable actors.[2] To be sure, it is almost impossible to conceive of democratic government without elective institutions and actors playing a dominant role in that governance. Beyond that, however, the functionalist approach provides a framework for identifying conditions that are critical to the political system but leaves the issue of agency open. James Rosenau makes this point clearly: "To presume the presence of governance without government is to conceive of functions that have to be performed in any viable human system ... Among the many necessary functions, for example, are the needs wherein any system has to cope with external challenges, to prevent conflicts among its members ... to procure resources ... and to frame goals and policies designed to achieve them" (Rosenau, 1992:3, quoted in Stoker, 1998).

The challenges of governance in the early 2000s look quite different compared to those of the mid-1900, yet some degree of institutionalization of governance is critical to the long-term sustainability and legitimacy of governing. Also, the previous discussion demonstrates that the organization of governance is both a proactive and a reactive process. Proactive processes seek to anticipate societal changes or aim

---

[2] We base this normative argument in democratic theory which ties public authority closely to democratic accountability.

at designing governance in ways which reflect the governance ideals of the incumbent political elite. The emergence of the Thatcher government in Britain or the Reagan administration in the United States entailed profound changes in the governance of the two countries, albeit more so in the United Kingdom than in the United States. This change was not confined to a preference of new policy instruments or a new strategy of financing the state; it referred to a shift across the board from the state toward the market in terms of problem definition and problem solution. Government was believed to be inefficient or unable to solve contemporary political problems, largely because it was government itself and the state-centric governance that were now seen as major sources of political and economic problems.

Until these developments, there had been a substantive overlap of government and governance, particularly in Britain and Western Europe. As postulated by liberal democratic theory, government – the state – was the undisputed center of governance enjoying whatever financial and institutional resources and capabilities necessary for the state to govern society and to impose its will on society. The new model of governance that emerged during the 1980s emphasized different forms of public–private partnerships, market-based arrangements of public service production, market liberalization and a political emphasis of the regulatory role of the state while downplaying the material, service-producing role of the public sector. This development dovetailed with the emergence of New Public Management which prescribed a very similar reform strategy.

In terms of organizing governance, Reagan and Mrs. Thatcher sought to place priority on economic growth by "unleashing" the market and to relieve government from its responsibility to provide extensive services to large constituencies. Citizens should no longer look to the state for aid and assistance. "There is no society, only churches and families," as Mrs. Thatcher put it (quoted in Pierson, 1994). Phrased in a somewhat different way, this strategy also sought to solve the problems of government overload and ungovernability. The overload problem would be solved as soon as citizens realized that the state in this new model of governance no longer provides the range of services and programs it had hitherto delivered. Similarly, the ungovernability problem would disappear because the state no longer sought to steer society but rather to provide a regulatory framework that fostered economic growth.

The governance shift in the United States and Britain also tells us much about how deeply entrenched models of governance are. One conceivable reason why we have seen so few debates on governance-related issues could well be that any major, paradigmatic changes in governance are very rare indeed. No governance arrangement is likely to be sustainable unless it is anchored in an institutional framework explicating some common meanings and symbols. Over time, governance is shaped not only by those institutional arrangements per se but also – and arguably more importantly – by society's adaptation to institutional reform.

Congruence Politics. Both supply and demand issues in governance raise the issue of the need to match patterns of governance with the surrounding society and economy. Harry Eckstein (1963), for example, argued that democracy was unlikely to be successful in societies in which the society was itself undemocratic. Effective democracy required underpinnings in the family, the educational system, and other aspects of social life that would provide citizens with a sense of efficacy for participation. Robert Putnam's (2002) research on social capital makes a similar assumption about the necessity of democratic societies for effective political democracy.

For governance, there must be analogous congruence between the desire for, and acceptance of, steering from the state and the capacity of the state for such steering. If societies, such as that of the United States, do not readily accept command and control styles of governing, then other options such as the greater use of markets are likely to be more successful. Likewise, societies with high levels of participation in social organizations (Scandinavia and the Low Countries) are likely to find other interactive forms of governance such as social networks more acceptable than étatiste styles. In short, governance will be occurring in all settings, and therefore the important question becomes how, and who plays the central roles.

This matching of governance styles and national patterns of governing is also an evolutionary process. Both political systems and the mechanisms for governance continue to change so that there are new opportunities and new challenges. Further, failures of one style of governance (Peters, 2014) may lead to the development of alternative formats. Governance is not static but represents a continuing pattern of adaption to opportunities and circumstances.

Governing in the Shadows

When discussing the use of networks and other delegated forms of governance, Fritz Scharpf (1997) developed the concept of the "shadow of hierarchy." By this Scharpf meant that although state actors may make extensive delegations of authority to non-state actors, they always have the capacity to withdraw those delegations and to reassert their hierarchical authority. This conception of delegation emphasizes the power of state actors, but it also points out that delegation need not be considered as threatening to state actors. This understanding therefore can actually help to facilitate governance through non-state actors.

The shadow of hierarchy is not, however, the only "shadow" that can be seen as operating in the selection of governance styles. First, there is the "shadow of society." If governments fail, as they do all too often, then social actors may replace government. This replacement may occur through creating network governance, or it may be through social actors such as the church, or community groups, providing services that the state might normally provide. Christian Lund (2011) has examined the operation of these informal social institutions in Africa, describing them as "twilight institutions." He argues that in these cases public authority does not work just through the state, or even primarily through the state, but rather through social actors working at the very local level.

And even if the state remains capable of providing services, social actors may still be engaged in governing and providing public services. We should be careful, however, not to assume that this shadow of society is necessarily positive. Street gangs, for example, provide a form of governance in their areas in cities, albeit not one that most citizens would choose if there were an alternative. And clientelism in less-developed countries can also be seen as a form of society-based governance (see Piattoni, 2010) in which social relationships replace law and hierarchy within the public sector.

There is also a shadow of the market that may function to replace, or to augment, governance being created through the state. For example, in many failed states market actors provide a governance of sorts, providing a range of public services in order to support their own activities as well as to provide more general public services. While many citizens might not consider this a positive form of governing, other ways in which the shadow of the market is exercised may be even less positive. For example, the Sinola cartel in Mexico provides a form of governance in its territory in order to regularize the life of the local citizens.

Finally, there can be a shadow of expertise. State actors may not want to make decisions about scientific or technical issues, and therefore decisions may be delegated to experts. This may be done casually, as when governments seek out policy advice. Or it may be done in a more institutional manner, in which decisions are delegated to "non-majoritarian institutions" (Majone, 2002) that can make decisions relying primarily if not exclusively on their expert knowledge. But again there may be more negative results of this reliance on expertise, with the loss of political control over important public decisions.[3]

In summary, the alternatives to governance through the state are more extensive than sometimes understood. The options for governance go well beyond networks and can include a range of social and economic actors. Each of these alternatives can contribute to the achievement of public goals, but they also involve risks. These means of governance are also more difficult to hold accountable than are more conventional means. Therefore, the shadow of hierarchy may have a broader range of implications than was originally understood.

Organization of the Book

This brief, introductory analysis of changes in governance in the western democracies does not in any way claim to exhaust the topic. The preceding discussion has primarily used the United Kingdom and the United States as illustrative cases of the points we make but subsequent chapters will show that these models have a wider empirical relevance. Chapter 2 elaborates on the functionalist approach to governance while Chapter 3 focuses on what we see as the key function of governing – decision-making. Chapter 4 then places this model of governance in the context of comparative politics in order to demonstrate the empirical validity and strength of the functionalist governance model. Chapters 5 and 6 are devoted to analyze the intrastate ramifications of different external governance arrangements;

---

[3] There is an extensive literature on the dangers of "technocracy", beginning some decades ago, supplanting democratic controls over policy (Meynaud, 1964).

Chapter 5 discusses the multilevel governance and Chapter 6 analyzes public management and governance. We then zoom out again, so that Chapter 7 focuses on governance failure and Chapter 8 addresses processes through which governance and governance functions change. Chapter 9 summarizes the book.

2 | *The Theory of Governance*

It is very easy to say that all societies require governing. It is also easy to say that governance is about steering the economy and society. Those statements are largely truisms, and they beg any number of questions about how exactly that fundamental task required by society is to be accomplished. Governments have been in the business of governing for some centuries, but the hierarchical, linear conception of steering that is inherent in a traditional state-centric model of governance is far too simple for the social and political complexity that now confronts any would-be system for governance. Governments now confront a seemingly endless sequence of "wicked problems" that require some form of response, even if any enduring solutions may be impossible (Head, 2008), and they may be facing those problems with diminished legitimacy and resources (Fukuyama, 2014).

These complex problems pose distinct challenges to governments and to business as usual within the public sector. The complexity and indeterminacy that confronts would-be governors today also makes it improbable to assume that the autonomous social actors who have been advanced as an alternative to the conventional state-centric model can provide effective governance on their own. Contemporary governing requires linkages across institutions within the public sector and between the public sector and actors (market and nonmarket) who exist outside the public sector.

Given the complexity of the task of governing and the complex relationships between civil society and the formal institutions of the public sector, we will first need to build a general model of governance. Such a model will identify the functions required to govern, leaving aside which sets of actors will actually be performing those tasks. This governance model will also be sufficiently general to be able to include the range of variation that may exist for each of the elements of governance identified in the analysis and therefore can be used as a template for comparative political analysis. Governance generally has been discussed in rather absolute terms – it exists or it does not – but the extent and manner of governance does vary across societies, and we consider governance as a fundamental approach to political analysis.

The model of governance developed here is also sufficiently generic to be able to be applied to both democratic and nondemocratic forms of governance, although our emphasis will be on democratic forms and the rather extensive range of governing styles that may exist even within the category of democratic governance (Keman, 2002; Lijphart, 1999). This focus on more democratic systems not only reflects a bias in favor of such regimes on our part but also is a reflection of the greater complexity involved in maintaining effective democratic governance. Further, there is sufficient variation in democratic forms of governance to fill this one book, as they already have any number of times,[1] so we will leave less humane forms of governance for another time. That said, the model of governance developed here can be applied to nondemocratic regimes, given the generality of the functions included in the model.

The model of governance that we will be developing is unashamedly functionalist. Although functionalism has been widely criticized as an intellectual approach to the social sciences (Dryzek, 1986; but see Lane, 1994; Giddens, 1975), that basic approach to social and political analysis appears well suited for examining governance. First, governance is a crucial activity for any society and it is indeed performed in some manner in every society – the question is how it will be performed. In the classic Parsonian analysis of society, the goal attainment function was ascribed to the polity, pointing out the need for carrying out that function and the central role of the state. Even if governance has been associated with the state, it can be performed in a variety of different ways and involves different sets of actors in those different settings (see Knill, 2004).

Both Parsons (1975) and Merton (1957), as the two major functionalist theorists in sociology, have argued that they developed their various list of requisite functions for societies through a combination of sociological theory and empirical observations of society. We are

---

[1] This model will, however, consider a much wider range of factors than many significant studies of variation in democratic politics such as Lijphart (1984, 1999) and O'Donnell (2001).

doing the same thing here concerning governance. This analysis of governance is informed by existing theory, especially process approaches in public policy. This analysis also relies in part on the comparative politics literature, to the extent that it also does consider political processes. In addition, the governance literature itself, including that focusing on networks and so on, talks about the same types of activities that we do.

Aberle et al. (1950) make another interesting argument about defining functional requisites for a society. They argued that a function is requisite; if not performed, it would lead to the failure of society. In our case, we are arguing that not performing any of the functions developed below would lead to governance failure. Having observed governments for some years, we have some confidence in this analysis of what has to be done to govern. It is difficult to see what has been left out, or what has been included that is not relevant for effective governance (see below, pp. 30ff).

It is very clear that functionalism is not a causal model defining the actions of governments and their partners. Functional models can, however, be considered the precursors to developing models that do have greater potential for making causal statements about governance. That absence of causation in these theories is compensated in part by the generality of the models and the capacity to apply a common framework to a wide range of cases.

Further, governance must be considered in a contingent manner. Different forms of governance are more or less successful in different settings, defined in terms of social and cultural underpinnings of the political system, the existence of social capital, or other social and economic characteristics. Also, the various approaches to governance that we develop later also will be more or less successful when confronting different challenges. Finally, the level of theoretical development in this field is not yet sufficiently advanced to permit the development and testing of hypotheses about governance, although that should certainly be one goal of development in this field.

Establishing a functionalist model generates a mechanism for examining governance in a wide variety of settings, so that this rather generic model will be useful for comparative analysis. In contrast, concepts of governance that posit a particular format for governance define away alternative forms of steering society and hence narrow the investigation prematurely. For example, if the model of governance is dependent upon high levels of interaction between state and society, then it may not be suitable for political systems outside the more advanced democracies (Torfing et al., 2012).

The process of governing has, we will argue, several crucial requirements that must be taken into account in any consideration of social steering, and identifying these functions facilitates the process of comparison. Rather than being forced to cope with governance as an undifferentiated process or just as an outcome, this functional model will facilitate comparison and will help to understand how various segments of governing do fit together into more or less coherent patterns. This approach therefore can link the process of governing to specific institutions and processes that facilitate comparison.

We will also argue that the failure to conceptualize governance in this relatively general and functionalist manner has been the source of a good deal of the confusion that appears in the contemporary literature on governance (see Offe, 2009). Most importantly, the tendency to equate governance with the absence of, or at least a minimal role for, the official public sector in steering society begs one of the central comparative questions in governance. Therefore, by asking what is needed to govern, and then who performs those tasks, we can develop more encompassing conceptions of governance.

Further, discussions of "good governance" put forth by several international organizations (Kaufmann, 2005; but see Andrews, 2008) have concentrated on corruption in implementation rather than more general questions about the capacity to steer (see Doornbos, 2004). That aspect of good governance is important but does not answer if governance can actually reach its goals no matter how clean the government involved may be.[2] We could proliferate examples of the tendency toward premature attempts to narrow the discussion on governance and to place somewhat arbitrary boundaries around a concept that is inherently broad, complex, and multifaceted.[3] The fundamental point is that we

---

[2] Indeed, some scholars have argued that a certain amount of corruption may actually facilitate governing by reducing transaction costs among the actors involved. See, for example, Alam (1989).

[3] In terms of comparative conceptualization, it appears more appropriate to develop some "radial categories" of governance (Collier and Mahon, 1993), for example good governance, rather than excessively limit the general concept of governance. By adopting such a strategy, we will expand the opportunities for comparison and also have a concept of governance that can more readily travel across a range of types of political systems.

pursue a more open strategy of inquiry in the pursuit of a mechanism for comparing the governance performance of various political systems.

Although the model of governance developed here is functionalist, it will be significantly dissimilar to the structural-functionalist models that had characterized the study of comparative politics (Almond and Coleman, 1960; Almond and Powell, 1966) during the 1960s and 1970s. The most important difference is that this model, and any other contemporary governance model, will be obliged to focus on just those elements that those structural-functionalist models tended to ignore. The decision-making processes in the public sector tended to be considered a "black box" in the structural-functional models of the political process, and little interest was expressed in the "through-puts" in the social systems model.[4] In part because comparative politics prior to that time had been characterized by the study of formal institutions almost exclusively (Eckstein, 1963), the models developed at that time largely ignored these formal structures in favor of the input institutions. In the following chapter, we will expand the focus on decision-making and discuss how to relate standard models of decision-making to governing and more broadly to governance. In addition, unlike other functionalist models that have been used in political science, this model of governance does not contain any assumptions about homeostasis, nor does it have a teleological element, as did funtionalist models of political development, e.g. that of Almond and Powell (1966).

In the structural-functional models then developed for comparative politics, the process of making public policy appeared to be an almost mechanistic one, In this model, inputs are rather automatically converted into outputs, with the processes in the "black box" being of little apparent interest. In fairness, these models did differ from much of the history of comparative political science in that they directed some attention to the outputs of the political process, and hence made scholars in the discipline think more about what governments actually

---

[4] This focus on inputs into the political system and the de-emphasis of the choices made by governments were in part because so much of political science before the development of these models for comparative politics focused almost exclusively on the internal structures and processes of government (see Eckstein, 1963). The structural functional model reversed that focus on the formal aspects of government, but perhaps overshot the mark by ignoring those formal institutions.

did.[5] However, this emphasis on the actions of government was not so much about steering the society – the central concern of our governance model – as we will be discussing in governance terms. Rather, policy was conceptualized in the structural-functional models more as merely responding to the demands being articulated from the society. Thus, in much of the literature that emerged at this time, public policy appeared to reflect a range of other socio-economic factors more than it did the political forces. The governance approach is not oblivious to the importance of social and political inputs into the process, especially given our focus on democratic forms of governance. But neither do we consider those inputs to be converted directly into policies; they must be processed through the decision-making systems internal to governance arrangements

We argue that any mechanistic approach is inadequate for understanding governance. The mechanistic assumptions about translating inputs into outputs contained in the structural functional models of the 1960s were troubling for several reasons. The most obvious problem in the approach was that a good deal of the analytic capacity and substantive knowledge in political science was totally ignored by adopting such an approach to making public policies. If there was one thing that political scientists at the time knew, it was how the formal institutions of government functioned, and those institutions were generally given a limited role in these models. This avoidance of formal institutions may have reflected an attempt to make a clean break from the past but it did not reflect the reality of governing then or now.

Further, the direct translation of inputs into outputs provided little means of reconciling the multiple demands that were pressed on any political system. In political systems with deep social or economic cleavages (at the time of that writing the Netherlands and Belgium, not to mention Northern Ireland, would have fit into that category), those cleavages might have been thought to produce demands that were irreconcilable, but the functionalist assumptions produced an easy flow of decisions and policies (see Brettschneider, van Deth, and Roller, 2002). In reality, government institutions are designed to reconcile

---

[5] Harold Lasswell had argued some years previously (1936) that politics was about "Who Gets What," but that fundamental point was, and still is, often forgotten. Thus, as we consider governance we will be concerned with the capacity of actors–public and/or private–to make decisions that reach collective goals about what citizens can expect.

the irreconcilable, but the simple focus on inputs would not make that capacity for coping with conflict evident. Constitutional rules and other guides for collective decision-making can produce a decision in most instances; it may not be a perfect decision, but it is a decision (Hardin, 1989). Therefore, we will place a good deal of attention on decision-making in the public sector as central to understanding how governance is actually created.

Finally, this body of structural-functional theory ignored the state as an actor in the process and assumed that state actors – notably public bureaucracies (but see Heclo, 1974; Peters, 2009) – did not have interests of their own. The state has now been brought back into political science several times (Almond, 1988; Evans, Rueschmeyer, and Skocpol, 1985), an especially important intellectual occurrence for American political science. The governance model in which we are interested focuses on the role of the state, *in conjunction with society*, in governing. In part, the inadequate attention to the role of the state as an actor in governing was the result not only of not having a clear conception of the state, but to the extent that it did exist it was undifferentiated and unitary. The inadequacy of these rather simplistic conceptions of the state has become increasingly evident as the study of governance has expanded.

The governance model we are developing will thus provide for more complex interactions between state and society than that existed in the structural-functional models. In those earlier functional and systems models of politics, the society was conceptualized as pressing wants and demands (see Easton, 1965b) on the public sector, but the models being used at that time posited a relatively distinct boundary between those two elements of the overall social system.[6] In particular, in the social systems model popular in comparative politics at the time, the

---

[6] Part of the developmental argument of Almond and Powell (1966) was that the differentiation of the political system from other aspects of the social system represented one of the important markers of modernity. In this view, the increased intermeshing of state in society in contemporary governance would represent a retrograde development of the political system. Further, the Almond and Powell model was formulated on the basis of the Anglo-American experience and hence ignored the level of interaction that already existed between state and society in many Northern European countries at that time (Rokkan, 1966; Rothstein, 1988) and that continued to progress toward broader ranges of involvement.

concept of "boundary maintenance" was considered to be a measure of success for the political system (see Easton, 1965b).

In the contemporary social sciences, scholars tend to consider strict boundary maintenance both undemocratic and potentially inefficient. Strict boundary maintenance would be uncongenial toward social networks (Koppenjan and Klijn, 2004) and associated forms of collaborative governance (Skelcher, Mathur, and Smith, 2004) that have assumed a significant position in the literature of political science and are also readily apparent in the real world of governing. For the advocates of network governance, these linkages between state and society provide a more effective form of democracy than contemporary representative systems (see Sørensen and Torfing, 2003) and also may enable governments to be more efficient in reaching their policy goals (Bogason, 2000).

In our model of governance, as indicated in Chapter 1, high levels of interaction between state and society will be assumed as a central component of the governance process in most contemporary governance systems, and governance is very clearly a result of that interaction. Social actors do not simply express their demands and then go away; they are intimately involved in the process of making and then implementing public policies, and therefore are involved directly in governance. This involvement of societal actors in the model of governance to some extent reflects a changing social and political reality. At the time at which the structural-functionalist models were developed for political science, the distinction between state and society was more widely accepted, especially in the United States, than it is now. There certainly has been greater activation of societal interests than in the past. As well as some changing reality, the more direct inclusion of societal actors in these models of governance reflects the growing recognition in academic circles of this involvement. While Continental European scholarship had recognized these interactions for some time (see Heisler, 1974; Pierre, 2009), Anglo-American scholarship was somewhat slower to come to this recognition.

The above paragraph implies a convergence of models of governing in Europe and North America at an academic level (see Milward and Provan, 2000 but see Kopstein and Steinmo, 2008), but there also appears to have been some convergence in practice. This convergence has been most noticeable in reactions to the economic crisis beginning in 2008 (see Peters, 2012c). The reactions of the United States to the

crisis was relatively quick and very interventionist, with first a program
to support banks and other firms with "troubled assets" (TARP), then
a large (if not perhaps large enough) stimulus program, and then
a major regulatory reform for the financial sector (Dodd-Frank).
In contrast, the European response has been largely austerity – reducing
public spending and removing flexibility in fiscal as well as monetary
policy, thereby making the state a much less effective economic
manager.

We have been arguing above that the earlier functionalist models
ignored the nature, and central position, of the institutionalized state
in governing, and we are concerned that some contemporary models
of governing are tending to drive the state back out into the cold.
As already noted, some of the contemporary governance literature
places private sector actors in a dominant position in policy and deni-
grates the role of public actors. In these models, the lack of adequate
treatment of the state is not so much the absence of interest that
appeared to characterize the structural functionalist models. Rather,
the argument being made in some of these models (Kooiman, 1993,
2003) is that the state is largely ineffective in governing and that networks of private sector actors are more capable of regulating themselves. Other analysts argue that the state is ineffective because of the
power of international markets (Strange, 1996; but see Weiss, 1998)
and hence focusing on governance through traditional state action is
likely to be disappointing.

We are attempting to develop a model of governance and to find an
intellectual stance that at once will assign an empirically valid role to
government structures but will also have a place for a vigorous private
sector (both profit and nonprofit sectors) that is involved directly in
governance. More than just being involved in policy-making, these
private sector actors are directly linked to the public sector and play
crucial roles in the design, implementation and legitimation of public
actions. The involvement of these actors, and the manner in which
they are involved, will be one of the principal points of comparison
when we begin to apply this model of governance to real-world
political systems.

Further, there are important differences in the manner in which the
profit and not-for-profit elements of the private sector are involved in
the policy process, and hence these differences will constitute a second
dimension of comparison in these models of governance. For

example, in some instances, social actors have been legitimated as central actors in the policy-making process, while in others they must work diligently to be involved. Thus, unlike many state-centric conceptions of politics, we do not assume that societal actors are irrelevant, nor like some contemporary models of governance do we assume that societal actors are dominant. Rather, this is an empirical question with an implicit assumption of marked variation in the amount and style of involvement. And these differences among varieties of governance systems constitute the second pillar of our analysis of contemporary governance.

A General Model of Governance

Having now attempted to contextualize the contemporary study of governance theory in the development of the discipline of political science, as well as in some of the contemporary debates about the role of the state in governance, we will proceed to develop our own model of governance. Rather than concentrating on the actors, as do both the traditional state-centric models of governing (Bell and Hindmoor, 2009; Dryzek and Dunleavy, 2009) and the network models of governing (see Torfing and Sørensen, 2007), we are more concerned with the underlying *processes* of governing. With the functionalist perspective, we will first ask what must be done to govern, rather than who are the principal actors. Once the dimensions of the process are established, the involvement of different types of actors, and the way in which they are involved in governing, becomes an empirical question and a foundation for comparison rather than an assumption.

Beginning with a clear view of the processes of governance also provides us a higher probability of sorting out the substantial, and growing, complexity of contemporary governance. Not only do actors from the private sector play significant roles in governing, but the public sector itself has developed alternative modes of making and implementing policy. There have been in fact two basic shifts in the style of governing. The first has been some movement away from the state being the actual provider and deliverer of public programs toward a model in which the state often sets the conditions for the delivery of services, provides some funding for the delivery of services, and works with nongovernmental actors to provide the services. These arrangements involve partnerships, contracts, networks, and a host of other mechanisms all of which involve the state delivering its services "at a distance" (Kickert, 1995).

In addition, governments have been shifting from the command and control style of governing typical of regulatory states and begun to use a variety of "enabling" or "soft law" approaches (Brunsson and Jacobsson, 2000; Mörth, 2004; Salamon, 2001) that depend more upon voluntary cooperation from the regulated, rather than on more Draconian means of enforcement. Rather than the public sector attempting to coerce action, the style in many policy areas has become one of encouraging action through agreements, benchmarking, and a host of other means. Thus, rather than a "regulatory state," we have an "enabling" state (Botsman, 2001; Page and Wright, 2006) that attempts to facilitate action rather than to force action.

This shift in the style of governance is perhaps particularly interesting because it appears to contradict part of the logic justifying the claims being made by the advocates of network governance models. That is, those advocates of networks as almost inherently superior to governments have argued that social actors would be more successful than would government actors in regulating society. Their argument has been that the rigidity of the legal instruments central to regulation prevents government from achieving its ends (see Bardach and Kagan, 1982; Lundqvist, 1980). Even if that critique had been valid at one point or another in time, it appears less so in the early 21st century. Governments have altered their modes of making decisions and implementing decisions so that they have proven themselves capable of responding more flexibly to changing social conditions, and changing political demands.

The Governance Functions

We will be arguing that governance requires some set of actors in society to perform five major functions, and to do so in a reasonably integrated manner – decision-making, goal-selection, resource mobilization, implementation, and feedback, evaluation and learning. As already noted, we are agnostic about which among the range of possible actors will perform these activities, and what actors can perform them best. We tend to consider cooperative arrangements between public sector actors and social actors being the most likely to produce positive outcomes, but that is an empirical question. We therefore remain open to a range of solutions being capable of producing effective governance. Further, we are arguing that some form of central direction may be necessary to make governance work as effectively as citizens would like, and everything else being equal, the public sector will be better prepared to perform that overall coordination and direction function (see later).

As we argued early in this book, we see decision-making as the fundamental activity in governing. This is partly because decision-making permeates all other functions and activities of the state in governance. Also, given our earlier criticism of previous functionalist approaches to governance for their lack of interest in the black box of the political system, that is to say the decision-making phase of the policy process, we want our analysis to pay particular attention to how decisions evolve (see Chapter 3). That said, we can conceptualize decision-making as one component of the governance model. This function is pervasive, but still need to be considered separately as a means of understanding how governance actors make the choices necessary for effective governance. And, in particular, we are concerned about the manner in which law and law-like statements are made within the public sector, and in conjunction with actors in the private sector.

Decision-making. Decision-making should, according to democratic theory, be a task where government plays a leading role. Decision-makers should be elected officials acting on a popular mandate and being held accountable by the electorate in general elections. Goal-selection and decision-making are the tasks of governance where responsiveness and accountability matter the most since these are inherently political tasks. Decision-making is, not only normatively speaking but also empirically, a core government task. David Easton's definition of politics as the authoritative allocation of values identifies decision-making as a fundamental government role in governance (Easton, 1965b; Riker, 1962). Again, in a functional perspective, nonelected actors could play (and frequently do play) a more or less prominent role in decision-making. The key criterion on democratic governance is the degree to which elected officials control these tasks.

The relationships between political decision-making, governance, and allocation of values are however less self-evident than they might appear. First, there are contexts where major decisions in society in terms of the values allocated are made not by government but by other actors. In unstable or emerging democracies, political decision-making can at times be made either by the military or in its shadow (Houngnikpo, 2011). Furthermore, the decision-making capacity of political institutions at all levels of the political system can be severely constrained by private actors. For example, the urban political economy literature is replete with accounts of the submissive and anticipatory strategy of political leaders in order not to challenge powerful economic actors (Crenson, 1971; Jones and Bachelor, 1993). Similar accounts from other institutional levels are provided by the globalization literature (Camilleri and Falk, 1992; Hay and Rosamond, 2002).

Thus, state-centric models of governance argue that goal-selection and decision-making are the most obvious tasks for the state. In more interactive governance arrangements, particularly in networks, decision-making tends to be removed from political institutions and into more opaque settings. In these cases, decision-making caters primarily to the interests of the involved actors who have little incentives to factor in the preferences of absent actors. In our more inclusive conception of governance, decision-making is pervasive and its location is an empirical question, with the state playing a central role in some instances but not in others.

Political goals are generally statements of good intentions, but need to be translated into action if indeed any steering is to occur. We discuss goal-selection as one of the principal functions of governance, but developing the means of reaching those goals is also important for the success of any effort at governance. While many people in the society may agree on goals such as international peace and economic growth, there is likely to be substantially less agreement on the appropriate means for reaching those goals, and statements of the means may be even more divisive politically than the statements of goals. Despite those inherent political problems, however, governments must develop the means of reaching their stated goals.

We will discuss models of decision-making more generally in the following chapter, but at this point we are discussing the importance of decision-making in policy design and formulation (see Howlett and Lejano, 2013). The selection of means to pursue the ends already selected through a political process tends to move governing from high levels of generality into less abstract pursuits. Naturally, the actors involved in this aspect of governing also change, with political parties and political leaders at the level of presidents and prime ministers tending to give way to the individual sectoral ministers and also to public bureaucracies. The action of designing public programs and then beginning to put them into effect is a more specialized task than advocating and selecting broad goals, and this requires putting some meat on the bones of the pious hopes that are often the content of goals. Designing public programs also requires the expertise and experience that are contained in public bureaucracies. That said, given the tendency of power to move upward toward prime ministers, policy formulation may now involve the prime minister and his advisors (Eichbaum and Shaw, 2010).

The selection of a set of mechanisms for reaching policy goals generally requires acceptance of some model of causation for the problems being addressed, and the goals being pursued (see Linder and Peters, 1984). For example, if the societal goal being pursued is economic growth, then program designers must have some idea about what causes economic growth. Further, these would-be program designers have multiple alternative models for causation available to them as they make their decisions. In economic policy, for example, Keynesian ideas are still popular in some quarters (Hall, 1989), while monetarism and neoliberal ideas (Arestis and Sawyer, 2004) have gained substantial credibility for decision-makers in many systems. The selection of one or the other of these models will provide policy-makers the foundation needed to design a program, and for justifying the particular interventions into the economy and society that are to be undertaken.

The selection of means to pursue policy goals is often path dependent, and the selection of one model of causation or one instrument will exclude the pursuit of the goals through other means. For example, if economic growth and job creation is being pursued through public works and large-scale public investment, then the resources that might otherwise be made available for private sector investment (supply-side economics) or for creating effective demand in the economy by the public will be exhausted. When we move to even more micro-issues in program design, the path dependence of the selections becomes even more apparent. Building a public pensions program, for example, will make movement to a privatized pension program more difficult, if not impossible. Individuals will have paid into the public scheme all their working lives and will expect a return from that, not to be faced with a new form of pension.

The means chosen to pursue the goals of society are probably more contentious than are the broad goals for collective social action, and they may also be more visible to the public. Therefore, the means selected to pursue goals may be as important for the political success of a president or prime minister, as is the selection of the goals. That impact on the political fortunes of a leader may be present even though the means are more often the product of decisions taken at lower levels, and the political leader will have relatively little direct involvement with the final decisions. The selection of means is therefore just one of many points at which political responsibility and accountability become diffused in the process of governance, and hence a point at which the feedback instruments discussed below become crucial both for the internal management of governance and also for the accountability of these systems to the public.

As already noted, the literature on governance has been deeply concerned with the relative importance of state and non-state actors in steering society. We have argued that the process of goal-selection is perhaps the peculiar province of state actors, but when we begin to think about the selection of the means for achieving those ends, non-state actors may become significant players. State actors are still central actors, but non-state actors may be important in the selection of the means for achieving ends, and indeed may be the repository of many ideas about policies and programs. Indeed, non-state actors are often the means of delivering public services and have strong commitments to particular mechanisms for steering (see Lodge and Weigrich, 2015).

State actors are not necessarily inert actors, however, and public sector organizations are often important advocates for policy ideas and use these ideational resources as the basis for policy, and also as components of their arguments over the definition and control of policy. The usual logic of bureaucratic maximization (Niskanen, 1971) is that organizations want more budgets and more personnel in order to maximize their own position, and the well-being of the leadership of the organization. Even if that model had more empirical and theoretical support than it appears to have (see Blais and Dion, 1991), the bureaus would need some means of pressing for the financial support, and ideas are often that means. Even if public organizations do not use ideas to advance their own interests, they may have commitments to policy ideas and have their own ideologies about policy (see Beland and Cox, 2011).

The bureaus, and other policy entrepreneurs, therefore should be conceptualized as involved actively in constructing and advocating policy ideas. Most social programs are not pre-packaged, given the number of alternative approaches to reaching particular goals. Therefore, one of the most important parts of the political process, and hence of governance, is providing an acceptable and operational definition of the problem. Further, this process may extend to the identification of problems that had not been previously understood as impediments to reaching social goals. For example, the goal of creating greater equality in the society, and that of creating a more secure society was being undermined by spousal abuse and child abuse. That behavior, however, had not been conceptualized in many societies as being illegal, but rather just a part of normal life (Nelson, 1984). Thus, in order for this issue to get placed on the agenda for public action, some form of policy entrepreneurship is required.

The agenda-setting process, described here as a means of considering the range of possible mechanisms for achieving policy goals, may be an especially important point at which the societal component of governance comes into play. The networks and other social actors that support a public organization are often sources of ideas for programs, and indeed public organizations may have their ideas shaped through their involvement with their social partners. If we continue to think about the development of economic policy, there are networks of economists, think tanks, and significant economic actors that surround ministries of finance and central banks and help to feed ideas into these policy-makers.

As well as being the source of ideas, those social actors also are major sources of legitimation for the ideas used to achieve goals. The members of networks and other social partners for public organizations may have ideas about social goals, but tend to be more committed to more proximate questions about policy. These actors generally want to ensure that their particular clienteles and their interests are being served by the programs of government, and perhaps also that there are possibilities for involvement of those groups in decision-making. Further, those social actors are often as committed to the means for achieving public ends as they are to the broader goals. For example, they may consider participation in the processes – playing the game – more significant than actually winning the game.

To this point, we have been discussing the means of achieving policy goals in the abstract, but we should also think about this aspect of governing in somewhat more concrete terms. We have been using the familiar term "program" to describe the mechanisms of achieving goals, but that is more a structural description. The operational elements required for achieving the goals can best be conceptualized as instruments (Hood, 1976a; Salamon, 2001). These tools are means of bringing together the resources of government to produce an identifiable result. Programs as discussed to this point may use multiple instruments to achieve their ends. For example, a program to enhance the opportunities of young people to attend university may use direct grants to students, loans, loan guarantees, grants to the universities for programs such as work-study, tax credits, and perhaps regulations to limit increasing tuition costs from the universities. Each of these individual instruments has some capacity to aid in achieving the policy goal, but may be able to help different types of students in different settings.

In summary, in some ways deciding upon the societal goals that should be pursued may be the easy part of governance and steering. Although there will be disagreements about the interpretations of goals and the relative priority of goals, there is likely to be greater disagreement about the means that can be used to reach those ends. Those goals are often abstract and future oriented, while the development of the means to reach those goals are more likely to directly help or harm social interests. Those programs and mechanisms involve ideas and those ideas also separate people, perhaps as much as the programs that are derived from them.

Goal-Selection. Like decision-making, goal-selection is a task which democratic theory would assign to government since this is a governance function where democratic accountability is paramount. The first requirement for governance is that a common set of goals for society must be developed and articulated. If governance is about steering, it is helpful to know what the collective direction of the society is meant to be. While it may be possible to find some very general goals on which citizens and their political leaders might agree, when we move from the very general to more specific targets and programs that consensus is likely to erode very quickly. The consensus is likely to erode even more quickly when the means for pursuing those goals are considered. A large majority of citizens may agree that economic growth is a goal, but may disagree about whether public ownership or neoliberal tax cuts are the best means of achieving those goals. Politics is about conflict, and also about resolving conflict, and governing reflects much of the same fundamental conflict over the means and ends of governing.

The conception of goals for government action and the nature of the end states that the public sector will pursue have been explored relatively little in political science or policy analysis. The one aspect of goal-selection that has been pursued extensively has been agenda-setting (Cobb and Elder, 1972; Kingdon, 2003). There is by now an extensive literature on how actors attempt to have their concerns placed onto the active agenda of governance actors and institutions. And in some cases, the nature of events in the environment of governance structures pushes those events onto the agenda with relatively little action by agents (see Birkland, 1997).

Our perspective in this model of governance is that agenda-setting is a necessary but not sufficient condition for goal-selection. Having an issue on the agenda of government does not mean that it will in the end be selected as one of the active goals for the process. There are simply too many things that can, and even should, be done through collective action and the resources of governance actors – including time – are limited. Therefore, those governance actors must *select* some goals for further action while declining to act upon many others. This does not mean that the issue is dead for all time, but only that it is not acted upon in present time.

The temporary nature of agendas and goal-selection is emphasized in the literature on punctuated equilibria in the public sector (see Baumgartner and Jones, 2009). In large part through the rather fleeting attention of the media to issues, those issues move onto and then off the active agenda rather quickly. An issue may return but often unless acted upon positively during its brief stay will become dormant for some time. In terms of our governance model then, the governance goals implied within that issue would not be selected and any resolution of the concerns would have to wait or be performed through private action.

The need to have issues placed on an agenda for action points to a crucial point about goal-selection in governance. If issues can be excluded from an agenda, then they will not be acted upon and have no opportunity to be selected for governance actions. This now familiar "second face of power" (Bachrach and Baratz, 1962) demonstrates the power of more conservative social and political actors to constrain governance activities and maintain the status quo in public policies.

The majority of the literature in the policy sciences has tended to assume that goals are largely exogenous to the policy process and to governance. The goals for governing reflect societal aspirations, or the ideologies of leaders and political parties. They may be put forth in political manifestos or can be expressed in campaign speeches, but have been little analyzed by political scientists. Further, for political science, goals are assumed to be primarily instrumental, functioning as a means to get elected, rather than having much intrinsic meaning of their own. This interpretation of policy goals was shocking when advanced so clearly by Anthony Downs (1957) in the 1950s, but now is the conventional wisdom about politics. For policy analysis, the goals tend to be given, and the interesting part of the analysis is to find the means of reaching those goals in the most effective and efficient manner possible.

However, when we begin to think analytically about governance, goals become a central component of the analysis. In most democratic political systems, the problem confronting the political and social elites who would steer society is not the absence of goals; it is the presence of too many goals. That presents governing institutions with the need to select among the goals that are on the agenda and to find the means of making the goals operational. Further, the selection of one set of goals may preclude opportunities to pursue other sets of goals, for budgetary reasons if no other. The familiar scarcity argument, therefore, can become a reason not to select some goals that might otherwise be worthy of action. Policy, and the goals to which it is related, is generally path dependent so that the opportunities for prompt reaction to changing social conditions and changing public demands may not be available to governing actors.

Social and political goals present several interesting analytic problems. First, there is time and the path dependence of the goals pursued by governments. Most of the outcomes that citizens might list as goals for their society are very broad, and generally long term (Jacobs, 2011). Most people want at least some level of material security (or even affluence), peace and security, a just society, and some level of personal freedom (see Inglehart and Welzel, 2003). Those goals are rather vague, subject to interpretation, and will require a good deal of sustained effort to achieve. In addition, at least some of these goals, e.g. environmental management, may not be obtainable by any one country alone but will require substantial levels of cooperation. The good thing, however, is that these goals are largely compatible.[7]

Individual goals are not, however, the only goals that are operative within governance processes. The organizations involved in governance, including public sector organizations, also express a set of goals that may or may not be aligned with the goals of their constituents. We have known for some time, for example, that the leadership of interest groups and the leadership of political parties may have different policy goals than do the activists (May, 1973). Likewise, public bureaucracies often have well-defined goals that may be linked both to their own survival and to their own definitions of desirable outcomes for society (Goodsell, 2011).

In addition to the individual goals and specific policy goals held by public organizations, there may be goals coming from within the public sector that cut across organizational boundaries. For example, most governments now require policy-makers to consider environmental impacts, impacts on gender equality, racial equality, and number of other cross-cutting goals when making their policies (Pollack and Hafner-Burton, 2000). These may be in conflict with the goals pursued by the individual policy-makers, or perceived to be irrelevant, but they do generate some greater consistency across the entire system of governance.

Although goals are often stated vaguely, reforms associated with the New Public Management are tending to force greater specificity. The logic of performance management (Bouckaert and Halligan, 2007) involves developing measures for the performance of public programs, and to do that requires specifying the goals being pursued with the program in operational terms. While there are numerous problems with measurement of performance, at both the individual level and the organizational level, still this managerialist innovation has forced organizations to clarify what they are doing and what their goals really are.

---

[7] But perhaps not. High levels of economic growth may not be compatible with a broad social goal such as environmental protection (Feiock and Stream, 2001). Further, certainly for neoliberals the creation of a more egalitarian distribution of resources in society may not be compatible with economic growth.

There are several important comparative aspects of goal-selection. Different types of political systems will approach the question of establishing societal goals in different ways, as a function of their institutional structures as well as their political cultures. At the extreme, the process of goal-selection can appear rather simple for authoritarian regimes, especially dictatorial regimes. The leadership of the regime in an authoritarian system can simply choose the goals for society, and presumably will have the means to enforce those goals. Buchanan and Tullock (1962) discussed the selection of goals in terms of the costs that the selection imposed on members of society. On the one hand, there are costs from having one's preferences excluded from the final decision about goals and policy. In a dictatorship, those costs are very high, as almost all people's views are excluded as the leader imposes his views. On the other hand, in a decision-making requiring unanimity, e.g. the consensus style of some Nordic countries, exclusion costs are close to zero for the participants.

Decision-making costs are the other type of costs involved in selecting goals in the Buchanan and Tullock model. The more individuals and groups that have to be involved in the decision, the higher the decision-making costs will be. Not surprisingly, decision-making costs are the mirror image of exclusion costs. For a dictatorship, the decision-making costs are extremely low, and the leader can rule through his/her whims. On the other hand, in a consensus system the decision-making costs can be extremely high, and bargaining will have to continue until that desired consensus is achieved. While difficult for outsiders to understand, consensus is valued sufficiently in some societies to make the decision-making costs required acceptable to the public (see Kvavik, 1976; Goodin, 2003). The costs are manifested through slower and perhaps less innovative decisions within the public sector (see also Scharpf, 1988).

Even in this type of system, governing can be more complex than implied in the usual description of authoritarian control. For example, many memoirs and studies of the Third Reich (Speer, 1981) and of the Soviet Union (see Urban, 1982) point to the internal differentiation and needs to create and defend common goals. Single hegemonic party and authoritarian leadership can generate substantial commonality among the contending actors within their governments, and the closed nature of the systems will maintain a greater sense of unity in the policies being adopted than might actually be the case. Still, some of the same divisions that exist in any government may make governance more difficult than would normally be expected.

Democratic political systems provide for very different and more problematic forms of goal-selection. For example, Richard Rose (1975) confronted the question of goal-selection in attempting to understand how political parties are able to impose their control over government. He argued that two of the conditions for party government are that the political party must articulate a set of goals that they will pursue once in office, and secondly that they must allow voters to understand what mechanisms the party will use to achieve those goals. Party platforms and the campaign for election are used as means of informing the public about these likely policy consequences of their choosing one party of another.

Even within democratic systems there may be marked differences in the style of selecting goals and the willingness to bear high decision-making costs. Arend Lijphart (1984, 1999) distinguishes between *majoritarian* and *consensual* styles in democracies. In majoritarian systems, most notably the Anglo-American systems, the expectation is that a single political party will win and will have a clear mandate to implement its policies. It will then be judged retrospectively (Fiorina, 2002) on the success or failure of its policies at the next election. In such a system, the decision-making costs are relatively low, although the political parties in these systems tend to be coalitions of various internal factions that have to be rewarded after the election. Hence, cabinets in the majoritarian systems are not as united as they might appear simply from party labels. For example, the cabinets of Tony Blair and Gordon Brown in the United Kingdom were often divided between allies of those two leaders. Still, the members of the cabinet all do have that single party label and have the incentive to maintain their party in office and the party is able to punish members who do not cooperate in office. Conversely, exclusion costs may be rather high for members of the losing party or parties, who will simply have to wait until they get a chance to try out their own programs, and exclude the other party.

This variation in party control of government in majoritarian systems and the tendency of the public to make their assessments of parties and governments retrospectively raise some questions about goal-selection within these systems. One argument would be that the differences among the parties are less than they sometimes appear, and the catch-all parties (see Duverger, 1951; Mair, 1997) that have been typical of majoritarian systems may have broad agreement about goals and policy. That argument would have appeared valid during the period of postwar consensus, but that consensus appeared to have been broken during the Reagan and Thatcher years in the United States and the United Kingdom, and if anything, the differences between the parties continue to increase, so that elections are now more about stark choices about the future (Fiorina and Abrams, 2008).

A second argument is that voting is less retrospective than it is sometimes assumed to be. Economic conditions are a reasonable predictor of voting, and of the fate of a government, but by no means the sole predictor, and the public appear to make some prospective judgments about parties and about their candidates (Lewis-Beck, 2008). Those judgments are not always very sophisticated, but they will be made. Further, the past behavior of parties in office often is a good predictor of their future behavior so that voters with some memory of the past will be able to guess what goals a party running for office will pursue if elected. Unfortunately, as party dealignment continues and political parties tend to come and go more than in the past (Mair and van Biezen, 2001), this information is becoming less available and less valuable.[8]

Following from the above argument, new political parties have been emerging, even in majoritarian systems that offer different sets of goals to the public. These parties often offer extreme platforms on the left or the right, or raise issues that the conventional political parties have chosen to ignore. Again, even in some majoritarian systems, these parties may be able to affect the goals being pursued by government, even if they are not likely to form governments. Perhaps, the clearest example of a party like that would be the Reform Party in Canada (Laycock, 2002). This party has gone from being a small, seemingly radical party in Alberta to being the second-largest party in the Ottawa parliament. Although perhaps incapable of forming a government in the foreseeable future, this party has been successful in raising a range of issues and in altering the discourse of Canadian politics, having been largely absorbed into the Conservative Party (for European parties, see Spoon, 2011).

---

[8] The same political elites, however, may go from one party to another so the more astute voter may be able to make some predictions about future goals.

Finally, there is a continuing argument that parliamentary systems, and especially those of the majoritarian systems, are becoming "presidentialized" (Poguntke and Webb, 2007; Savoie, 2010). In these arguments, goal-selection in the public sector is increasingly dominated by prime ministers and cabinets, and ordinary members of parliament have had their opportunities for affective governance diminished. In this view, goals have become more political than governmental, with leaders attempting to ensure their reelection, if not their beatification, through controls over the media and controls over the remainder of government.

In consensual democratic systems, the political styles are substantially different. In consensual systems, governments are almost always coalitions, sometimes coalitions of numerous parties. Further, coalitions are increasingly drawn from across the political spectrum, as in the "Rainbow Coalitions" in Finland, or the Purple Coalitions in the Netherlands.[9] Not only are these cabinets coalitions but the style of governing in these systems tends not to exclude the nonmembers so much as would be true in the majoritarian systems. In addition, there are a range of other political institutions that provide alternative venues for influence for the interests not represented in the government.[10] Thus, in these coalition and consensus systems, decision-making costs may be high, but exclusion costs will be rather low. In these systems, the overall systemic goals being pursued through government will tend to be more predictable and constant than in majoritarian systems. Further, the goals being expressed through the political system are likely to be more congruent with the interests of a range of social groups than in the majoritarian systems.

One of the crucial elements in goal-selection in both of these political systems is the process of *aggregation*. If we return to the structural-functionalist models of politics mentioned (Almond and Powell, 1966) above, one of the functional requisites for a political system was interest aggregation. That concept focused primarily on bringing together the range of interests being pressed on the decision-making apparatus

[9] The Rainbow Coalitions included parties ranging from Communists to Conservatives, although dominated by the Social Democrats. The Dutch coalitions were deemed purple because they were composed of socialists (red) and conservatives (blue).

[10] Stein Rokkan's famous dictum (1966) on Norway was that "votes count, but resources decide."

into more coherent packages. For the purposes of a model of governance, it is more appropriate to think of putting together the numerous
alternative goals being advocated by parties or other sources of ideas
about governing. The interests in the previous models may have had
broad social goals in mind, but the conceptualization was largely one of
more immediate wants and demands.

The aggregation of goals may be more difficult than putting together
interests. In the first instance, goals are somewhat more amorphous
than are interests, but also may have more of an ideological or even
philosophical element. The interests being articulated toward the public sector were generally conceptualized as being more immediate, and
more amenable to being monetized (see Peters and Hoornbeek, 2005),
and therefore are more negotiable than ideational elements of goals.

Although we as analysts may consider aggregation of goals and
interests an important attribute in governance, many actors in the
political system are more interested in pushing a single issue or a very
limited agenda of items. The growth of single issue parties in many
political systems, especially in proportional representation systems
that make the representation of new political parties easier, has tended
to focus political attention on narrow goals (see Meguid, 2010). While
these goals may be important, and perhaps central, to some segments
of society, they rarely can provide the broader and more aggregative
social goals that we are assuming that are crucial for effective
governance.

In addition to the development of single issue parties, the increasing
use of referenda to resolve political issues also makes the identification
and pursuit of broader social goals and more coherent packages of
goals more difficult (Budge, 1998). Referenda have become popular as
a means of policy-making as the public has lost faith in the formal
institutions of government as effective means of making those choices
(Norris, 2011; Nye and Zelikow, 1997). Advocates of referenda see it is
a means of bypassing institutions that have become, in their view,
hopelessly bogged down in compromise and detail, and too subject to
influence from special interests. Even in cases such as Switzerland with
extensive histories of using referenda to legislate, this instrument has
become used much more extensively, at times producing results that are
inconsistent and hence virtually impossible to implement.

Given the limited capacity of the average citizen to cope with the
complexity of contemporary policy issues, and with the demands of

contemporary governing, the referendum is probably a very blunt instrument for setting collective goals for the society. This method tends to take issues one at a time and must find some rather simple yes or no answer to the perceived problem, often a rather complex one. Thus, goal-selection in this method of making decisions involves choosing one goal at a time, and making some popular choice about that goal, generally removed from context and generally also with few of the constraints – law, budget, personnel – that would trouble members of the formal institutions of government when they are making policy. Further, fundamentally the referendum is a majoritarian device, with winner taking all as a central feature. Hence, as this method becomes more widely used in consensual societies, it may upset the balance existing among the relevant social forces.

The most important element of the goal-selection process for our purposes is that it is to be a set of *collective* goals that emerge. A crucial aspect of our unfashionable interest in the more traditional institutions of government as an important component of governance is that these institutions are peculiarly suited for dealing with collective goal-selection. In particular, these institutions have legitimate procedures for selecting those goals from among the panoply of available goals. In most instances, it is the legislative institutions that are charged with reconciling a range of competing and perhaps also complementary goals into reasonable packages for governing. As already noted, however, in some societies those legislative institutions are supplemented by structures that link state and society directly, with the state then becoming one of a number of bargainers over policy. In the end, however, the state must certify the decisions made through corporate or analogous structures as being *the* decisions with the force of law, so it then must become something more than an equal partner in the governing process. It has been perhaps too easy for students of networks and similar structures to assume that because the state becomes one of many participants in bargaining that it has somehow ceded its role as primus inter pares. We are arguing, however, that the formal-legal role is still there and is little less significant than in a more hierarchical system of policy-making.

The most important of the mechanisms for resolving multiple and potentially conflicting goals in government is majority rule. The virtue of majority rule as a principle for resolving goal disputes is that it is widely accepted within most western societies (see Buchanan and

Tullock, 1962). Even though individuals and groups may be losers in the political process, they may still accept the outcome of majoritarian processes. Even in the consensual societies discussed above, the notion of majority rule is accepted for many aspects of policy-making. There may be mechanisms for compensation, and means of pursuing the goals of those who lose, but the implicit justice of the system may be accepted.

The additional advantage that the public sector may have for goal-selection is the very fact that it is indeed *public*. Increasingly, transparency is an element of public governance so that the winners and losers are more identifiable than in the less transparent systems for making decisions such as networks. Although the network model may have a great deal of legitimacy for the participants, that legitimacy may not extend to other members of the political system who are excluded from the process. Indeed, the members of society who are excluded from those processes may consider that the decisions are quite illegitimate, given that the authority of the public sector may be lent to private actors.

Even in cases in which the usual standard of majority rule does not appear suitable, constitutional and other compacts provide mechanisms for making decisions. In particular, issues of meta-governance – choosing rules about making rules – tend to require more than simple majorities, or may require majorities at several points in time, in order to be adopted. In some countries, such as Switzerland, very high barriers are presented to any would-be change in the public sector, in order to set broad social goals.

Resource Mobilization. Once the goals of governance have been set and the strategies to attain those goals have been designed, resources must be mobilized to sustain the collective projects. In theory, government is well positioned to extract resources from society. The history of the development of states tends to begin with the development of laws and institutions that allowed government to tax its citizens (see Finer, 1999). We see similar patterns of evolving resource mobilization today in many developing countries (Persson, 2008). Over the past couple of decades, however, tax fatigue has emerged in many of the advanced western democracies.

This growing critique against increasing taxes has driven government to explore alternative sources of funds to support collective action. Even within the tax system itself, there are shifts away from direct and more visible taxes toward less visible taxes such as expenditure (sales and excise) taxation. In particular, governments have tended to increase levels of "sin taxes" on alcohol, tobacco, and gambling, knowing that the demand for these commodities and "services" is relatively inelastic.

In addition to shifting the pattern of taxation, governments have also begin to utilize fees, charges, and instruments such as lotteries to raise money without raising taxes. These tend to be favored by citizens because they permit some choices – you do not have to go to the municipal swimming pool, but if you do, you pay the fee – and because they are directly linked to a service. Similarly, even for taxes, those revenue measures that are directly linked to a service – revenue from the state lottery in Pennsylvania, for example – goes only to fund services for senior citizens. Even in areas that tend to be averse to new taxes, these "earmarked" taxes generally will pass in referenda.

We should not, however, constrain thinking about resource mobilization by governments and their allies totally in terms of revenues for the public sector itself. Especially in developmental states such as the "Little Tigers" in Asia, governance involves leveraging actors in the private sector to pursue broad social goals as well as their own private goals. The public sector can utilize regulatory methods, as well as partnerships of all sorts, to generate investment and speed economic growth. These countries also have significant sovereign wealth funds that they use to pursue economic development through the private sector. These forms of action indeed fit neatly into the governance framework of interaction and cooperation between a range of actors in the pursuit of collective goals.

Implementation. After programs have been designed and integrated as more or less coherent packages, those programs must be implemented and made to work effectively. Program implementation has been a major component of the study of public administration and public policy, and this is also a crucial aspect of governance (Pressman and Wildavsky, 1974; Winter, 2012). There is little reason to invest time and energy in developing policy goals and the programs required for reaching those desired goals, if those programs cannot be made to perform adequately in the real world of governing. The implementation of public programs is rarely if ever easy, but when we relate this more directly to the other elements of governance, the inherent difficulties of implementation may be enhanced. That is, the governance model we have been developing is premised on a notion of setting policy goals and achieving those goals, while the implementation literature often demonstrates how and why that pursuit of goals does not occur in practice as it is designed.

The failures that have dominated academic discussions of implementation appear to arise in part from the failures of goal-selection in governments. While in a democratic state, the implementors should not necessarily tell the goal-setters what they should do, the goal-setters do not always pay careful attention to the nature of the implementation process and what will have to happen in order for their goals to be put into effect. The "backwards mapping" or "bottom up" (Elmore, 1979; but see Sabatier and Jenkins-Smith, 1993) approaches to implementation made this point, albeit in a rather different manner, some time ago, but the questions of how to relate goals to the implementation process remains. We will not argue, as the more extreme versions of the bottom up approach have, that goals are largely determined by the prospects for implementation. On the other hand, however, it seems naive to assume that goal-selection should not take into account some aspects of implementation.

Governments often do themselves great harm when they select more specific and immediate goals as means of elaborating the larger goals that have been selected (Tarschys, 2003). Much of the failure of programs has to do with goals that are vague, or unreachable, or simply unrealistic. The nature of politics is, however, such that rational designs and a cascading of broader goals into more operational goals, as might be expected in a system of strategic management, can rarely be achieved, if such a rationalist style of establishing goals runs counter to the political imperatives of coalition-building and bounded rationality that are better explanations for governing styles.

To a great extent, the linkage between goals and implementation reflects the process of designing programs mentioned above. Instruments are the means that link goals that governments wish to achieve with the actual delivery of services. Further, rather than being neutral instruments for implementation, policy tools have political dimensions of their own and reflect political coalition-building just as does the process of selecting goals (Macdonald, 2008; Peters, 2001b).

Of course, implementation failures also result from failings in administration. The majority of these failings are not willful sabotage on the part of civil servants but rather represent pathologies of formal organizations, perhaps especially formal organizations in the public sector. Christopher Hood some time ago (1976b) pointed to the "Limits of Administration" and the problems he identified there in managing and implementing public programs continue until this day. For example, the difficulties in managing information flows in organizations, and perhaps among organizations, in the public sector continue to reduce the effectiveness of public administration and to produce results that can only be deemed suboptimal only if one is being too polite.[11] Coordination problems of all sorts (Peters, 2015) limit the capacity of governments to pursue the broader public goals discussed earlier. The list could easily be extended but the basic point would remain that governance is dependent upon implementation, and successful implementation is very hard work.

The administrative reforms generally referred to as the "New Public Management" (Hood, 1991; Pollitt and Bouckaert, 2011) have been designed to address some dimensions of the implementation problems that arise out of formal organization in government, and their reliance on hierarchy, rules, and monopoly provision of services (Peters, 2001a). In particular, these reforms have been designed to bring the (presumably superior) ideas of managing from the private sector into the public sector to make government more effective and more efficient. The outcomes of these changes have not been unambiguous, and the results have varied across countries and across policy areas. However, the consequences of administrative reform in the implementation processes, as viewed from our governance perspective, are more mixed than the advocates of these changes might have wished.

One finding about these reforms is that it does appear that the adoption of NPM reforms, meaning here particularly market-based reforms, has made individual public programs and organizations somewhat more efficient, but, on the other hand, the focus on program by program management tends to divert attention from broader policy goals. This effect of NPM is apparent for both structural reforms such as the creation of autonomous public agencies (Pollitt and Talbot,

---

[11] The most egregious recent example of these failures of information is the intelligence failure before September 11, 2001 in the United States (Boin et al., 2005). While much of the information that might have been needed to prevent the disaster was indeed available, it was held by different organizations that did not coordinate their efforts and indeed attempted to use information as a resource in bureaucratic politics.

2003) and procedural remedies such as performance management. The structural reforms have tended to disaggregate government and to increase the transaction costs that are incurred when organizations have to cooperate with one another. The procedures have tended to focus attention on limited definitions of efficiency and therefore to make managers less concerned about governance taken more broadly.

The above having been said, there are certainly ways of using some of the fundamental ideas of NPM while at the same time attempting to implement a more comprehensive conception of governance for society. If, for example, we take performance management as an indicator of the styles of reform that are being implemented, then the public sector can develop broad measures of the performance of the public sector as well as the more sector-specific indicators that have attracted most of the attention in government. The government of New Zealand, for example, has developed "Strategic Results Areas" that capture performance in some broad areas of government, that can complement the "Key Results Areas" that are more closely tied to programs and organizations (Halligan, 1997). In the United States, the programmatic Government Performance and Results Act (GPRA) has been supplemented by some "government-wide" performance areas.

Another important aspect of the implementation process for governance is the linkage of public programs with the social partners in the networks that surround the public sector. This linkage is in some ways a major strength in governance, but in other ways it also presents a number of vexing problems for individuals programs and perhaps especially for the more integrated sense of goal-selection and goal-attainment process that we consider essential to governance. On the positive side of the ledger, the societal partners of government programs are important sources of assistance in implementation, just as they are sources of advice and information as goals are determined and the means for reaching those goals are designed (Howlett, Ramesh and Perl, 2009).

On the other hand, the linkage of interest groups to particular programs tends to isolate the programs and to exacerbate the coordination and coherence problems that are inherent in the public sector. If the implementation of the programs depends upon the beneficiaries in the form of the interest groups, then the goals of the programs may be displaced from more public gorals to more special interest goals.

This capture of programs may be especially characteristic of pluralist formats for governance (see Chapter 4).

Even when there are not the almost organic linkages between state and society assumed in the network literature social actors, these partners – groups, individuals, movements, etc. – can still contribute to the delivery of services. One of the most obvious contributions to governance can be in the delivery of services in a manner that may be more acceptable to the clients of the programs, and less expensive, than if the services are delivered directly by government. For example, immigrant groups often prefer social services delivered by nongovernmental organizations, fearing that their immigration status is being monitored along with the service delivery. This involvement need not be a total delegation of responsibility for those programs to the partners, but indeed may be a genuine partnership. Further, as we will develop in subsequent chapters, there are marked comparative differences in the ways in which state and society interact as they work to provide services. Even the language may vary, as Anglo-American systems tend to refer to the groups as "interest groups" while other systems may have more positive conceptions.

The negative potential of these relationships for governance is to some extent a result of the strengths. That is, the linkages between the state and social actors may involve diversion from the presumed goals of governance in favor of more specific goals that are linked to the groups (see Peters, 2014). The possible diversion of goals from the more general (and we hope democratically selected) goals is to some extent a price that is paid for the involvement of the groups. Further, the involvement of the social partners often is justified as a form of democracy. As Stein Rokkan (1966) argued with respect to corporate pluralism in Norway and other parts of Scandinavia, the involvement of social actors can be a separate form of representation that complements that provided through elected, territorial representation that is central to democratic governing. That may be true in some instances, but that representation may be effective in involving groups and individuals directly concerned with the policy area but may exclude others. This will, in turn, produce outcomes that may satisfy those participants in the process but those results may be less desirable from broader social perspectives.

This tendency of governance processes to reward the participants is reflected in part in the segmentation of governments in general, not just in the manner in which they interact with their social partners. The segmentation of governments into ministries and agencies tends to segment policy-making activities, with some narrowing of focus and the use of expert advice from a relatively narrow range of sources. While specialization certainly creates some benefits for governance, it also limits the capacity to address larger and more comprehensive issues (Bouckaert, Peters, and Verhoest, 2010).

Evaluation, Feedback, and Learning. The final requirement for effective governance that we have posited is that there must be adequate mechanisms for accountability and feedback. After the public sector acts, with or without the involvement of their social partners, there is a need to assess the consequences of those actions. This need for external assessment of public action is especially evident for governance in democratic regimes, but it is also important for less democratic means of steering society.[12] We are arguing, therefore, that any adequate governing process must be designed in a way that provides its participants with some understanding of how they have governed in the past and hence some more information about how they should govern in the future. For the less democratic forms of governance, the feedback may be used primarily to make the policy choices more effective, rather than for responsiveness to public demands, but even for those regimes there is some level of policy failure that may engender popular reaction.

The location of this element of political life in a central position in this model to some extent differentiates governance from the earlier structural functionalist models of politics. While it is true that the systems models that were in part coupled with structural-functionalism (see Easton, 1965b; Finkle and Gable, 1973) did contain an element of feedback in their conceptualization of the political process, that linkage was assumed to go back into the input side of government, and to have its effects primarily through the usual mechanisms of inputs – wants and demands from the public. The governance model does include some elements of that reasoning, but it also permits a more direct connection between the mechanisms of accountability and feedback and the public sector itself. Thus, in the governance model we develop here, the public sector can act more autonomously from social actors in coping with its

---

[12] For nondemocratic governments there is still some need to maintain legitimacy, so that making good policy is not unimportant. Given that these governments would have few procedural mechanisms for maintaining legitimacy, the substantive ones of making good policy may be all the more important.

reactions to its own actions than might have been the case for structural-functional models and their allies.

The notion of governance we are developing here is to some extent cybernetic. That is, we consider it important to assess the extent to which governments are conscious of their own actions and respond to the failure, or even success, of their policy choices (see Bovens, 't Hart and Peters, 2001). This perspective on governing involves a normative stance on what constitutes "good governance" (see later), believing that more responsive governing systems provide better governance, but it is also an empirical question. To what extent have governments organized themselves to receive feedback, and to what extent are they predisposed to maintain established policy paths, even when confronted with information that indicates the undesirability of those established paths? These questions and others like them will say a good deal about the steering capacity of governments.

This notion of cyberneticism within government should not be taken, however, to imply a pursuit of equilibrium as has been true for most systems models of politics (see Peters, 2014). Rather, we are concerned with the ability of the governance arrangements to receive, process, and act on information received from the society. At one level, this cybernetic quality of governance might be manifested as "evidence-based policymaking," while at a higher level, it may be manifested in changing goals and overall orientations to policy-making.

Accountability and feedback for governance does have the two basic, and somewhat distinct, purposes. The first purpose is to provide for accountability, and again especially for democratic systems. The public should have some means of determining what actions have been taken in their name, and whether those actions were what was intended as a result of the previous election, or perhaps whether they were appropriate despite any previous elections. They should be able to determine whether the actions taken were even legal, no matter what their standing as responsive to popular demands. In contemporary democracies, as important as elections and other forms of representation are, output democracy, based on evaluation of government performance, may be at least as relevant as input mechanisms (Weiler, 2012). The argument is that the prospective nature of voting and even interest group representation is substantially less certain than assessing the actual behavior of government.

The importance of output democracy in contemporary society emphasizes the importance of direct government contacts with society through the bureaucracy, and through actual program delivery. The average citizen is unlikely to encounter his or her elected representatives on a regular basis, but will encounter public servants on almost a daily basis. These "street level bureaucrats" (Lipsky, 1980; Meyer and Vorsanger, 2003) are arguably the crucial links between state and society for the average citizen, but that role is often poorly understood by both citizens and by people in government. These interactions are important for both stylistic and substantive reasons. How citizens are treated by the bureaucrats whom they encounter (see Goodsell, 2000) is likely to influence their assessment of government more generally, and therefore this aspect of governance again is crucial for determining how contemporary democracies perform, at least in the mind of the public.

Substantively, public employees at this level of government have substantial discretion, and the manner in which that discretion is exercised will make a good deal of difference for the outcomes of the policy process for individual citizens (Huber and Shipan, 2002). Political science tends to focus on major decisions made by parliaments or by political executives, and these decisions are certainly worthy of our concern, but the vast majority of decisions made by government are actually made at the very lowest level of the public bureaucracy. These decisions are in general the "mere application" of the law, but still there is discretion involved. Which law will be applied, and how stringently or how leniently will it be applied? Further, this discretion is exercised with respect to a particular case, meaning an individual citizen, and often in a face-to-face situation with that citizen. Again, for many people that contact with the bureaucrat, and that decision, is government, and governance.

The importance of these direct linkages between service providers and citizens constitute another part of the logic for using nongovernmental actors in service delivery, and therefore part of the logic for the "governance without government" approach we have been discussing. Although the rigidities of public organizations are sometimes exaggerated, nongovernmental organizations often do have the capacity to respond to popular demands in more flexible ways than might be possible if the laws governing the decision are to be followed in any meaningful fashion. Therefore, if service delivery can be contracted out, or performed in a collaborative manner with actors in the private sector, then the provision may be more acceptable. That enhanced acceptability of not-for-profit providers may be important in social policy and immigration policy, for example, because of fears that arise when the socially excluded have to confront the public bureaucracy (Benn, 2002). Regulatory activities may also be a natural domain for this style of governance, with the view to using more for-profit contractors than the not-for-profits more common in the social service sector.

As well as the strictly evaluative element of this feedback and accountability in governance, there is an important substantive and cognitive element as well. That is, how have programs performed, and are there ways of improving that performance? This cognitive element is closely linked with several approaches to administrative reforms already discussed. Performance management, in particular, has emphasized the evaluation and assessment of programs (Bouckaert and Halligan, 2007). As discussed above, however, the emphasis has been largely on administration, and enhancing efficiency when public sector programs are delivered. As we will discuss it here, however, performance management can also be concerned with both a means of evaluating government that can assist citizens in their democratic endeavors and also aid government in their attempts to not only deliver programs well but also hold programs and their personnel accountable for the choices they make in delivery.

While many systems of performance management have a high technical content and are suitable to discussions among professionals in government and in specific policy areas, there can also be a public element of these systems as well. For example, "scorecards" (Gormley and Weimer, 1999) and league tables (see Hood et al., 2004) can be developed through performance management techniques and then made available to the public. The public then can decide if, for example, they want to mobilize to deal with a failing school, or with an unsafe hospital, or whatever type of inadequate service they may be receiving. This use of information is the democratic side of feedback to government that can supplement and perhaps supplant the more official forms of interaction, that are perhaps more central to the use of performance indicators.

As we consider the democratic elements of performance and the relationship to the development of mechanisms for feedback and control, we need to think about the implications of relying upon information as a principal source of control over government (Hood et al., 2004). We are arguing that information devices such as those contained in "No Child Left behind" in the United States are necessary but not sufficient for managing accountability (Linn, Baker, and Betebenner, 2002). Further, placing a great deal of emphasis on performance-based mechanisms such as this has significant class implications. The assumption of information devices for accountability is that once parents learn that their children's school is substandard, they will immediately rush to organize and exert effective pressure on the appropriate officials to make improvements in the school. That assumption is probably true for middle-class parents, but probably much less true for working-class and underclass parents who may lack the organizational and communications skills necessary to produce the needed political pressures. Given this potential problem, and perhaps other, in the too facile reliance on mechanisms of feedback for addressing problems of accountability, we have been placing somewhat greater emphasis on internal processes within government processes itself.

Performance management is important as a means of judging how government is performing, but it tends to assume that the goals of the governing process are accepted and appropriate. As we consider the governance of societies, we need to think somewhat more about not only changing the day-to-day administration of public programs but also changing the goals toward which we are steering. Thus, the feedback elements of governance may involve learning not only about the performance of government and its programs, but also about how realistic (and socially acceptable) are the goals being pursued by the government. We intimated above that coping with goals is one of the most difficult aspects of the governance process, and certainly it is for the analysis of governance. Coping with goal change may be even more difficult, as aspirations are likely to continue and individuals and their organizations are likely to continue to press for certain types of programs. The programs themselves will have a strong inertial tendency, in part from sincere commitments to goals and in part from an instance for self-preservation. Therefore, thinking about successive iterations of policy-making and their impacts on goals will require developing a stronger political capacity than most countries can muster.

At a more extreme level of using information in the public sector, we can conceptualize the public sector in cybernetic terms (Baumgartner and Jones, 2015; Deutsch, 1966; Peters, 2012a). In this perspective, governments can be conceptualized as utilizing feedback from their policy initiatives to guide further policy interventions. This style of governing, in turn, requires developing sensitive information gathering and processing capacities within the public sector. This development is not conceptualized primarily in a technical sense, i.e. "E-government," but more in the sense of the capacity of public sector institutions to process information effectively and understand the implications of their previous actions for future governance.

In contemporary governance, much of the discussion of this capacity of the state to learn and to build on its previous interventions is expressed as "evidence-based policymaking" (Sanderson, 2002). In this conception of governance, the public sector can learn from policy innovations in other settings and therefore can reduce their own chances for error and poor policies. That said, however, governments are generally rather poor at learning from other cultural and political settings, tending to make assumptions that these conditions are not particularly relevant for implementing programs. In reality, however, the success and failure of policies, and governance more generally, depends upon the congruence of policies and the environment within which they are being implemented.

Caveats on the Model

The model of governance we have presented to this point is analogous to stages models of the policy process (see Jones, 1984; Hupe and Hill, 2006). Like those models, when presented in a simple descriptive form, the governance model appears excessively linear and also appears to assume that one phase of the model neatly and easily follows the other. While this apparent simplicity is necessary for presentation purposes, we do recognize that the real world of governing is substantially more complex and that there are dynamics involved that do not conform to the linear presentation. There are multiple connections among the stages and among the actors involved in the stages that move governance away from any simple linear process.

In the first place, the real world of politics may mean that actors may intervene at any of the phases of the model in order to produce action. For example, if we utilize the logic of the garbage can (Cohen, March, and Olsen, 1972) then goals may arise from action, rather than actions arising from goals. Similarly, the accountability and feedback stage of the process is the natural beginning of a new round of governing, as the actors involved learn from their prior success and failures and attempt to improve the quality of subsequent governance. Indeed, most policy-making and governance should not be conceptualized as beginning with a tabula rasa, but rather as attempting to intervene in a governance space that is already crowded with existing programs, policies, and institutions (Carter, 2012; Hogwood and Peters, 1983). That crowding can help to legitimate the policy but may also limit the number of possible policy choices.

The simple linear model of governance (as is true for the stages model of policy) can be argued to be devoid of agency. As we think through the application of this model to real-world political systems, it is crucial to consider the role that actors play in moving governance initiatives forward and making decisions about each of the functions involved. Much of the discussion of governance has been about institutions and structures, but we need also to understand how actors are involved and how the roles that they play in making governance function. This is as true for the roles of social actors as it is for the role of government actors in the process.

Finally, we must ask if there are any crucial elements of governance that have been excluded from this model. Although we could disaggregate the model even more, and enumerate a number of additional sub-functions, we believe that the functional categories contained in this model do capture the essence of governance. We cover the process from the initial formulation of goals through the evaluation of the success or failure of the programs. Further, as developed these functions can be utilized to describe and compare governance in a wide range of political systems.

Conclusion: What Must We Do to Govern and to Govern Well?

This chapter has advanced a set of functions that are crucial for governance and described some aspects of the political processes involved in governing. As already noted, this analysis is clearly functionalist. We are arguing that there are some activities that must be performed if governance is to be said to have been delivered to society. Much of the debate about governance in political science has involved defining whether one way or another of performing these functions should be defined as governance, or whether one version or another is more democratic or more effective. We are arguing, however, that answering those questions requires us to begin at the beginning, and ask what activities must be performed in governing the society. We can then proceed, as we will in subsequent chapters, to consider what actors are involved, and the consequences of difference constellations of actors.

Although we have not settled on a single format for governance, or even a single desirable format for governance, the question of "how" is far from unimportant – indeed it is so important that we leave it open for multiple formats, and use those multiple formats as a basis of comparison. Governance provides an approach to comparison that focuses on the activities of the public sector (and its social partners). The concept of governance certainly is concerned with processes involved in making decisions that generate the outputs, and approaching basic political processes from the perspective of governance provides greater insight into how governments work, alone and in conjunction with other actors. And it is also concerned with the capacity of these processes within countries to provide effective public services to their citizens.

This model of governance appears to focus heavily on the capacity of those involved to make and implement public policy given that our principal concern in governance is making decisions and implementing changes in the economy and society. That said, governance does involve a wider range of concerns than does most policy analysis, given that we are concerned with the political institutions through which goals are established. Further, we are also concerned with the comparative dimensions of governing, so that the nature of political regimes as they govern becomes crucial to the analysis.

We will now proceed to study decision-making more in-depth before we apply this basic framework for studying governance to five types of governance systems existing within democratic political systems. We will thereby attempt to demonstrate that this approach to governance can be a fruitful mechanism for comparative political analysis. The analysis of the various formats for public governance will be done largely through the development of ideal types, and the examples will be drawn from a limited array of cases, but the analysis will still demonstrate the utility of this approach to governance for comparison, and indeed the need to bring a governance perspective to comparative politics.

3 | Decision-Making
The Essence of Governing

We argued earlier that governance is about governing, and governing is primarily a matter of decision-making. The functionalist approach typically includes decision-making as a core function of government, and the definition of politics in systems theory as the "authoritative allocation of values" also identifies decision-making as the essence of governing (Easton, 1965). Unfortunately, much of the structural-functionalist and systems theoretical work of that period tended to treat decision-making in the passive voice. That is, saying "decisions are made" does not really provide a great deal of understanding of how decisions are made or who makes them.

Decision-making is action, not debate. It is about making final priorities and allocating public resources to various programs and purposes, but it is also about settling disputes, enforcing rules, and bringing closure to issues. Again, we need to consider how those decisions are made and the manner in which different types of actors are involved. Perhaps most importantly, there is no single answer about the who and how of decision-making, and our comparative analysis of governance becomes all the more important as a means of understanding the varieties of governance available.

We will argue that in order to understand the linkage between decision-making theory and governance theory, we need to think of decision-making not just as a formal or legal process designed to facilitate debate and formal decisions but also as a societal process where governing institutions set priorities for society and impose regulation and other authoritative measures to involve society in the pursuit of those collective priorities. Some time ago now, Riker (1962: 10–11), echoing Lasswell (1936), pointed out that "if, as Easton asserts, politics is the authoritative allocation of values and if ... 'allocation' refers not to a physical process but to a social process of deciding how a physical process shall be carried out, then the subject studied by political scientists is decision making." This perspective on decision-making emphasizes the centrality of decision-making, both in governance and in the study of politics. The focus on decision-making is not an artifact of the functionalist approach to governance; the argument is rather that decision-making is the critical, defining phase of the policy-making process and in governance more broadly.

Furthermore, Riker's argument that decision-making is both a "physical process" and a social process highlights the societal embeddedness of governing. Government decision-making always takes place in an interactive societal context; most decisions aim at steering or regulating society in some aspect, and most decisions are informed by a dialogue between government and societal actors and interests. We suggest that the concept of a formal process captures the first aspect of decision-making better than Riker's notion of a "physical process" as both the governmental and interactive dimensions of decision-making tend to be very concrete and formalized processes. Thus, throughout this chapter, we will be discussing the formal and social processes that comprise decision-making.

So far, we have discussed decision-making as one of several functions of governance, assuming no hierarchy among these functions. There are three basic ways to think about decision-making in a functionalist analysis. One perspective, following the previous discussion, would be to argue that decision-making is the dominant function of government actors in governance. The system of government is essentially a decision-making system. The stages model of policy analysis (Hupe and Hill, 2006) highlights the procedural logic of public decision-making from goal-selection to evaluation. The functions elaborated in this book follow the same sequence, from goal-selection via resource mobilization and decision-making to implementation and evaluation, feedback, and learning.

First, we can, as was done in Chapter 2, discuss decision-making primarily as a formal process, virtually synonymous with policy formulation. This is certainly an important aspect of governance and does involve making difficult choices about policy instruments and other modes of intervention. While that is indeed important, we will also need to consider how decisions are made throughout the governance process and therefore must consider confining a consideration of decision-making to only policy formulation as somewhat inadequate.

A second option, looking at decision-making as the dominant function of government within governance, suggests that all other functions are subordinate to decision-making and that they, in different ways, represent stages of a decision-making process either preparing decisions (goal-selection, resource mobilization, and feedback and learning) or implementing decisions (implementation). This perspective represents an important analytical question for governance and policy. How can we integrate all the numerous decisions that must be made in all the stages of governing into policies and overall governance outcomes? That appears to imply rather detailed process-tracing for each aspect of governance (see Bennett and George, 2005). That may be useful for the analysis of specific decisions but perhaps not as a more general manner of assessing governance. This approach draws on both the formal and social dimensions of decision-making.

The third possible perspective on decision-making is to consider it as a function permeating all other functions of governance. On reflection, it appears clear that functions such as goal-selection, resource mobilization, and implementation all entail significant elements of making decisions. Indeed, each one of these stages involves multiple decisions. Goal-selection clearly involves decision-making and setting priorities; resource mobilization requires answers to questions about who should pay for, and who should benefit from, collective projects; and implementation is fraught with difficult operative decisions (Lipsky, 1980; Pressman and Vildawsky, 1974; Winter, 2012). Further, each of these stages may involve a variety of actors who will interact in a variety of ways to produce the final governance outcomes. Thus, this perspective brings forth the social, interactive dimension of decision-making although there is also attention to the formal process.

The distinction between these latter two perspectives is central to governance analysis. If we adopt the first of those perspectives, defining decision-making as the dominant function of government, we may appear to define away much of the significance of the exchange between government and societal partners which is fundamental to governance. If governance is all about decision-making and government monopolizes that function, what roles remain for the governance partners and how important are those roles? If we, on the other hand, accept the view that decision-making is a feature of all aspects of governing, we also allow for taking into account the importance of exchanges between the state and societal actors throughout the policy process.

Observing decision-making as a function that in effect shapes all functions of government thus opens up the analysis for a wider and more encompassing governance analysis compared to the previous perspective on decision-making. Thus, although we discuss decision-making as a separate function, as already observed, it can be found in all the other functions such as implementation and resource attachment.

Thus, emphasizing the formal dimension of decision-making may appear to privilege or exaggerate the role of government in governance. Even in the latter perspective where decision-making is an omnipresent aspect of all functions of government, it might appear as if this approach would be the undisputed hub of governance. While we argue that government is central to governance, as previous chapters have shown, we do emphasize the societal aspect of decision-making, i.e. the collaborative and inclusive nature of governance. As a result, and particularly when drawing on the wider definition of decision-making, we do not believe that this will tilt the analysis toward a more state-centric view than the empirical reality of governance cases may warrant. If formal, political decision-making is still controlled by government, the type of decision-making that takes place in goal-selection and implementation, for instance, is far more reflective of the wider societal involvement which is typical to contemporary governance. And in perhaps less obvious ways, these actors also influence evaluation and especially feedback from governance decisions back into the process. Again, we should think of decision-making as both a formal and a social process. The two types of processes are to some extent related. Governments which make decisions without any consultation with key societal actors, i.e. focusing only on the formal process, may find that the implementation of those decisions will be more challenging compared to decision-making which combines such a formal process with social consultation, i.e. a social process.

Therefore, we argue that decision-making provides insights into the processes of governing that cannot be obtained through more formal and static conceptions of governance. At the same time, we argue that it is essential to analyze the formal and societal aspects of decision-making in their political and institutional context and not to define away contextual factors which may hold a significant part of understanding decision-making processes and outcomes. This perspective does not, as it might appear, privilege any set of actors but rather asks questions about the range of actors involved and the manner in which they become involved. This is a more dynamic conception of governance than can be provided through assuming that one set of actors or another is dominant and further assuming that the manner of involvement may be relatively invariable.

But saying that decision-making is essential to understanding governance is only the beginning of the analysis that is necessary. How are these decisions made, and what intellectual models can be used to understand how decisions are made in governing? Further, how do we integrate the political dimensions of decision-making into models of decisions that tend to be focused on more formal actors and formal styles of making decisions? We will be assuming that as well as attempting to cope with the policy challenges facing governments, there will be a need to respond to social and political demands. Thus, we will now explicate some of the central models of decision-making in governance and how they relate to overall collective choices.

Approaches to Decision-Making and Their Relationship to Governance

Having said that we need to place decision-making at the center of a study of governance, we must now proceed to discuss how we understand the processes through which decisions are made, and the manner in which individual decisions are linked across the governing process. Political science and public administration are inherently about making decisions and there is a range of models to consider after having made the seemingly simple statement that we need to consider decisions more carefully. However, the literature on decision-making is mainly concerned with the formal process of making decisions (Zeitz, 1999). There is a tendency to define away the political and institutional context and state–society interactions that shape decision-making in governance.

Rationality. For contemporary political science, the usual manner in which to begin considering process of making decisions about governing would be to think of these as a rational process in which the actors involved attempted to maximize their personal or organizational utility (Hindmoor and Taylor, 2015). That rationalistic perspective can be developed either in a rather simple descriptive sense or in a more formal manner. In either version of rationality, there are a set of assumptions that are fundamental to the approach and which at once strengthen the analysis produced and place constraints on the range of decisions that may be taken.

For our purposes, the first and perhaps most difficult of these assumptions is that there is a known order of preferences and these preferences are transitive. That is, if a decision-maker prefers A to B and prefers B to C, then he or she will prefer A to C. This appears to be a rather simple condition for ordering preferences, but in complex political and strategic governance situations this condition may not hold. This is in part because governance decisions involve multiple dimensions so that having to choose A or B or C involves actually making choices about a number of factors – goals, instruments, budgets – that may not all vary together in the preferences of a decision-maker.

A second assumption about rationality in governance decision-making is that all the actors involved will have the same set of preferences, or at least that their preferences will be based on roughly similar foundations. The functions of governance discussed earlier involve a range of actors, all of whom may want different things out of governing, and they may not even be thinking about the same factors. The leader of a bureaucratic agency may be thinking about maximizing the prestige or budget of the organization while the political leader may be thinking about reelection or even the best way of serving the public. These conflicting rationalities then need to be integrated in some ways through the process of governing (see later). Likewise, the inclusion of numerous social actors into the governance process may also introduce a range of preferences that are quite distinct from those held by actors within the public sector itself.

A third assumption would be that the actors involved have perfect information so that they can make rational choices among the available alternatives. And indeed, there is an assumption that the actors are aware of all the options, so that they can make the appropriate choices among them. In the real world of policy-making, there is generally very incomplete information and incomplete understanding of the options (or even of the problem being addressed, see Peters and Hoornbeek, 2005). Thus, in this setting, the possibilities for making fully rational decisions are limited, even if the actors involved are attempting to be as comprehensive as possible in their analysis. Further, with multiple actors, there may be alternative information available to different actors, further complicating reaching a collective decision. Thus, everything else being equal, we can assume that the larger the number of actors involved in decision-making and the greater the heterogeneity among those actors in terms of information, the more complex will decision-making become. This would be a defining feature of decision-making in interactive forms of governance or governance where networks are the predominant actors.

Fourthly, this model of decision-making would assume that the outcomes of a process can be assessed on a common utilitarian scale of benefits and costs. In the world of politics and governing, however, process may count for as much as substance, and image may trump reality. In the terms of March and Olsen (1989), the logic of appropriateness may be at least as important as the logic of consequentiality in understanding how to evaluate decisions made in governance. If this is the case, then decision-making may involve a set of incommensurable dimensions of evaluation, and different sets of political and policy values, which renders making a reasonable decision difficult.

Finally, a rationalistic model of decision-making for governance would assume that the consequences of the choices being made are predictable and reasonably stable. Unfortunately for policy-making and governance, making predictions about outcomes is difficult. There is, for example, a large and interesting literature on the unintended consequences of decisions made in governance, as well as on the massive failures of programs and policies (Bovens and 't Hart, 2001; Sieber, 1981). Thus, even if we were able to provide unambiguous rankings of preferences for outcomes, the ability to link those outcomes with specific governance choices may be limited, especially when considered over time.

While the assumptions about rationality discussed above give some cause for concern about this approach to understanding decision-making for governance, we can still gain some useful insights by acting "as if" the assumptions could be sustained and then looking at the ways in which decisions are being made. The simplest of these ways of understanding choices are relatively simple utilitarian models of choice and evaluation. For example, cost-benefit analysis and risk-benefit analysis assume that actors should make decisions on simple utilitarian grounds. Can we compare that criterion with the actual decisions to understand to what extent policymakers are acting in a "rational" manner?

It is important to notice in these discussions of decision-making from a rationalistic perspective that the emphasis tends to be on the formal aspects of decision-making and on single decisions rather than on the complex chains of decisions that are inherent in governance. Likewise, the emphasis is on *a* decision-maker, or a limited number of decision-makers who make bargains among themselves. These bargains are generally conceptualized as one time deals based on a particular set of preferences. Governance, on the other hand, is a continuous, societal process so that reducing transaction costs among the participants may be as important for the success or failure of the process as the rationality of any particular choice. And actors may be willing to cede potential gains at one point in time in anticipation of gains at some future (if perhaps unspecified) time, depending on differences in the intensity of their preferences. Thus, the formal and societal dimensions both offer explanation to actors' behavior in decision-making processes. Not only do different types of actors have different objectives and different degrees of intensity in their preferences; the logic of the societal process is that the process of making decisions is influenced by the actors who are the targets of those decisions and sometimes even the agents of implementing the decisions.

Analyzing decision-making in different governance arrangements shows how some models appear to perform better than others in terms of accommodating different preferences among the actors involved. In étatiste governance (see Chapter 4), the state actors will largely decide for themselves on policy with only a minimum of societal consultation. The process of making decisions is regulated in detail and societal interests have extremely limited possibilities of influencing public decision-making. In interactive governance, on the other hand, policies and decisions evolve through more or less continuous societal consultation, and the decision-making process is characterized by much less formalization and fluid participation of the actors. In terms of interest accommodation, governance models where there is a high degree of consistency in terms of who is involved in the decision-making can accommodate divergent interests by compromises over a number of issues. However, the higher the degree of turnover among actors, the less efficient such accommodation will be to resolve conflict.

One of the most familiar examples of rationality in the literature on governance is Graham Allison's study of decision-making in the Cuban

Missile Crisis (Allison and Zelikow, 1999). He examined the behavior of American and Soviet decision-makers during the crisis using three alternative frames, one of which was full rationality. This version of rationality was, however, rather informal and the conditions that would underpin that approach to governing were not fully specified. This crisis also contained multiple individual choices with tacit bargaining between the two sides. Similarly, Yehezkel Dror (1986) examined the rationality of decision-making under adversity in governance.

A more detailed set of models about the application of rationality to governance decision-making can be drawn from the literature on decision science, seeking to quantify the payoffs of making choices under risk. For example, what should a decision-maker do when faced with an event (the landfall of a hurricane) that is to some extent uncertain? There are costs and benefits associated with any action (evacuation or sit tight) and therefore we can consider the likely costs of any action given different sets of probabilities. The typical cost-benefit analysis associated with policy analysis produces the same type of analysis albeit generally without consideration of the probabilities of events.

More formal models of rational decision-making such as game theory contain most of the formal assumptions mentioned earlier. Individuals are assumed to have a set of preferences to which they can rank and can assign ordinal if not cardinal values. These models are largely based on the interaction of two or more actors who make choices in the absence of knowledge of the choices of the other participant(s) in the game. For governance, these game theoretic models are not particularly valuable because they assume actors with conflicting preferences and the absence of direct bargaining among the participants. The world of governance tends to involve multiple actors with some competing and some compatible goals engaged in long-term interactions with one another over programmatic choices. Where the game theoretic approaches do help for governance is when they are considered over an extended period of time and also involve repeated interactions and learning (Axelrod, 1984).

Models of coalition formation in the public sector also provide some insights into decision-making in governance from a more rationalist perspective (de Swaan, 1973). This perspective assumes that there are several political parties attempting to form a coalition to govern. Each political party has a set of policy preferences. These actors must then find a majority that maximizes the utility of the participants. For governance, an analogous process can be seen among actors seeking to provide some direction to government. In this way, social actors involved in a network structure with governmental actors may negotiate among themselves and with government to produce a winning coalition, i.e. a coalition that can agree upon how to manage a policy domain. That agreement may be short-lived and easily upset by defections of parties involved in the coalition, or by changes in context.

In summary, while we have an ingrained expectation, or at least hope, for rationality in decision-making, producing rational decisions is difficult. It is especially difficult in governance when there are multiple sets of preferences, actors may not even agree on the definition of the decision situation, and there is limited and often biased information. Given these barriers to comprehensive rationality, students of governance need to consider alternative models if we are to have a more realistic understanding of the manner in which decisions are made in the public sector, and through the interactions of actors in and outside that public sector.

This rather linear and formal thinking about decision-making may be even more difficult to attain in a governance setting than in a single organization, i.e. when we consider not just the formal dimension of decision-making but also the societal dimension. The multiple actors interacting to make decisions, as well as the chain of stages, going from goal-selection through implementation, and then evaluation almost certainly precludes any comprehensively rational form of decision-making. Further, the bargaining among the actors may be on a variety of different dimensions – the content of policy, institutional power, etc. – that further complicates the pursuit of rational solutions. All that said, however, the fundamental governance notion of steering toward a target appears to require at least some attention to rational planning and execution. Many of these problems are encountered in models of policy-making, especially stages models, and any useful approach to governance will need to be able to cope with the inherent complexity of these decision situations.

Bounded Rationality. All the problems with a comprehensively rationalistic perspective on decision-making for governance lead rather naturally to consideration of *bounded rationality* and means of making decisions that reflect more accurately the complex realities of governance. Indeed, some of the assumptions behind bounded rationality represent contradictions of those of comprehensive rationality in making decisions. These assumptions are, of course, also subject to criticism, and whereas comprehensively rationalistic models may be too well-specified and produce excessively neat answers to governance problems, bounded rationality may provide answers that are too indeterminate and not adequately precise.

Bounded rationality is usually associated with Herbert Simon and his studies of public administration. Simon (1947; see also Jones, 2001) argues that most of the assumptions about decision-making by "economic man" – the perfectly rational decision-maker – are not sustainable in reality. As already noted, in the public sector (or indeed in the private sector) preferences may not be transitive, and individuals may not really know their own preference orderings until confronted with specific decision situations. Likewise, the information available to decision-makers is far from perfect and indeed if individuals waited for perfect information or a full array of possible decisions they might never make a choice.

The alternative that Simon (1947) proposes to the seeming severe requirements for economic man is "administrative man." This decision-maker wants to act rationally but also understands that any decisions would inevitably be made within a set of boundaries on information and analysis. Therefore the decision-maker is well-advised to make smaller, less comprehensive decisions. These decisions should be good enough for the time being – they "satisfice" rather than maximize.

The logic of satisficing is also that the decision is good enough for the time being and can be revised continually as conditions change, new information becomes available, or new actors become involved in the governance process. This version of rationality may therefore be more suitable for governance than is the comprehensive rationality described earlier. Bounded rationality tends to recognize more that decision-making is being conducted in a much more complex world than that assumed by many of the rationalistic models of decision-making. Further, it assumes a more continuous process of making policies in which there can be some learning and some adjustment.[1]

In addition to satisficing as an acceptable, and again desirable, goal for the outcomes for a governance decision-making process,

---

[1] In fairness some later versions of rational actor approaches to policy and governance do allow for learning and more continuous adjustment of decision-making.

bounded rationality also tends to emphasize routines and standard-operating procedures as means of institutionalizing these formats for making decisions. The role of routines within the processes can be seen perhaps better in March and Olsen (1989) than in the original work by Simon. March and Olsen argue that the logic of appropriateness within organizations involved in governance is defined by a series of factors such as symbols and routines (see also Berger and Luckman, 1967). These routines tend to simplify the decision-making process by establishing bounds on what will be considered, when they will be considered and the like. Rather than writing on a tabula rasa as might be understood from the rationalistic perspective, decision-makers in governance are writing on a slate that is already crowded and within which only relatively minor adjustments are likely to be successful.

Although not in the direct intellectual lineage of bounded rationality, the logic of incrementalism (Hayes, 2013) has many of the same features as does bounded rationality. Perhaps most importantly, there is the rejection of the possibility, or even desirability, of synoptic decision-making in governance, and with that rejection the acceptance of continuing processes of "partisan mutual adjustment" (Lindblom, 1979) to make decisions. This model of decision-making therefore explicitly accepts that there are multiple perspectives on policy and governance held by multiple actors (the partisan element) and that decision-making in this context is never finite but continuous.

Advocates of bounded rationality and of incrementalism will argue that this form of decision-making may in fact be more rational than the synoptic attempts at rationality described earlier. They argue this on the basis of two elements affecting decision-making. The first is that comprehensive decision-making may uncover a solution for a governance problem, but it is perhaps more likely to fail, given the complexity of the decision-making situations involved. When these "rational" decisions fail, they tend to fail in a large and visible manner which is bad not only in substantive policy terms but is also undesirable from a political perspective. If politics is indeed about blame avoidance (Hood, 2011), then making large-scale comprehensive decisions may not be the best approach.[2]

---

[2] But sometimes this is the only viable approach to the issue being confronted (Schulman, 1980).

The other way in which incremental solutions may be more rational is that they can minimize decision-making costs. Even attempting to make decisions in a comprehensive manner requires marshaling large quantities of evidence and analysis, and even then it will almost be inevitably inadequate for the complexity of most governance decisions. Therefore, making a series of smaller decisions, assessing the impacts of those decisions, learning, and then adjusting to the evidence, better decisions can be made with less investment in the decision-making. Of course, the danger is that this more conservative style of decision-making will never reach more demanding goals, so that governance fails in small ways rather than in larger, more dramatic ways. And those smaller failures may also be less visible to citizens and therefore produce less political mobilization for change.

Whether in the lineage of Simon and other members of the school of bounded rationality (see Jones, 2002) in the incrementalist school, decision-making for governance is being conducted within a set of constraints that tend to privilege certain types of decisions. These bounds are in part cultural, so no American president would think of nationalization as a mechanism for addressing economic policy problems.[3] The boundaries may also be organizational. Simon's bounded rationality model is a model of intra-governmental processes with only very limited attention to the societal dimension of decision-making. Governance is conducted primarily by organizational actors, and organizations tend to have their own internal logics that they utilize to shape their internal dynamics as well as to present themselves to the outside world (Goodsell, 2011).

The emphasis on organizational actors in governance points to the need to consider the internal dynamics of organizations involved in governance (Jacobsson, Pierre and Sundström, 2015). There is a tendency, especially in the rationalistic models, to consider organizations as unitary actors with a single perspective on policy and governance. That internal integration is not necessarily evident either for public sector organizations or for social actors that interact with governments to facilitate governance. Individual members of those organizations may have divergent views (see for example the organizational culture

---

[3] Except, of course, when they do. Both George W. Bush and Barack Obama partially nationalized automobile manufacturers and banks and insurance companies in response to the financial crisis beginning in 2007.

literature) that at times intervene into the decision-making, and decentralized organizational structures may enhance the internal variation of values within an organization.

Thus, there is a need to consider any set of positions taken in a bargaining situation around governance issues to be a temporary equilibrium within the organization and hence subject to change. Indeed, the process of decision-making itself may produce some alteration of perspectives if not of fundamental values. Even if the information being exchanged in bargaining is imperfect, it may still be new information that will alter the perspectives of participants in the process.

Having mentioned Graham Allison's study of the Cuban Missile Crisis above with respect to rationalistic models of the governance process, we can also think of his "Organizational Process" model as to some extent a version of bounded rationality. In this analysis of decision-making, the decisions were not structured so much by rational calculation as they were by routines and institutionalized processes. A decision-maker, such as a president, would have to find means of overcoming those institutional routines if he wished to have the governance conducted differently. These routines were seen by the participants as means of minimizing costs and of producing predictable responses to situations, whatever that situation may be.

In summary, bounded rationality represents a seemingly more applicable approach to decision-making for governance than does the comprehensive rationalistic model. The bounded rationality approach assumes that decision-making involves actors who are constrained from making any comprehensive by the complexity of the situations, the absence of complete information, and the routinization of decisions within organizations and established processes. Further, this model is not in any way remorseful over not being able to make comprehensive decisions but rather posits that ultimately higher quality decisions can be made through this more incremental and bounded process.

We have been singing some hymns of praise to bounded rationality as an approach to decision-making for governance. There are, however, several considerations about the approach that do cause some concerns. One is the assumption that decisions can be made over again and again, so that any decision made is reversible. The problem in the public sector is that once organizations are created, personnel hired, and clients being served, remaking the program becomes more difficult than assumed in these models. Indeed, the very logic of routinized and path dependent decision-making would seem to make continuing replacement of programs very difficult for organizations and managers. The difficulties in reversing decisions may be even more pronounced in interactive forms of governance because multiple social actors will also have been committed to the decisions.

Indeed, there is to some extent a paradox in the bounded rationality perspective on decisions. On the one hand, there is the argument that organizations or other decision-makers will learn from their own mistakes and adapt. But if their decisions are viewed through the perspective of the bounds of their own culture and values, then they may be resistant to information that does not correspond to their institutionalized conceptions. This difficulty may be evident for initial adoption of programs, but even more so once initial decisions have been made and with them some understanding of the policy area institutionalized.

Further, the bounded rationality approach may be conservative and prevent rapid adjustment to changing social and economic conditions. The basic logic of bounded rationality is gradual adjustment of policies to the environment, through trial and error and learning. That is suitable for problems that are not severe or which change gradually, but not at all suitable for crises or rapidly changing processes. Therefore, as we will develop below, this model and indeed the others need to be understood and evaluated in context. A slow adaptive approach may be well-suited for affluent countries with functioning governance arrangements but ill-suited for developing regimes requiring more significant transformations of the social and economic systems.

Although the bounded rationality perspective on decision-making does assume less structured decision situations than does the rational perspective, it still is not especially well suited to the multiple players and interactive involvement that characterizes much of contemporary governance. Much of the discussion is of the bounded rationality of a single, and generally governmental, actor, whereas any realistic conception of modern governance is that it involves multiple players who may or may not have the same set of intellectual bounds, and who may well not conceptualize the decision situation in the same way as other actors involved. These interactions among actors, each with their own bounds and own values, do not fit easily into the more monolithic model of bounded rationality. Therefore, we will not be able to fully understand decision-making in governance by focusing only on the formal decision-making process. In an interactive governance perspective, objectives and preferences emerge through exchanges among a wide variety of actors involved in decision-making and implementation (Torfing et al., 2012). In this model, the formal and societal dimensions of decision-making influence each other, or, as some might say, they are mutually constitutive.

Finally, and to some extent related to the point about conservatism of the bounded rationality perspective, some problems require large-scale interventions. There is a tendency for bounded rationality approaches to disaggregate policy problems and attempt to solve them piecemeal. But large-scale and complex problems need to be addressed more comprehensively, even if the approaches which are adopted may not be comprehensively rational in any useful meaning of that term.

While bounded rationality may appear a more appropriate approach to understanding decision-making within governance, there may still be significant problems for making good decisions for governance. The multiple actors, each with its own bounds on rationality, may still have difficulties in agreeing on a common frame for decisions. The bounds may involve not only different understandings of policy issues but also different time frames for making decisions. And what is "good enough" for some actors may clearly not be good enough for others.

Multiple-Streams and the Garbage Can. If we move even further way from the model of comprehensive rationality in governance, the logic of multiple streams and the garbage models can provide a perspective that introduces a good deal of randomness in decision-making. Although written from somewhat different perspectives and for different reasons, the garbage can model (Cohen, March, and Olsen, 1972) and the multiple streams model (Kingdon, 2003) share many of the same assumptions and appear to have relatively common implications for governing.

For both of these models, there is an assumption that decision-makers do not so much seek to make decisions as they have decisions thrust upon them. While even in the bounded rationality model there is an assumption (a principle of intended rationality in Simon's terms) that individuals and organizations responsible for governing are engaged in responding to perceived need to govern a particular domain or to solve a particular policy problem, the actors in the multiple streams perspectives are somewhat more passive. They appear to realize that governing is difficult and efforts to intervene into the complex chains of action involved in governing are fraught with dangers for the unwary (see Mucciaroni, 2013).

Given those difficulties, the decision-maker in the multiple streams approach tends to wait for a "window of opportunity" to emerge. In these windows, the several streams hypothesized to be necessary for an effective decision come together. In the garbage can model, these various elements of decision are conceptualized as swimming about in some primeval decisional soup, and when they come together, there is the opportunity for decisions, and especially opportunities for decisions that are likely to be successful.

There are several elements that must come together for the decision to be made. The first of these is problems. Clearly, both policy-making and governance involve addressing problems. Whereas for the models above these problems are almost inherently prior to the initiation of a decision process, in this model they are initially merely there and become activated as the source of action only when joined with the other elements. The second of the elements involved in a decision is the solutions. These may be conceptualized as a set of policy instruments (Hood and Margetts, 2007) or as programs integrating resources and law, but in either case, these are possible means for solving policy issues.[4]

For governance, the third element of this primeval soup may be the most significant for explaining when decisions are actually made. This third element is meetings where decisions are made and the politics of those meetings. The problems and the possible solutions can swim around for very long periods of time until there the political element aligns with the other two elements. Although these three elements tend to be discussed as relative equals in the decisions, politics create the opportunities for attempting to solve the problem. This activation of the political element may be a function of a "focusing event" (Birkland and DeYoung, 2013), or changes in the governing coalition, or even the result of the charisma of particular leaders (Helms, 2012). The fourth element, finally, is participants.

---

[4] Solving may be an excessively optimistic word. Most policy areas, and domains of governance, are never really solved but represent overlays of multiple attempts at solution (Carter, 2012; Hogwood and Peters, 1983).

Above we noted that the confluence of the three elements of decision explains, or at least describes, the timing of decisions. Unless and until the necessary elements come together, there is unlikely to be a decision. It is important to note here that this confluence of events is not particularly adept at explaining the content of the decisions. The content of the decision tends to be a function of which problem met up with which solution by whom and in what political context. This random element of the decision process may be extremely unsatisfying for anyone attempting to impose a governance style on a policy area, but in this perspective such "intended rationality" should not be expected to be successful.

In John Kingdon's conception of the multiple streams approach, the confluence of events represented a "window of opportunity." When these windows opened, there decisions were possible. This decision need not, however, be made on a conventional ends-means conception of making decision. Rather, it is equally likely that solutions will chase problems as much as vice versa. For example, we know that organizations and individuals have favorite policy remedies (see Linder and Peters, 1983) and these actors may be looking for problems to which their favorite tools can be applied.

Although the above discussion has emphasized the passivity of decision-makers in the multiple streams approach, they are also characterized by Kingdon and others as "policy entrepreneurs." The conception that scholars working in this perspective have is that these actors may have ideas about good policy, or good governance, and are merely biding their time until they are likely to be successful in having their ideas adopted and implemented. When the opportunity arises, these entrepreneurs need to be ready to go through the available windows and push forward with a decision.

The multiple streams approach represents an interesting confluence of possibilities about decisions within itself. On the one hand, there is the underlying assumption that decisions arise when there is a virtually random meeting of various streams required for the decision. On the other hand, at least one version of this approach assigns a significant role for a more activist entrepreneur to help shape the decisions. Indeed, one could conceptualize the availability of an entrepreneur as yet another one of the necessary elements that must come together in order for a decision to be made.

For governance, the multiple streams perspective may offer more possibilities for explanation and understanding than the previous two approaches. As is the case with the garbage can model, this perspective emphasizes the societal dimension much more than the formal dimension. The logic of multiple actors interacting across a range of functions within the process appears to invite this less deterministic conception of decision-making. That said, however, the randomness involved here may also make the steering conception of governance more difficult to sustain. Multiple streams converging makes any continuous steering toward a target easy to ignore as opportunities open for action that may or may not be part of the intended direction of action.

The multiple streams approach does not have as strong a steering approach as might be desired for making this model of governance work. We have emphasized the role of goal-selection in governance, and in this model the goals do not appear as a dominant feature. Indeed, the goals appear to emerge from action, and from the confluence of the streams, rather than from more purposive action. Thus, as a normative approach to decisions in governance, this approach may have significant deficiencies.

The Advocacy Coalition Framework. A fourth model for decision-making in governance has been described as the "advocacy coalition framework" as developed by Paul Sabatier and Hank Jenkins-Smith (1993; see also Weible, Jenkins, and McQueen, 2009). This approach to decision-making is based more on ideas than are the others discussed earlier. The model is also based more on policy change than are the others, but as noted in several places most governance interventions and most policy-making actually involves adjustments to existing policies.

The fundamental assumption of this model is that there are a set of core ideas that define a policy, or perhaps the governance of a particular sector of society. Although there is a core of ideas, these ideas vary in terms of their centrality for the policy (or governance area) in question. An organization or other actor will attempt to protect their core ideas against change, but will be willing to change more derivative ideas at the perimeter of their policy space. This change will come about when confronted with a challenge to the programs from some other actor that has ideas that to some extent overlap and to some extent contradict the dominant set of ideas being acted upon within the governance domain.

As implied above, this approach to policy change and governance assumes that subsystems are the dominant arenas for governing. Much of governance theory tends to look at whole systems of governing and to make assumptions about them, but the advocacy coalition framework focuses on more tightly defined subsystems, with actors involved having their core beliefs that tend to be stable.[5] Thus, there are some similarities with the multiple streams approach in that shifting away from the status quo tends to be difficult. However, unlike the seemingly random nature of the multiple streams perspective, governance here is more purposive, and more driven by conflicting ideas than by the random confluence of events.

This conception of decision-making may be especially useful for the more interactive versions of governance we are including along with more state-centric conceptions of governance. In these cases, we would conceive of the social actor – be it market or nonmarket – as presenting some ideas that challenge the status quo. Although in most cases this status quo will be defined by an actor within the public sector, it may also be that the dominant approach to governance is defined by other social actors, or a coalition of public sector and social actors. Whatever the source of that dominant governance arrangements, there will be challenges, and those interactions between the status quo and alternative solutions to the same problems must be understood to understand governance.

The interaction of the dominant governance arrangements and the challenges emerging from external actors, whether they are state or non-state actors, in the process of producing a new equilibrium should be conceptualized as a decision-making process. In this view, the actors tend to bargain over changes in the status quo, but more importantly they learn from one another and from their interactions. This conception of decision-making in governance is therefore more open than many, and assumes that interactions among actors produce the capacity for improvement in governance.

The advocacy coalition model of decision-making adds to the other approaches discussed here by bringing in the need for bargaining more explicitly. The other approaches appear to have a more hierarchical conception of the manner in which decisions are made, differing primarily in the extent to which rationality, in any comprehensive sense, can be expected to emerge from the process. The Advocacy Coalition Framework (ACF) assumes that there are at least two possible policy coalitions available, each with a set of beliefs about policy and

---

[5] The emphasis on subsystems is visible in a good deal of the political science literature on public policy, beginning at least with the work of Theodore J. Lowi.

governance. Through a process of negotiation and learning, a dominant coalition will be able to impose some or all of its wishes on the area. That said, the process through which that bargaining is conducted is not specified as clearly as it might be.

Like the other approaches to decision-making, the advocacy coalition framework provides some insights into the decisions made when attempting to provide governance, but also leaves some questions unanswered. Perhaps most importantly, this model does address change more clearly than do the others, but like the others tends to focus attention on a single institution or a single decision rather than the chain of decisions required for governance. Also, the identification of an existing policy approach appears to recognize the steering aspects of governance, but at the same time the presumed changes of that core also makes steering more mutable than it might be thought to be.

Contingent Models and Choices

We have now identified several important models for decision-making in governance. We have made some allusions to the settings in which any one or the other may be particularly useful, but in this section we want to expand that discussion and attempt to make even closer linkages between governance and decision-making. We should point out here again that we are making as a central claim for this book that decision-making is the essential feature of governance, and the remainder of our discussion will be focused on the manner in which decisions are made in different policy areas and in different institutional settings.

The examples drawn from the Cuban Missile crisis point to one important dimension of variation – the extent of real or perceived crisis (see Boin, 2004), but there are a host of other variables that might be included. As Chapter 4 focuses on differences in decision-making across different political systems, this section will place greater attention to the role of particular types of issues, and the role of different types of situations, in shaping governance. This list will not be exhaustive; given the wide variety of influences, there may be over governance, but it is intended to provide some insights into the variability of decision-making for governance.

The most fundamental difference among governance issues is the extent to which they are programed (see Simon, 1947). That is, to what extent are the actors and the premises for decisions well-established through law or through institutionalized patterns of interaction? Some of the models of decision-making above assume such structuring, while others, such as the multiple streams approach, do not. Even when decisions are not well-programed, they must still be considered within the bounds of steering toward broad governance goals. The formal dimension of decision-making assumes a high degree of programing, whereas the societal dimension highlights the many contingencies in public decision-making that stem from broad societal consultation. Other things being equal, the stronger the societal aspect of decision-making, the less likely that decisions will programed.

As mentioned above, crisis may be the antithesis of programed decisions. Crises tend to reduce the capacity for rational decision-making, given that preferences may not be knowable in a fluid situation and the range of decision premises will not be constrained. To some extent, crises are examples of decision-making through multiple streams, with the crisis being analogous to a window of opportunity in which the demand for decisions may force bringing together solutions with the problem presented by that crisis. Crises may, however, reinforce some of the fundamental goals for a society, calling for some return to the established path of governance goals (see Peters, Pierre, and Randma-Liiv, 2011).

In summary, although decision-making is central to the processes of governance, most existing models of decision-making used in political science and policy studies have notable deficiencies as explanation of that decision-making. While this is in some ways disappointing, it does point out that thinking about governance requires an even more comprehensive approach than thinking about public policy. Governance involves the linkage of multiple actors engaged in a variety of governance functions that have to mesh well in order to produce effective steering. Any one of these models of decision-making may assist understanding at any one stage, but the more comprehensive functionalist frame is required to understand governance as a whole. Further, understanding that each of the models provides some insights into decisions made in governance enables us to consider how hybrid understandings, if not formalized hybrid models of decisions, can advance the study of governance.

Decision-Making, Governance, and Comparative Politics

We see, to reiterate a point made earlier, decision-making as the critical, defining element of governance. Whether we look at the allocative nature of decisions or their capacity to resolve conflict, this is the essential element of governing and, by extension, an aspect of governance which is central to political science.

We mentioned earlier that the centrality of government in governance is a key factor in understanding decision-making in governance. In a conventional perspective, decision-making is seen as a process conducted entirely within government. In more interactive governance contexts, on the other hand, there is uncertainty in terms of both preferences and the range of actors involved in the decision-making process, and indeed of the process as such. There may also be ambiguity in terms of both the substantive nature of the problem and who decides and how (and with whom) policy can be implemented, although this ambiguity.

The key point we make in this chapter is that understanding decision-making in a governance perspective requires firstly that we are aware of the degree to which different models and theories conceptualize substantive issues and the fluidity of actors and process. There is a continuum from rational choice to garbage can where the rational choice theory side emphasizes process and actors with little consideration to substance or context, to the garbage can model which is almost completely about substantive issues and rather little about process and actors. The advocacy coalition framework and bounded rationality fall somewhere between these two extremes.

Furthermore, we develop the distinction between the formal and societal aspects of decision-making where the formal aspect highlights the actual decision-making, whereas the societal dimension focuses on the interactions between government and societal actors in collective goal setting. As subsequent chapters will discuss in some detail, different institutionalized governance arrangements accord different significance to such consultation. Unlike more formal analyses of decision-making, the societal dimension helps explain the contingencies that real-world decision-makers face. These accounts substantiate the importance of context and uncertainty and there a distinct pattern that the stronger the focus on actual decision-making, the stronger the rejection of rationalist decision-making theories.

This is not to suggest, to reiterate a previous point, that decision-makers in complex, interactive settings are any less rational than those who make decisions in more secluded contexts. It does, however, suggest that as we bring in the societal dimension of decision-making, leaders become exposed to a set of contingencies and patterns of resource dependency which ultimately will have an impact on the way in which they make decisions and which considerations become salient in that process. Collaborative governance must, by necessity, include making joint decisions about the objectives of that governance.

A central element of the comparative analysis of governance therefore becomes how decisions are made, and the mixture of formal and societal elements of decision-making. As we will demonstrate in the following chapter, there are a range of different styles of governance that affect the manner in which governance is created and the success or failure of governance. In all of these models, however, the fundamental question may be how decisions are made, and indeed for some whether decisions can be made.

4 | Governance and Comparative Politics

We have argued that, as well as having general theoretical relevance for the study of politics, governance theory has particular relevance for comparative politics. By positing a set of requirements for governing, this approach provides the foundation for comparing how different political systems perform these functions. Very much like the older structural functionalist approaches to comparative politics, this model argues that by understanding how different political systems perform the tasks necessary for supplying governance, we have a clear foundation for comparison.

Unlike the structural functionalist approaches, however, we are more concerned with the processes of governing within the "black box" rather than the relationships existing between those "conversion functions" and their environment. The analysis of Almond and Powell (1966) focused much of its attention on the mechanisms for moving wants and demands from the environment into the political system, and somewhat less on how decisions were actually made within the system. Clearly, we do not ignore those connections with the socio-economic environment of the public sector, nor would we want to, but we are more concerned with the choices that actors inside and outside the formal public sector make when attempting to steer economy and society. The study of governance has been to some extent been built around the link between the public sector and social actors (Torfing et al., 2012), but these relationships are about how governance is conducted rather than merely expressing wants and demands.

In this regard, the relationships between state and society in governance theory are often conceptualized in a more utilitarian and strategic manner than those that have appeared in Almond and Powell's (1966) analysis. For example, although the use of societal actors in networks and other interactive structures does to some extent involve the processing of their demands for programs from the state, the direct involvement in the construction of the programs tends to emphasize the actual performance of the governance tasks rather than a more remote "articulation of interests."[1] We are, of course, concerned with the legitimacy of governance arrangements but are perhaps more concerned with their effectiveness (see Przeworski, 2003) and the extent to which full legitimation of governance structures and processes enhances governing effectiveness.[2]

For comparison therefore, we want to examine the manner in which governments and their collaborators in the private sector (both market and nonmarket) go about the process of making and implementing public policies. This comparative examination is in many ways a monumental task, so we will employ a number of ideal types or models to discuss these differences (see Mahoney, 2004). Although the models presented in this chapter are conceptualized as ideal types, they will have real-world referents, and these will be illustrated with real-world cases. These case materials will draw heavily on the experiences of the industrialized democracies, but we will also attempt to explain how these models can be applied in rather different selections with rather different governance challenges.

Further, although the primary function of this analysis is empirical, there are also normative questions that arise in the context of discussing governance. That is, not only must we be concerned with how these governance functions are fulfilled, but we also are interested in how well governance can be conducted using the different alternative models. While to some extent the choice of institutions and processes for governance is a function of historical circumstances and national political cultures, we can also ask to what extent these alternatives are successful, and to what extent alternative formats for governing are likely to be more successful.[3]

We have to this point been using words such as successful and effective with relatively little specification. We should first distinguish

---

[1] The idea of the articulation of interests is by no means unimportant in governance models. As we will point out later, some versions of governance depend heavily on the more indirect involvement of social actors in the processes than do the interactive versions that have the center of much of the discussion of governance.

[2] Legitimacy and effectiveness have long been recognized as being closely related, so that legitimacy can build effectiveness, and vice versa. Creating such a virtuous spiral is crucial for successful democratic transitions.

[3] Success is difficult to define for governance, as it is for public policy. See McConnell (2010).

between political success and substantive success (Bovens, 't Hart and Peters, 2001). While these forms of success and failure might be thought to covary, they often do not, and political constructions of failure in particular can be crucial for a policy (see Zittoun, 2014). We should also distinguish policy success from governance success, and again note that these may not necessarily covary. A policy may, for example, be beneficial for the society but not really reach the intended governance goals.

Thus, our ultimate conception of governance success is reaching the intended goals of the actors responsible. This does not mean, however, that these goals will be desirable from a normative perspective. Some of the most successful governance regimes have had profoundly evil goals. While stating that reaching posited goals is a measure of governance success is relatively easy, measuring the outcomes is much less easily done. Goals stated in the public sector are often rather vague. Likewise, how much attainment of the goals is sufficient to declare success? Success is not a simple dichotomy but rather is a dimension with more or less attainment.[4]

Components of the Models

We could approach the comparative dimensions of governance in a variety of ways, but we have chosen to build ideal-type models to understand the dynamics of governance in a variety of comparative contexts. Given that the intention of utilizing governance as an approach to comparative politics is to demonstrate patterns within the complexity of the numerous real-world cases, the use of ideal-type models is a middle-range strategy between universalistic but vague models and highly detailed studies of individual cases. Ideal-type analysis provides a set of standards against which to examine the real-world cases, while also making some theoretical statements about that reality.

To perform that ideal-type analysis will require beginning with the five components of any model of governance developed in the previous chapters and linking them to empirical realities to understand their complex interactions. Our perspective on governance has a number of

---

[4] On the dangers of "degreeism" and making dimensions into simple dichotomies, see Sartori (1991).

moving parts, and those various components appear to have varying importance in different national selections. Further, even within a single country, there may be marked differences among levels of government or different areas of public policy. For example, decisions in policy areas such as health care may be dominated by professional groups while others, e.g. defense, may be dominated by political parties and elites rather than interest groups and will be more dominated by internal forces of the state rather than by the social actors that will be more influential in social and economic policy. Further, in times of crisis or stress, patterns of governing may change, with state actors in general becoming more powerful (Boin et al., 2005; Peters, Pierre, and Randma-Liiv, 2011).

Therefore, to understand governance in a comparative manner, we use the essential components of a general model of governance and determine how they apply in different political arrangements. These essential elements are the actors involved in governing, the processes through which these actors perform their governance tasks, and some understanding of the outcome of those processes. Some approaches to governance may define themselves through the sets of actors involved, e.g. interactive governance (Torfing et al., 2012). A second version of governance may define itself through processes, e.g. legalistic conceptions emphasizing the formal processes (Jayasuriya, 2006). Still a third approach may be defined largely through policy outcomes and performance, e.g. strategic governance and coherence. A more complete understanding of governance will require some integration of these three dimensions.

Although the first two of those three elements might be considered, "independent variables" and the third the "dependent variable," part of the logic of governance is that these elements may be so intertwined that isolating a neat causal chain may be both difficult and counterproductive. The outcomes that are being sought through governance processes may in turn invoke particular sets of actors. For example, if a country is pursuing the "good governance" associated with the World Bank's governance programs (see Rothstein, 2012; Rothstein and Teorell, 2012), then legal actors will be central to the governance process.[5]

---

[5] In this conception, "good governance" involves creating the rule of law, reducing corruption, and enhancing the regulatory capacity of governments. It is less concerned with goal seeking and effective implementation.

We will use the governance functions described in some detail earlier in this book to structure our analysis of the governance models. As we apply these functions to different models of governance, it is essential that we escape the static nature of those functions as their execution involves a great deal of dynamics, both within the political system and also in its relationship with society. Let us therefore briefly rehearse the governance functions, emphasizing their dynamic dimensions.

Goal-Selection. The first aspect of governance is identifying the collective goals of society. The analogous aspect of the policy process is problem identification and agenda-selection (see Dunn, 2008). The important difference in the governance context is that this is a more normative process, with the crucial element being to decide *what* society wants, rather than deciding simply which issues will be processed at any particular time. Agendas will to some extent be derived from goals. As already noted, this stage tends to be highly governmental, given that the public sector may be the only legitimate means of selecting the collective goals for society.

Resource Mobilization. Resource attachment reflects the need for the actors interested in the program to identify and mobilize public and private resources to reach their goals. Thus, a particular set of instruments may have been adopted, but if there are not the resources necessary to make them function properly, then those instruments are almost certain to be ineffective. Also, although financial resources are crucial, personnel and, perhaps most importantly, legitimacy are also important elements of the resource base for governance. Further, non-state actors such as NGOs or contractors may be available to supplement the activities of the public sector in resource mobilization, perhaps especially in providing personnel for implementing public programs.

Decision-Making. The next part of the governance process is making decisions about how to reach the goals that have been established. As we discussed in detail in the previous chapter, this function is central to governance and the most important of the governance functions we study. This function too is often performed within the public sector, albeit generally with a good deal of input from the private sector. This aspect of the process involves, among other things, the selection of instruments and the selection of a mix of public and private action that is deemed most appropriate for reaching the goals. Even more fundamentally, this stage of governance implies legitimating the programs selected to pursue the goal, and legitimating the very involvement of the public sector in pursuing that goal.[6]

Many approaches to governance that depend upon a set of assumptions about the principal actors in the process tend to ignore the importance of decision-making in governing. Theoretically this is a crucial omission because without understanding the logic of the decisions being taken, important questions about the fundamental logics of governance will be ignored. As scholars working in the perspective of analytic sociology (Hedström and Swedborg, 1998) have argued, it is crucial to have some understanding of the micro-foundations of choice, whereas most governance approaches have worked entirely at the macro-level.

Implementation. The implementation process is a crucial component of the governance process, although it is sometimes relegated to the category of "mere administration." We noted above that the choice of policy instruments is part of decision-making in governance, and at the implementation stage, these instruments are then made to perform and to produce the effects intended. These instruments (even in more state-centric models) often depend upon private sector actors so that this can also be a point at which there is substantial loss of control over policies. In the shift to "the new governance" (Héritier and Lehmkuhl, 2008; Salamon, 2001), there is decreasing dependence on command and control instruments and increased emphasis on interactive instruments involving the private sector.

Feedback and Learning. The final part of the governance process is feedback, with the actions of instruments in the past being evaluated and put back into the decision-making process.[7] Governance has the same root word as "cybernetics" and hence implies some connection to the environment and a continual adjustment of instruments (and perhaps even goals) in light of the success and failure of actions taken in the past. Most policy-making is indeed remaking of existing policy, with

---

[6] In the terms of the agenda selection literature (Cobb and Elder, 1972), this can be considered placing an issue on the systemic agenda of the public sector. That is the collection of all issues considered appropriate for the public sector to act upon.

[7] This component of the governance process is rather similar to the ideas of systems analysis in which feedback was a crucial aspect of the presumed processes of political systems. We also noted above the possibility of conceptualizing some aspects of governance in a cybernetic manner, with the system developing patterns of response to changes in the environment.

governments learning from their past actions and (one hopes) improving their policies in subsequent rounds of action (Hogwood and Peters, 1983). The learning literature has now become especially concerned with the capacity for "evidence-based policy making," using evidence from other cases to improve policy formulation.

Ideal Types of Governance

Having in mind how the basic governance model can be used as an approach to comparative politics, we will now proceed with the five ideal-type models. We need to emphasize again that although these do have referents in the real world of governance, they are still abstracted from that reality and are intended to emphasize some of the crucial points of governance as it is practiced. We should also emphasize at this point that the five models developed here are ideal types so that no single real-world case will fit the model perfectly (Mommsen, 1989). The use of the cases will help to demonstrate that these models do indeed have some relevance to the real world of governing.

Also, we should mention that although these are four stylized models of governance at the national level, they are likely to be manifested primarily at the local level. Local politics is obviously embedded in a national culture and institutional framework but deals with issues that are inherently more interactive than those typical to national politics (Pierre et al., 2015). What differs is the nature of those interactions; some models are clearly more hierarchical than others just as some models emphasize social consultation and involvement more than others.

Étatiste Governance

The stereotype of the role of government that many governance scholars have used as a straw person to advocate models of governance more defined by social actors is, for us, an étatiste model. Within this model, the state is the primary and virtually sole actor for providing governance (see Hazareesingh, 1994). Although this model of governing can indeed be a straw person, it is also at times a real style of governing. Although some governance scholars have written governments out of the script for steering economy and society, they are still alive and well and actively involved in governing. Indeed, as the ramifications of the fiscal crisis beginning in 2008 continue to appear, the role of the state in governing is if anything being strengthened, even in countries with extensive involvement of social actors in governing (Kickert, 2012).

At the extreme, authoritarian regimes are clearly étatiste, whether they are single party regimes, military regimes, or perhaps traditional monarchies such as Saudi Arabia. In these governance systems, the state tends to rule hierarchically and to suppress any attempts by social actors to become overtly involved in governing (Gandhi, 2008). That said, these regimes may still utilize some mechanisms for social involvement to legitimate their actions, but even that involvement may be hierarchical. For example, the Spanish Falangist government created their own "syndicates" to control the labor sector without any meaningful participation (Anderson, 1970). Likewise, Schmitter's discussion of "state corporatism" (1974) points to the desire of some strong political regimes to attempt to control social actors, and potential rivals for power, through involving them directly in governance processes.

As well as the authoritarian regimes dominated either by a personalistic leader or by a hegemonic and ideological political party, in some instances a strong state and the associated étatiste style of governing result from the absence of governance capacity within the society. Joel Migdal (1988) has argued that opportunities for governance depend upon the relative strength of state and society. If the society is weak[8] and cannot support the state in governing, then the state will have few choices but to supply the necessary governance. Again, there is a clear functionalist logic in this analysis, with the assumption that there is a need for governing that must be fulfilled through one means or another.

The étatiste style of governing is not, however, confined to authoritarian or traditional governments. The state may be the dominant actor in democratic as well as in nondemocratic regimes. The obvious difference is that virtually all nondemocratic regimes are étatiste while

[8] For governance purposes, weaknesses in the society may be manifested in several ways. One would be the absence of effective social organizations that can perform public tasks and can also channel demands upward into the public sector. Alternatively, when the society is divided along racial, linguistic, or other lines, then the presence of strong organizations may in fact further limit the opportunities for governing (but see Lijphart, 1999).

relatively few democratic regimes are dominated by the state any longer.[9] The étatiste style may have been the dominant approach to governing historically, but as societies have evolved and as demands for political participation have increased, governments find it more difficult to exercise control over the processes of governing.

There are perhaps two dominant examples of étatiste styles of governing among well-established democratic regimes. The clearest example would be France (but see Page, 2012), and the perhaps less clear example would be Japan. Within more recently democratized regimes, countries such as India, Brazil, and the "Little Tigers" in Asia would appear to be significantly étatiste in their style of governing. Indeed, the role of the state in economic and social development in these regimes emphasizes the dominance of state action.

In order to understand the étatiste style of governing, we will now proceed to examine the three major components of our model as they function within these states. In so doing, we will not describe the various actors involved as these will be relatively similar in all cases. What is more important is how these actors work through processes in order to produce outcomes. As noted in Chapter 2, the institutions are important but are more important in action than as static structures. We will focus on the French and Brazilian cases when discussing the étatiste model, but also utilize examples from other analogous states to illustrate the analytic points we are making.

We also must remember that although we characterize several countries as governing in an étatiste manner, almost any system may govern in this manner in particular circumstances and in particular policy areas. For example, in wartime, governments tend to centralize and to impose their priorities on the economy and society. The United States is usually conceptualized as the antithesis of an étatiste system (but see below, p. 103) but during World War II, and after September 11, acted in a very étatiste manner (see Boin et al., 2005). Similarly, the economic crisis beginning in 2008 provoked a number of governments to become substantially more intrusive in economic affairs than expected from the prevailing neo-liberalism of the period leading up to the crisis.

---

[9] The Italian and French governments during the postwar period were cases in which the bureaucracy dominated governing, given the weaknesses of other aspects of the political system.

Goal-Selection. Perhaps the most important difference between the étatiste model of governing and the other models is the extent to which goal-selection is dominated by government. This is certainly true for the authoritarian regimes but is also true for more democratic versions of étatiste governance. In many of the cases of this strong state model, the principal goals imposed on society have been for development. If one remembers the roots of French government in the Napoleonic model, the state was conceived as a developmental actor.[10] The creation of the *Grands Ecoles*, for example, was to a great extent to provide the state with the talent necessary to develop the economy and the society.[11]

For Brazil and the Asian Tigers, economic development was the principal goal for governing and required difficult choices about the allocation of resources that could perhaps be made only through a hierarchical system (Kriekhaus, 2002). Although we have been discussing the étatiste version of the state as it is encountered in France and other Napoleonic states, much of the same pattern can be identified in the developmental states of East Asia (Johnson, 1982; Okimoto, 1988). These states have tended not to develop Welfare states in the pattern of other industrial systems but rather to focus on "productivist welfare states" (Kim, 2012) that emphasize accumulation rather than distribution. These arrangements enable governments to promote economic development while at the same time also providing some social protections, and substantial educational and training opportunities, for the public.

Also in étatiste systems, goals can be more consistent across time than in other forms of governance. Rather than responding to immediate democratic pressures and short-term goals of incumbent political leaders, the étatiste style of governing relies more on goals emanating from the bureaucracy or, in the case of autocratic regimes, those goals that come from the autocrat. Especially in the developmental states mentioned earlier, maintaining that consistency is important. That said, the goals for the governance system may not always be as consistent as might be expected. As already noted, the bureaucracy itself is far from monolithic, meaning that different components of the system

[10] Although not necessarily operating in the developmental style of France, other countries within the Napoleonic tradition may have many of the same general administrative and governance styles (Ongaro, 2010).

[11] This role was especially true for the technical *ecoles*, e.g. the *Polytechnique*. See Armstrong (1973).

may be pursuing different goals with little or no reference to other components of the state.

One important version of goal-selection in state-centric systems is technocracy and agenda control through expertise. The agenda of the public sector would in many cases be determined more by rational pursuit of elite priorities rather than through more democratic processes. For example, the French tradition of economic (and to some extent also social) planning was central to the postwar economic development but also implied a strong central state willing to replace its own judgments with those of the market (Dreyfus, 2013). The same technocratic style of planning has been found in the Asian Tigers and in some countries of Latin America (Markoff and Montecinos, 1993).

We need to be careful to include a second set of goals in this process, which is the maintenance of some level of social accord. Thus, difficult decisions must be made about the level of resources to be allocated to the consumer segment of the economy and also about levels of inclusion in the political process. The creation of welfare-state programs, for example, may be means not only of benefiting the public but also of purchasing social peace in order to support the superordinate goals for development and change.

Resource Mobilization. In this model of governance, with a commonly occurring emphasis on development and social transformation, the decision-making and resource allocation processes are to some extent intertwined. The public sector always has limited resources and must make decisions about how to reach goals within the constraints of that resource base. All governments function with limited resources but the developmental goals of these systems require even more careful use of both authority and monetary resources.[12]

The étatiste governance model singles out to some extent in this regard since the state tends to mobilize the resources necessary to sustain its prioritized projects. The more cautious resource strategies that are typical to several of the other governance models do not apply to etastiste governance since the state sees little reason to decline important projects out of fear that it would trigger societal opposition

---

[12] Perhaps in reaction to the étatiste style of governing, local governments in Brazil have been among the most innovative internationally in using participatory forms of budgeting (Wampler, 2007). The creation of these methods has to some extent also assisted in the creation of a more viable civil society and has fostered the developmental goals of the government.

to increased taxes. Thus, the resource strategy which is common to many neoliberal regimes – sharing costs with market actors, forging public–private partnerships, and so on – is not attractive to the state in this governance model. Those strategies entail contingencies on market or societal consent, and étatiste governance sees very little societal influence on the state.

This capacity for resource mobilization in étatiste systems is perhaps especially important because these regimes have tended to be developmental states. Napoleon and subsequent leaders used the state as a means for developing France and that role has been very evident for the Little Tigers in Asia, and for Brazil (Montero, 2005). Further, in addition to the usual means of raising financial resources through taxation, other mechanisms such as banking and state-owned enterprises have been, and often continue to be, important mechanisms for raising the resources needed to govern.

Decision-Making. In étatiste governance, decision-making rests solely with the state. There are often procedures of consultation and dialogue with major societal actors as part of the deliberation process although such dialogue serves more to ensure smooth implementation than to shape decisions. This does obviously not mean that the policy-making process is consensual although many cases of étatiste governance display a lower rate of party competition than is typical to less state-centric governance models.

Although most discussions of decision-making in the public sector tend to discount rationality as an effective or even desirable approach to making public policies, more étatiste political systems do tend to strive for greater rationality of action (Zittoun, 2014). Traditions of planning and technocratic policy-making tend to push these systems in the direction of searching for comprehensively rational decisions, even while often understanding the improbability of such a result.

Implementation. Étatiste governance systems tend to rely almost exclusively on their own resources for implementation. One aspect of the strong state is to utilize, in so far as possible, its own bureaucracy for implementation, or in the case of more authoritarian versions of this model to also employ the military which may be a relatively modern element in many less-developed societies. These states tend to be characterized by powerful bureaucracies, even if not always the most capable, e.g. those of Italy and Greece (see Stolfi, 2013). As well as a preference for utilizing their own bureaucracy, these states may be constrained because of the absence of other alternatives. The absence of strong civil societies, and a relative dearth of social organizations that could assist in implementation, places much of the onus on the bureaucracy.

Utilizing their own bureaucracy is important not only for the actual implementation of the programs but also for exercising control over the society more generally. Indeed, these administrative systems may utilize prefectural officers in order to ensure uniformity across the country (Cole, 2011). The logic of prefects is to provide the Ministry of the Interior, or other central ministries, with an additional mechanism for control over the actions of local governments and devolved officials of other central government ministries. In the former Soviet states, the dual lines of control with party and government bureaucracies exercising oversight over each other provided another dual authority system to ensure some degree of conformity across the system (Fairbanks, 1987; Hough, 1965).

Given the emphasis on control within the étatiste system, and the general absence of concern with popular involvement, the instruments used for governance tend to be "command and control." Phrased differently, étatiste regimes tend to rely on authority and on organization (Hood, 1976a) to implement their programs and tend less to use "softer" instruments such as information and monetary incentives (Salamon, 2001). In authoritarian versions of the étatiste systems, the organizations involved may be the police and the army, while in more democratic regimes it will be a powerful state bureaucracy. The use of these more authoritative instruments is quite logical and necessary, given the emphasis on uniformity as well as control within these regimes. Given the centrality and respect of the state in society, government often does not have to use very coercive instruments to implement policy. As Chalmers Johnson argues in his study of the Japanese Ministry of International Trade and Industry (MITI), MITI only had to present "visions" or subtle recommendation to ensure compliance among the big Japanese corporations as they knew well that there was an iron fist inside the velvet glove (Johnson, 1982).

Outcomes of Étatiste Governance. The outcomes of governance processes in étatiste models of governance are less inclusive than might be expected in other styles of governance. Pluralistic approaches to politics tend to be associated with liberalism and a minimal role of the state in social and economic affairs. Therefore, despite the policy capacity of these governments when they do become activated (van Waarden, 1995), the general commitment toward liberal ideas produces a more reactive policy style (see Richardson, 1982). One obvious manifestation of this liberal ideology is the minimalist, residual form of the welfare state (Esping-Andersen, 1990), in contrast to the more extensive welfare systems of other industrial democracies.

The selective nature of involvement of social actors and interest organizations in governance also contributes to the lack of inclusiveness of policy choices made by these states. The clientelistic relationships that exist between public sector organizations and interest groups mean that there are limited amounts of information available to decision-makers and the interest groups involved tend to reinforce the preferences of the public organization. In the extreme, the public sector organization will be involved in licensing and even creating organizations that will support their own policy perspectives.

Liberal-Democratic Governance

A second ideal type of governance will be discussed as a liberal democratic governance model. The state in this model remains a powerful actor, albeit not as dominant as that described earlier for the étatiste model. However, the state still tends to operate more autonomously from social actors than would be true for the more interactive versions of governing encountered in corporatist or corporate pluralist systems (Molina and Rhodes, 2002), or in network forms of governance (Torfing et al., 2012), both of which will be discussed later in this chapter. Although other types of regimes may fit into this general model, the clearest examples of the liberal-democratic style of governing are encountered in the Anglo-American systems, with their associated pluralist approaches to governing.

The basic idea of liberal-democratic governance is closely analogous with pluralist theories of governing. The standard pluralist approach to governance is that the state is an arena in which various social actors engage in contestation over policy and over power (see McFarland, 2007). Although governance here does involve social actors, those organizations are functioning primarily outside the political system itself and may indeed be considered essentially illegitimate participants in the process. This somewhat ambiguous role for interest groups and other social actors creates competition among the organizations for access to decision-making and with that access the capacity to influence policy to the exclusion of other actors.

The politics of gaining access for interest groups tends to create close, symbiotic relationships between an individual interest group that has been successful and the public sector organization.[13] These relationships provide the groups very close collaboration with an organization within the political system and enable them to exclude their competitors from effective access to government. These close relationships with an interest group, or a limited range of groups, on the part of public organizations exchange rights of access for political support. Rather than being regime support, however, the support provided here is for individual organizations and for their policies.

In the liberal-democratic model, the social groups involved may be as much "pressured groups" as pressure groups. That is, in this pattern of governance, the public sector organizations often have their own ideas and ideologies about good policy and therefore search out partners in their relevant environments that can support these views (see Goodsell, 2011; Page, 2010). Thus, the interest groups involved in policy-making in this model are not as autonomous as assumed in some other models of governance but rather are often co-opted by government. Of course, the co-optation may be mutual (see Duran, 1998), with the two actors forming their own network independent of the rest of government and other interest groups.

This pattern of governance in liberal democratic systems is also highly segmented. The control over access in this style of governing functions through involving the social actors in symbiotic relationships between an agency or ministry and one, or a limited number, of groups. Thus, while social groups may be involved with the public sector, that involvement is closely circumscribed and their influence extends only to one area, often a very tiny area of policy; the classic example was subsidies of honey in the United States (see Gray and Lowery, 2005).

Although we will be developing a general model of the liberal-democratic governance style, there are some marked differences among these systems. For example, a number of the Anglo-American political systems are federal, with strong involvement of subnational

---

[13] These relationships have been deemed clientelistic, indicating an exchange of support for some political or policy considerations (see Peters, 2009).

governments in governance. These systems were thus engaged in multi-level governance long before it became a popular concept in the literature (Bache and Flinders, 2004; Piattoni, 2010) and continue to rely heavily upon subnational governments for a good deal of the implementation of public programs. Likewise, the American presidential system and its rather extreme commitment to liberalism mark it as significantly different from other systems of this type. And at the extreme, the United Kingdom remains a highly centralized and virtually étatiste system (see Marsh, 2008) despite its generally pluralist style of politics (Richardson, 1982).

The other interesting variation on this style of governance is found in the former British colonies in Africa, the Caribbean, and Asia that have inherited many of the basic forms of Westminster democracy but must implement them in vastly different contexts (see Braibanti, 1966; Lodge, Stirton, and Moloney, 2015). Both the lack of economic resources in most of these systems and the deeply seated social cleavages in many of them require substantial adjustments. The obvious path for many of these systems has been to move more toward an étatiste style of governing, as the developmental and social challenges to governments lead them to attempt to impose their own directives on the society. Thus, they maintain some of the formal constitutional logic of the liberal-democratic regime while actually functioning differently.

These governance arrangements are in the paradoxical situation of being state-centric yet having a contractual foundation that tends to limit the power of the state (Dyson, 1980). This paradox is largely resolved in that these governance systems tend not to be very active in the full range of social and economic policies, but for those areas in which they choose to become involved they are powerful and often effective in governing (see King, 1976). Thus, although their range of activities may be limited, they are powerful within those areas.

In addition to their state capacity, when it is sought to be exercised, the state in this model tends to operate through its own institutions for governing. If its own institutions are not used, it may attempt to make clear delegations of powers that attempt to create "tamper-proof legal instruments" that can control the actions of the agents granted the delegated responsibilities. That control over agents, and indeed even agents within the state itself, is in part a function of the perceived distinction between politics and administration, as well as between state and society.

Some of the strength of the liberal-democratic governance model comes from its being largely majoritarian (Lijphart, 1999) in the manner in which governance is created. That is, in these regimes, there is a tendency for one or a limited number of political parties to control government and to then to be evaluated by voters at the next election. In contrast to consensual governments (see later), there is rather clear alternation in office by different parties or stable coalitions. While in office these majority parties can control the machinery of government and voters have a greater capacity to assess the performance of the dominant party than would be true in consensual regimes. The major downside to this arrangement is that this alternation can create "stop-go" cycles of policy that may be detrimental to effective policies. This pattern may also impede economic growth when investors become uncertain about the longevity of a particular regulatory framework (Gamble, 1994).

In addition to the pluralist relationships with interest groups and other social actors, the liberal democratic model of governance is characterized by mechanisms designed to limit the role of government. These limitations are especially apparent in the United States with the system of checks and balances (Conley, 2003). For Westminster regimes, the limits on government are less formalized, and in the extreme may be rather weak; the concept of parliamentary sovereignty tends to confer very broad powers on parliament and more recently on the government of the day, and even more especially on the cabinet and prime minister (Foley, 2000).

These limitations on the role of the state in liberal-democratic systems create a rather paradoxical position for these regimes. On the one hand, these regimes are relatively autonomous from the society, at least in terms of the formal role of social actors in governing. On the other hand, however, the emphasis in government on holding those potentially autonomous public organizations to account produces more continuous scrutiny of the actions of these governments than might be found in other systems.

Goal-Selection. One of the central challenges for interest groups in pluralist political systems is getting issues onto the political and policy agenda. In the étatiste model, there is little such competition for access to decision-making, given that the principal actors involved in making policy are within the political system itself. There may be competition among organizations within the public sector for agenda time and for the shaping of collective goals, but these conflicts are among organizations functioning as components of the state (Ashworth, Boyne, and Delbridge, 2009). Functioning from within the political system is always easier than being on the outside looking in and attempting to influence decisions.

The competition among groups within pluralist politics may be especially important at the agenda stage (Baumgartner and Jones, 2009; Cobb and Elder, 1972), given that policies have little or no possibility for adoption if they cannot be placed on the policy-making agenda. The competition for selection of collective goals is therefore to some extent a competition of ideas. The "ideas in good currency" (Schön, 1983) that are involved in making policy do not achieve this status simply because they are good ideas. Rather, there is competition for the agenda, and to some extent the ability to place items on the agenda is a function of good fortune and the almost random opening of opportunities (Kingdon, 2003). The pluralist approach might argue that this competition for being on an agenda is relatively open, while the power of money in politics appears to be closing many opportunities for less affluent actors and less popular ideas.

Decision-Making. In the liberal-democratic model of governance, decision-making is not so state-centric as in the étatiste model, but yet the public sector actors tend to be dominant. This focus on the public sector is in part because of the general absence of legitimacy of societal actors as legitimate participants (at least in the formulation aspects of policy-making). The pluralist and clientistic pattern of interaction between state and society means that groups tend to fight significant battles over access to the political process, but the state continues to control that access and the resultant influence.

Decision-making in liberal democratic systems also is highly segmented. All administrative and policy-making systems tend toward segmentation and specialization (Bouckaert, Peters, and Verhoest, 2010) but the liberal democratic systems do so to a greater extent because of the tendency toward clientelistic links between interest groups and bureaucratic agencies. This segmentation tends to result in a set of governments in these systems rather than a unified system characterized by coherent action. And much of the institutional politics in these regimes involves protecting one's policy domain from the intrusion of actors challenging the understandings within that domain.

And again, there are differences within this category, and perhaps more for decision-making than for the other functions. Decision-making in the United States is perhaps the extreme case of segmentation and clientelism, a factor reinforced by the segmentation of the Congressional committee system and the links of the committees and individual members to interests. On the other hand, the United Kingdom in particular, in large part through the accretion of power into the hands of cabinet and prime minister, is more capable of creating coherent patterns of governance.

Finally, the multiple checks and balances that characterize at least some of these systems (notably the US) tend to be conducive to incremental and multiple streams forms of decision-making. These patterns mean in turn that governance in this system, and to some extent other systems such as Canada or Australia, may experience difficulties in making broad-scale policy interventions that involve planning. Again, governance may be confined to the specific silos and even then be incremental.

Implementation. In the liberal-democratic model of governance, implementation is primarily a public sector activity, although private sector organizations may also become involved. As with other aspects of the model, the state is very selective about the roles given to the interest groups or other social actors. However, the interest groups which are involved in implementation are often granted substantial powers to manage some important social sector. For example, state-centric and liberal-democratic governance arrangements tend to grant a great deal of power to professional organizations to manage their own affairs, including professional licensing.

Liberal-democratic regimes also have the somewhat paradoxical character that although they tend to do a great deal of their own implementation, they may also rely heavily on multilevel governance and their subnational governments for implementation. Although these actors may be within the public sector, broadly defined, they may not be any easier to control than the social actors found in the state-centric and interactive forms of governance (see later). Indeed, given that subnational governments may be controlled by different political parties than the central government, these partisan conflicts may lead to overt conflicts over policy and the implementation of national policies.

Feedback and Learning. The segmentation of liberal-democratic regimes and the multilevel nature of most of them are both a strength and a weakness for learning and feedback. In the first instance, the segmentation of the system makes learning somewhat easier and it is being done largely by experts with limited domains of concern. Actors will share a common understanding about the nature of policies and the goals being pursued. But conversely that segmentation makes learning broad lessons about governing more difficult, so that governance can paradoxically be effective at a small scale but inadequate at the larger scale.

Learning can also be enhanced by the multiple points of access into the policy-making system. The federal nature of many of these systems provides more opportunities for experimentation and feedback than would more monolithic governance arrangements. But the veto points and veto players that may make decision-making difficult may also make learning effectively difficult, especially if there are lessons that are applicable for more than one segment of the governance apparatus.

Outcomes of Liberal-Democratic Governance. As we noted earlier, liberal-democratic governance is characterized by several paradoxes, for instance related to societal contingencies in implementation. This argument can be extended to most state–society relationships. Liberal-democratic governance accords the state a very significant role in governance but at the same time emphasizes that state and society should, normatively speaking, be separate spheres. This arrangement would suggest that the state has the capabilities to govern with only a minimum of institutionalized exchanges with societal actors but those capabilities are often not available to state actors acting alone. Liberal-democratic governance tends to accentuate regulation and distributive policies, none of which are very powerful instruments for societal intervention. Thus, as is the case with all the governance models we study, governance form defines some types of policy as more fitting to governance than others.

In addition, the outcomes of governance in liberal-democratic regimes appear to be more subject to segmentation and specialization than in other forms of governance. While some specialization is, of course, beneficial, it can also produce incoherence and waste within the public sector. Further, not all liberal-democratic regimes will be exactly the same with the combination of separation of powers, a segmented bureaucracy and federalism in the United States producing almost certainly the most incoherent patterns of policy.

State-Centric Governance

The third model of governance we will posit for comparative purposes is a "state-centric" model. This title may appear to be little different from the étatiste model discussed above, but there are a number of crucial differences, and indeed some differences that have been central to comparative politics for the past several decades. There are several other means of characterizing this style of governance. The most common of these has been corporatism (Schmitter, 1974; Wiarda, 2000). Although this style of governance legitimates the role of interest groups in the governance process, the state remains a central actor. The state establishes the rules through which groups participate in making policy[14] and also retains the possibility of revoking the participation of groups.

A somewhat less state-centric version of governance, albeit still operating within this general mold, has been referred to as "corporate pluralism" (see Rokkan, 1966; Olsen, 1983). While interests are provided legitimate access to decision-making in this model, the capacity of the state to limit access is further reduced. While the logic of corporatism is having a limited number of organizations involved – often only business and labor – the logic of corporate pluralism is to open participation to the full range of organizations in society. That said, the public sector remains the decision-maker, albeit with the social actors exercising substantial influence over the choices being made (see pages pp. 109–13).

The third variant of the state-centric model is the clientelistic state (Briquet and Sawicki, 2000; Piattoni, 2003), also referred to as neo-patrimonialism. In this conception of governing, the principal actors are not interest groups but rather political *patrons* who utilize their roles within the state to provide benefits for individuals and localities. These benefits are provided in return for the political support and allegiance of the beneficiaries. We conceptualize this approach as state-centric because it is the relationship of the *patrons* to the state than provides them with their capacity to induce their clients into the cooperation with the *patron*. In essence, then the patrimonial relationship is utilizing state resources to

---

[14] For example, the litany that Schmitter advances to describe corporatism describes the importance of state sanctioning of the participation of groups, and the demands for those groups to function as *Spitzenverbande* for the sector of society that they organize.

co-opt members of society into some stable relationship with the state, and with particular the dominant power-holders within the state.

In all of these versions of state-centric governance, there are some common elements, in relationship to the actors, processes, and outcomes. They all involve utilizing effective intermediaries between the state and the society in order to both allow some form of participation and also simultaneously to control society. These intermediaries may be interest groups in the case of corporatism or they may be powerful local political *patron* in the clientelistic arrangements. Despite the significance of these actors, however, much of the governance process remains shaped by the state, and all the actors involved remain dependent upon the state for resources and for access.

The cast of actors in state-centric governance is dominated by two sets of actors; those in the state and the civil society actors. What differs among these three models is the type and range of actors from civil society and the locus of interaction between the state and the society. Interest groups constitute one of the important sets of actors in these approaches to governance. In the corporatist model, the number of actors involved is constrained and largely determined by the state. If the actors will not play by the rules established by the state, then they will not be able to participate. Further, in some cases the state may create such actors where needed to fulfill the policy and legitimation demands of the corporatist arrangements. In corporate pluralist arrangements, the participatory opportunities are much greater and few if any constraints are applied to the social actors.[15]

In the public sector, the actors involved differ rather markedly among the three models of governance. For the classical corporatist model, the relationships between state and society are matters of "high politics," generally affecting central policy decisions, so ministers and often the prime minister would be involved. For corporate pluralism, the decision-making is occurring more at a ministerial level and may be dominated by civil servants as much as the political leaders. Finally, the clientelistic model involves political leaders who are at once social actors and members of the state. This involves their using their public position to build political power with society and to some extent using

---

[15] For a discussion of the extremes of participation within this model, see Heisler (1974).

their social and economic power to build and maintain their public position (Katz and Mair, 2009).[16]

Goal-Selection. Although these models of governance all involve social actors in some form of participation with the state, the goal-selection remains rather firmly in the hands of the state. Even in the corporate pluralist model, the social actors given significant access to government and substantial power over the final decisions of government are generally reactive. The issues that they will deliberate, or about which they will send their views to government, have been determined by government. Thus, the "second face of power" (Bachrach and Baratz, 1962) is very evident here with issues that might be of special concern to the social actors potentially excluded from the agenda.

Resource Mobilization. Two of the three versions of state-centric governance discussed here have deep involvement with resource mobilization decisions. Corporatism in its classic tripartite form tends to focus attention on major economic management issues, and in any contemporary economy, these decisions concern in large part the size and shape of the public budget. Likewise, patrimonial forms of government involve utilizing the public purse as a means of sustaining the positions of the actors involved, meaning that the budget is central to governance. The corporate pluralist bargaining tends to be more about substantive policy issues rather than about the use of resources (although in practices separating the two is difficult).

Decision-Making. Although the public agenda may be largely controlled within these variations on the state-centric form of governance, the decision-making processes are more open, and social actors may have something approaching a veto over decisions, except in the clientelistic version. The logic of tripartite corporatism is that a bargain must be reached among the three participants in order to ensure economic success and political cohesion. The same is true for corporate pluralism, although the greater number of actors involved here may slow decision-making significantly.[17]

Decision-making in patrimonial systems may be as closed as in étatiste systems, although there may be substantial bargaining among

---

[16] Although clientelism is usually described as occurring in less-developed countries, political machines, and even cartel political parties in Europe (Katz and Mair, 2009), have some of the same characteristics.

[17] Not surprisingly, this version of governance has been most successful only in rich and relatively homogenous societies.

the *patrons* themselves in order to reach an accommodation that preserves their positions within government and society (see Ames, 2001). In the extreme, these actors may have relatively common interests but as economic modernization occurs in many of these systems, the differentiations among elites become more apparent. Urban machines may complement the patrimonial power of rural elites and will require very different types of public programs in order to maintain their political positions.

Implementation. For the corporate and corporate pluralist models of governance, implementation is not a particularly contentious component of governing. The focus of this model is very much on involving nongovernmental actors in making decisions. There also tends to be substantial involvement of those groups in the implementation phase as well, but that is not a defining feature. Indeed, for the corporatist model, the major decisions made through the tripartite bargaining would be executed through the central agencies of government responsible for economic policy as much as through more differentiated structures. The clientelistic or patrimonial approach also is not particularly concerned with the implementation of policies.

If, however, we consider the corporate pluralist approach, then implementation becomes more of a concern. The involvement of multiple actors in goal-selection and in resource mobilization may co-opt them to become involved in implementation. This is especially the case given that implementation in almost all political systems now involves the use of significant numbers of non-state actors in implementation (see Chapter 6).

Feedback, Evaluation, and Learning. Feedback represents something of a problem for these models of governance. Clearly for the patrimonial model, feedback is not a particularly valued commodity, and the elites running these arrangements will attempt to suppress negative feedback, through co-optation or perhaps even coercion. Thus, while nominally democratic, the voters involved will be in the employ of, or receiving other benefits from, the *patron*, so feedback is not especially valued or valuable.

In the two variations on the corporatist theme, feedback is more important, but again may be somewhat stifled by the involvement of multiple actors in the processes of making the policy decisions. While these models of governance are conceptualized as alternative forms of democracy, the level of co-optation of social actors involved in these processes may inhibit autonomous and effective feedback. As these models generally are functioning in multiparty democracies, then the opposition parties can offer effective accountability, but the possibilities of social forms of accountability functioning may be restricted.

Outcomes of State-Centric Governance. As might be expected, the outcomes in state-centric forms of governance are neither as uniform nor as coherent as those produced by either the étatiste or the liberal-democratic governance arrangements. This relative incoherence is to some extent to be expected, given that there is increased involvement of social actors who themselves have different goals and different priorities. We have already noted that the agenda-selection within this model of governance is often conducted within the various substantive "silos," or through the influence of clientelistic connections. That said, there are some mechanisms involved in these forms of governance, e, g, extensive bargaining involved in corporate pluralism that can produce greater coherence.

The relatively lower levels of coherence characteristic of outcomes in state-centric governance are to some extent compensated through higher levels of inclusiveness and adaptability. Much of the justification for corporatist and corporate-pluralist forms of governance is the inclusion of a range of actors in decisions. The range of actors involved is not, however, unconstrained. In the case of corporatism, the range of actors involved is limited, while for corporate pluralism the range of actors is extensive. Even in the latter case, however, the state may exercise some control over the actors who are involved. Clientelistic relationships, on the other hand, tend to involve only limited numbers of actors who in turn "represent" a broader range of individuals.

Further, we would argue that the inclusiveness of the various actors in the governance process would enhance the adaptability of governing. The étatiste systems of governing and even the liberal-democratic regimes tend to be controlled more within the state itself, with the bureaucratic structures within the state tending to institutionalize policy choices and thereby limit the speed with which governance choices can respond to changes within the environment. The more direct inclusion of social actors in the state-centric model will tend to expedite reactions to environmental changes.

Finally, the accountability of governance within this version of governance can be conceptualized as involving a wider range of mechanisms than in the previous two versions. The difference is most marked with respect to the étatiste system in which accountability tends to be formalized, legalistic, and *ex ante*. By involving an increased range of social actors in the governance processes, there are more perspectives on the performance of these processes and on their success or failure (see Bovens, 't Hart and Peters, 2001). While the multiple perspectives on governance may provide more information about performance, the absence of a single, legal source of accountability may make enforcement difficult.

Interactive Governance

The fourth version of governance moves further away from the étatiste version of governing and emphasizes the role of societal actors in governance. The title for this version of governance emphasizes the interaction between societal actors and the public sector in the process of governing (see Torfing et al., 2012). At the extreme (see Rhodes, 1996), this version of governance has emphasized the role of the societal actors to the exclusion of the role of the state. We will not extend the argument that far, but rather will still emphasize the importance of societal actors in governing.

While corporatism has some of these elements of interaction between state and society, we will differentiate these models based on networks of social action and demonstrate their characteristics as systems of governance. The most fundamental difference between these interactive models and corporatism is that the latter versions of governance depend more on self-organizing networks rather than on the more direct role of government in creating the patterns of interaction. Even in the society-centric version of corporatism (Schmitter, 1974; Wiarda, 2000), the state structures the role of the social actors. In the interactive model, however, the state plays a significantly less important role, albeit it does continue to establish some of the parameters of action.

The interactive model of governance is based largely on networks and their structuring of interactions among social groups and perhaps individuals (Kickert, Klijn, and Koopenjaan, 1997; Marin and Mayntz, 1991; Sørensen and Torfing, 2005). The assumption is that these networks contain a range of social interests and interact among themselves to make decisions about policy and about implementing that policy. The networks operate either with a delegation of power from state actors or through their self-organization to address public problems that are not being addressed by state actors.

The advocates of network governance have made a number of assumptions about the virtues of these models of governance. These advocates tend to assume, for example, that the interactions of network members will produce better outcomes than will representative democracies and state bureaucracies and that they are more democratic because of their continuous involvement of the social actors in making the decisions (Sørensen and Torfing, 2005). Although we have some doubts about the accuracy of these claims, we will not evaluate them directly but rather consider the implications of the approach for governance within the framework we have been using for the other models of governance.

The very nature of the interactive model of governance is that it involves a wide range of actors in the process and legitimates the involvement of those actors in making public decisions. While some scholars might wish to assume that this model would essentially exclude the public sector, in reality even when networks are given substantial power they are always functioning within a "shadow of hierarchy," in which the state can always choose to withdraw its delegation (see Scharpf, 1997). Further, networks are not the only forms of interactive governance and some, such as public–private partnerships, provide a clear role for the state.

If we focus on the network version of interactive governance, then the actors involved in those structures are in many ways analogous to those encountered in corporate pluralism, albeit generally operating with greater autonomy. The groups involved in corporate pluralism are clearly working with, and to some extent for, ministers and bureaucrats in the public sector. In networks, these groups may be more self-organizing and working with less frequent contacts with the public sector. This autonomy in turn raises significant questions (see later; Torfing, et al., 2012) concerning the coherence and the accountability of the outcomes of interactive governance.

The delegation of activities to networks, partnerships, and the like may provide those groups with substantial autonomy, but other actors in the public sector may be involved in monitoring and controlling those networks. This responsibility typically falls on central agencies that utilize budgetary, personnel, and other instruments that can produce the control, often with minimal direct interference in the quotidian affairs of the network (see Dahlström, Peters, and Pierre, 2011). This "steering at a distance" (see Kickert, 1995) allows latitude on the part of the actors operating with delegation or devolution while maintaining some degree of control on behalf of the public.

It is also important to remember that interactive governance may involve a wide range of public actors as well as the private actors. Thus, the interactions may involve not only exchanges among private actors but also bargaining and negotiations among public actors operating with different goals. Much of this interaction will occur across levels of government, given that local government actors are often teaming with interest groups to make and implement policies that may have been made at the central government level (Piattoni, 2010). Thus, to understand the interactive model, we need to understand not only the behaviors of social groups but also the behavior of public sector actors.

Having some understanding of the actors involved in interactive governance, we now need to put those actors into motion and consider how they exercise governance. The same processes must be undertaken in the interactive model as in others, although the nature of the processes will be shaped by the nature of the greater variety of actors potentially involved in those processes, as well as by the norms that condition their interactions. These interactions open the governance system to a wider range of inputs but may also make the system less predictable than the others discussed here.

Goal-Selection. The other models of governance assume that much of goal-selection for governance is done by public sector actors. In the interactive model, however, goal-selection is more open to the involvement of social actors. In the extreme versions, the goal-selection is performed primarily through the actors themselves, although it is more reasonable to assume that the public sector remains important in establishing the parameters of action, through the budget if through no other means (Jensen, 2003).

The danger for goal-selection in these arrangements is that it will become as segmented as that discussed for the liberal-democratic form. The close connections of social actors with other participants in their networks may exclude outsiders from active involvement and make each policy subsystem focus on a limited set of goals. The participants within each subsystem may be greater than in other arrangements for governance but divisions will almost inevitably occur, thus undermining to some extent the claims made for inclusiveness and openness in network governance (Sørensen and Torfing, 2003).

Resource Mobilization. Any governance process involves making resources available, and interactive governance is no different. The difference, however, is that in the interactive model resources may come as much or more from the private sector as from the public. This utilization of private resources is especially true of the personnel resources necessary to implement programs. Financial resources may still be primarily derived from the public sector, but even here some mutual leveraging of money as well as other types of resources may occur. Indeed, some of the accountability issues that may arise in these forms of governing is that following the money involved in delivering services may be difficult.

Decision-Making. Many network models of governance assume that decision-making among network actors is relatively easy and noncontroversial. Membership in a network somehow is assumed to reduce the willingness of actors to pursue their self-interest. In reality, however, decision-making may not be as collegial as has been assumed. Part of reason for a social actor to become involved is to be able to pursue the interests of the group and its members. Further, many network structures do not appear to have *ex ante* decision rules actually reaching a decision may be difficult. Further, if decisions can be taken within the network, they may tend toward the lowest-common denominator with individual actors exercising something approaching a veto (see Scharpf, 1988). Thus, the capacity of networks to make high-quality, innovative decisions appears to be somewhat exaggerated by the proponents of the approach.

Implementation. More so than any of the other forms of governance, implementation and decision-making tend to be intertwined in interactive governance. Given the level of delegation that exists within this system, many policy decisions are being made at those decentralized levels by the same people who will be responsible for implementing them. This involvement does not mean that implementation will necessarily be of high quality. The same problems of multiple actors being involved that can be a difficulty for making decisions can also present problems for implementation.

Feedback, Evaluation, and Learning. Finally, the accountability of these governance processes is perhaps more important than for the other models, given the extent of delegation that resides at the heart of this approach. Feedback, however, may be more difficult to obtain given that level of delegation. The private actors involved may be reluctant to provide the degree of feedback common for public sector organizations. They tend to be more accustomed to responding to their own boards or their own membership rather to some external government organization. They do have, however, the incentive to report performance information in order to preserve their funding and their autonomy.

Outcomes of Interactive Governance. The final question about interactive governance is what sorts of outputs are likely to emerge from these processes. We can understand the nature of those processes, and the interests of the actors involved, but the most important aspect of governance here and in the other models, are what governance is likely to produce of citizens. The "what" being produced here is not only substantive benefits (and costs) but it also contains more political and administrative values such as participation and accountability.

The nature of interactive governance implies that it should perform very well in terms of the inclusiveness of the actors included in decision-making. The networks at the heart of most interactive forms of governance are assumed to include a broad range of interests concerned with a particular policy area and to involve those actors directly in making governance decisions. This inclusiveness is demonstrable, but only up to a point. As with corporatism (see earlier), it is not clear that those segments of society who are poorly organized and ineffective in articulating their own interests can be included in network decision-making in any meaningful sense.[18] Further, if the networks themselves define which groups are or are not relevant for the policy area, they are likely to become even less inclusive than mechanisms of governance constructed around representative democracy.

The relatively unstructured mechanisms for making policy in the interactive model may produce greater adaptability than that encountered in other forms for governance. Much of the logic of creating these interactive forms for governance has been to eliminate the rigidities associated with more conventional forms of governing (especially the étatiste model) and to permit policies to respond more quickly to changing social and political conditions. That said, the involvement

---

[18] There are some obvious analogies with deliberative democracy. Although the logic of this format for democracy is to involve all interested actors, their effectiveness once involved cannot be equal, given different endowments of communicative and analytic abilities (see Parkinson, 2003).

of numerous actors participating in these process may produce their own rigidities.

Everything else being equal, we would not expect high levels of coherence in the policy outputs in network governance. By empowering the networks to make their own decisions with minimal direction from the state, there are relatively few mechanisms for formal coordination and control over the numerous policy choices being made in the name of the government. Indeed, the assumption is that governance is superior when the various actors most directly involved in the policy area can make their own decisions.

However, there may be more informal mechanisms that can assist in creating more coherence. Indeed, the actors involved in one network may be involved in others, and hence provide some means of coordinating activities. Groups such as unions or farmers organizations may be involved in a number of different policy areas and can at least inform one group about the activities of others (see Peters, 2015). This may not be as effective as more hierarchical means of producing coherence, but it does compensate for some of the inherent weaknesses in coherence.

Networks are meant to provide an alternative form of democracy. The assumption about accountability is that the involvement of these numerous actors in the process will provide accountability simply because the actors most affected by the policies will be involved in making and implementing them. Further, the emphasis on social accountability taken more broadly, and participation of social actors, is assumed to allow ordinary citizens to exercise some control over the actions of the networks.

Although the problems of delegation and principal–agent relationships are endemic in implementation, they may be even more significant in the interactive model, and the assumptions about social accountability may be excessively optimistic. Therefore, the problems of accountability may be exacerbated (Considine, 2002). Given that networks and analogous structures are granted substantial autonomy in these models of governance, the chains of accountability are also attenuated and weakened. The felicitous assumptions of the advocates of network governance may not be sufficient to enforce accountability within interactive forms of governance. The level of delegation assumed in the interactive model makes monitoring of the activities of the networks and enforcement of accountability perhaps even more crucial than in the other models.

Processes and Actors: Understanding the Dynamics of Governance

The description of the governance functions provided above is important from a more static perspective, but adding the processes is crucial for putting that model into motion. Thus, we are arguing that to govern there are certain tasks to be performed, and that those tasks are in turn conducted through a series of processes that are linked to those functions.[19] We have also emphasized that these processes involve making decisions, and making chains of decisions, in order to govern.

A consistent pattern in the preceding analysis of the governance is the differences in the cast of actors that are typically involved and the types of processes through which governance and policy evolves. With regard to the actors, we have already pointed out that the two principal actors in each of the models of governance are components of the state and the society. That simple dichotomy, however, masks a great deal of underlying complexity. Merely saying state and society have institutionalized patterns of interaction is only the beginning in attempting to understand how governance functions.

This complexity is particularly evident for the role of the state in these exchanges. In much of the literature on the role of the state in governance, there is a tendency to treat the state as a unified actor and to act as if there is single entity involved in the political process. In reality, that is not the case in many, if not most, cases. There are numerous divisions within the state, with the most important for these purposes being the ministerial "stovepipes" defined by policy areas (Peters, 2015). Governments may also be divided by levels of government, with contemporary ideas concerning "multilevel governance" (see Piattoni, 2010; Peters and Pierre, 2001 and the literature cited therein) pointing out the need to bring together several levels of government in order to produce a relatively coherent set of public policies. There are strong pressures to create more coherent styles of governing both within and across levels of government, but it is still appropriate in most instances to think of a more divided and complex state.

---

[19] This is in part designed to overcome a common critique of functionalist and systems theories in political science. This critique has been that these models are reasonable descriptions of the reality of governing, but do not provide any means of understanding actions. We identify these processes and also provide some understandings of the basic mechanisms of action.

Just as the state is a differentiated actor so too is society. This differentiation is perhaps more easily understood than is the differentiation argued to exist for the state, given that we understand that there are often a series of competing interests in society that attempt to use the state as the arena for achieving their ends.[20] Further, as we discussed social networks earlier, the indeterminacy of the outcomes of these social structures means that there is a need to specify how they operate and the manner in which social actors make decisions on their own, or participate in public sector decision-making. While the state may be divided into "stovepipes," private sector actors within each policy area are themselves often divided and seek different outcomes. Thus, as we discuss society as an actor in governance, we need to exercise some care in how we assume "society" and its various components will perform.

Turning to differences in the governance process, this process involves a number of steps, not dissimilar to the familiar "stages" model of the policy process (Hupe and Hill, 2006; Jones, 1984). Like the stages model, this enumeration of processes contains at its heart a notion that authoritative decisions must be made that allocate values for the society. The principal difference is that governance does not have the public sector bias that the most of the policy literature displays, or at least is more willing to admit that the private sector may have a crucial role to play in the creation of governance. That means that the governance process takes on different forms and shapes and invites different forms of agency depending primarily on the centrality of the state.

Thus, taken together, variations in agency and process create a dynamic dimension of governance which a strict functionalist analysis would find it difficult to capture. At the same time, both the state and societal actors have interests in maintaining some degree of continuity in their exchanges as this reduces transaction costs and leads to a more efficient dialogue. The four governance models should be seen as institutionalized forms of governance featuring relatively little variation in terms of actors and processes but also in terms of policy instruments, state–society relationships, feedback and learning mechanisms, and so on. The governance models do change and states may gradually

---

[20] This pluralist conception of the role of the state (see below) emphasizes the differentiation within the society, but all of the models of governance.

transform governance from one model to another but these are very slow and incremental processes.

Limitations

We believe that these four models are useful depictions of some fundamental styles of providing governance to societies. As useful as these models are, they do have their limits for describing and explaining governance in real countries. First, as with any ideal-type models, no real case will be a perfect manifestation of the model. For example, although we have used France as a good example of the étatiste model, the model does fit perfectly as some aspects of French governing, e.g. the role of the Economic and Social Council (Chatriot, 2007) that has some elements of corporatism.

Another important limitation, implied by the discussion earlier, is that any one country may have manifestations of more than one of these models of governance. For example, Southern European countries (Sotiropolous, 2004) and Latin American countries (Acuña, in press) tend to have some characteristics of étatiste governance at the center of the regime, but that style of governing is supplemented by deeply institutionalized clientelism throughout the system. These may be formal and informal mechanisms of governing, or as Riggs (1964) argued in a developmental process, some traditional elements of governing may persist after formal institutions associated with modernity are adopted.

Multiple patterns of governance exist within individual countries (especially for local governments where clientelism is found even more commonly than at the central government level). Take, for instance, Southern European countries that may have a relatively étatiste style of governing at the center but may be characterized by rampant clientelism at the local level (Piattoni, 2003). Similarly, local governance in liberal-democratic regimes appears increasingly to have some characteristics of interactive governance (Sullivan and Skelcher, 2002), while national governance retains the liberal-democratic pattern.

As well as having different styles of governing in different parts of any individual country, different policy areas may be governed rather differently. As Gary Freeman (1985) has argued, the differences among policy areas in terms of their politics are greater than those of countries, and that a policy area, e.g. health, may be more similar in two countries than would health and agriculture (or some other policy) within the same country. Thus, there are multiple dimensions of comparison for governance that can provide rich understandings of how these processes function and how they perform.

Finally, although much of this discussion of governance has been concerned with the policy-making functions of governance, these models can predict the types of outcomes likely from governance (inclusive or not, etc.) but cannot really tell us the nature of the policies selected nor their likely success. This would involve moving the analysis down from this meso-level of actors, processes, and outcomes to consider much finer details of policy-making. This does not mean that this analysis of governance has no value, but only that it is one part, albeit a crucial part in our estimation, of the processes required to translate the wishes of the public and the wishes of political elites into policy.

5 *The Institutional Politics of Inter-governmental Relationships*

We have previously analyzed five key functions of governance; decision-making, goal-selection, resource mobilization, implementation, and feedback, evaluation, and learning. The same principal argument which was developed in Chapter 2 can also serve as a framework for understanding variations in patterns of governance between (and at) different institutional levels of government. Functionalist analyses of governing rarely address this aspect of government. We argue, however, that a full understanding of the performance of a political system as a whole is not possible without considering the degree to which different levels of contribute to systemic functions. For instance, the extent to which systemic goals and means of resource mobilization is controlled by the political center or dispersed across institutional levels is a fundamental aspect of the political system's coherence and, by extension, its capacity to provide governance.

We also put forth that many governance failures have their origin in malfunctioning and/or contested institutional relationships to deliver key functions of governing. Our argument here is not so much that the design of intergovernmental relationships harbors pathologies that cause the system to perform poorly. Rather, we suggest that these institutional arrangements and relationships have drifted from the original constitutional design, so much so that they now increasingly often cause governance failure. We see a growing tendency toward collective action problems and a tragedy of the commons in the relationship between the institutional levels of government.

The problems arising in governance at different institutional levels are compounded by the commitment of many international organizations, and many scholars, to a process of decentralization. Moving functions out of the center of government has become almost an ideology for many actors involved in designing systems of governance, but the assumed benefits are often unexamined, and the costs of such structural change are often ignored. Therefore, we will consider

119

decentralization very carefully as we assess the role that intergovernmental structures play in governance.

This analysis of governance at different levels is, however, more complex than it might appear since institutional governance roles and functions are frequently contested, negotiated, and unstable. This means that assigning functions like resource mobilization or decision-making or even tasks to specific institutional levels becomes a much less technical and objective exercise than could be expected.

Furthermore, assigning functions to different institutional levels of the political system would require that the universe of political systems were organized in rather similar ways which is of course not the case. We need only to consider the difference between unitary and federal states to begin to understand the heterogeneity of countries in this respect. Even within one of these categories, there is sufficient variation in the degree of subnational autonomy and scope of public service to make a general description of institutional roles and capabilities almost impossible.

Further, even within each of the conventional descriptions of governments as functional or unitary, there are marked variations. For example, federal governments vary in the extent to which the central government dominates policy-making, as well as the extent of coordination among the constituent units of the federal union (Hueglin and Fenna, 2015). For example, the coordinated federalism of Germany is in marked contrast to the less structure and more competitive federalism of the United States or Canada (Broschek, 2012).

In addition, conventional institutional hierarchies are less integrated and robust today compared to a few decades ago. It is probably true that the relationships between central government, regions, and cities have always been characterized by some friction related to issues of autonomy, financial responsibilities, and – in some cases – sustained political and ideological discord between the national and subnational leaderships (Harding, 1998; Muramatsu, 1997). More broadly, however, globalization and the increasing embeddedness of states in transnational institutions such as the EU is said to have driven a process of "rescaling" (see Brenner, 2004; van der Heiden, 2010). The domestic institutional hierarchy which was typical to the nation-state prior to globalization and international integration, according to this argument, is being replaced by a more negotiated, nonhierarchical institutional arrangement where subnational government position themselves in international arenas with or without the approval of central government. Higher-level institutions find it increasingly difficult to command or steer lower-level institutions. To put this in a slightly different way, the institutional hierarchy which once was ordinal has become nominal.

The continuing and deepening integration in the EU has also posed a major challenge to the domestic institutional hierarchy of its member states. In terms of institutional capabilities, integration has meant that domestic policy-making and regulatory institutions now find themselves embedded in a transnational system which has to a large extent taken over those roles. True, domestic institutions still enact legislation and regulations but it is now to be "harmonized"with EU rules which are transposed and inserted into domestic regulatory systems (Jacobsson and Sundström, 2006; Schmidt, 1999). The state, to put it in a slightly different way, is gradually transforming from having been a principal toward becoming more of an agent. That said, the nation-state may also be a principal in the shaping of European policy, especially when acting through the European Council of Ministers (Hayes-Renshaw and Wallace, 2006).

These developments in governance, particularly the increasing embeddedness of the state in international systems of institutions and norms and the relaxation of domestic institutional relationships, are central to the argument that governance is becoming more and more multilevel (Bache and Flinders, 2004; Hooghe and Marks, 2003; Piattoni, 2010). We will obviously discuss that concept in terms of our framework of governance, as well as governance differences at – and between – different institutions levels. For now, we will only make the observation that institutional capabilities at different levels and the relationship between those levels are contextually defined to a much higher degree than before. Also, the distinction between national and international institutional systems is becoming increasingly blurred as states surrender some control and jurisdiction to international institutions and regimes whose decisions and norms, in turn, are translated into domestic rules.

With these caveats and introductory observations on the increasing messiness of inter-governmental relationship borne in mind, this chapter will first discuss on a baseline level how the functions of governing play out at different institutional levels. Secondly, we investigate patterns of constitutional drift or the institutional politics of these inter-governmental relationships by studying how functions such as resource mobilization are de facto transferred from one level of government to another. From there, we apply the analytical framework outlined in this book to multilevel governance.

The functionalist framework draws on a distinct logic where the venue of different functions normatively speaking need to overlap. For instance, decision-making and resource mobilization are functions of governing which are closely related and therefore ideally should be placed in the same institutional venue. Placing these functions with institutions at different levels creates governance problems and raises questions about the quality of responsiveness and accountability in governance. That said, the real world of governance does not conform neatly to our demands and governance has become substantially more intertwined and messy.

Thus, we use our analytical framework to assess recent cases of constitutional drift. We will be using this concept to describe processes where the practice of governance gradually comes to deviate from constitutional norms. This does not necessarily mean that the practice of governance is in violation of those rules but rather that practice may move in directions not anticipated by the architects of the constitution. Most cases of constitutional drift tend to involve complementing the formal constitution rather than conflicting with it; constitutional drift which deviates from the normative foundation of the constitution is likely to mobilize constituencies in defense of those norms (Helmke and Levistky, 2004). Globalization, internationalization, and rescaling of domestic institutional relationships (see later) are examples of developments that constitutions normally do not consider or regulate. Constitutional frameworks are by definition static, whereas the practice of governance is highly dynamic. This tension between rules and practice leads to what we call constitutional drift.

Following that analysis, the chapter applies the analytical framework on multilevel governance. Again, while displacing or contextualizing governing functions might be a logical consequence of integrating subnational institutional levels with international institutions, it increases the risk of overlapping functions and issues of control. Most inter-governmental policy-making involves concurrent jurisdictions over policy domains, but those connections have become more pervasive and more difficult to map.

In this chapter, as the others, we will be emphasizing the role of decision-making. In this case, we will need to consider not only decisions made within each level but also the bargaining that occurs across levels. Conventional constitutional design tends to assume that the issues across levels are determined legally, but in reality every intergovernmental system requires continual bargaining, negotiation, and discussion to make decisions about the allocation of resources and responsibilities.

Governance Functions at Different Levels of Government

All developed democratic states display an institutional hierarchy although the differentiation among levels is not functional. Indeed, the relationship among institutional levels and the roles and functions of institutions on those levels vary considerably. Part of the reason for dividing public sector functions among different levels is simply efficiency. For instance, it makes little sense to have garbage collection or water and sewage systems maintenance organized by the nation's capital. Another important motive for an institutional hierarchy is derived from democratic theory, particularly the ideas that collective matters should be resolved at the lowest possible institutional level. This norm is also expressed in the subsidiarity principle which was a guiding principle in the early emergence of the EU. Indeed, the division of authority among institutional levels is often a reflection of the process through which a state was created (Dyson, 1980; Ziblatt, 2006).

A fundamental idea in both democratic theory and the subsidiarity principle is that the populace of a community should have a strong say on the public affairs of the locale and that only those decisions which affect wider interests and therefore require regional or central government decision-making should be handled at those levels. These norms are easy enough to comprehend but their implementation can be extremely complicated. How should, for instance, governing functions be allocated among institutions at different levels? What defines a national interest, and under which conditions is it legitimate for central government to override the will of local or regional majorities in the pursuit of that national interest?

Institutions at all levels of government engage in different forms of goal-selection, resource mobilization, decision-making, implementation, and feedback and evaluation. As we have argued in previous chapters, these functions are essential to all political systems although most systems allocated these roles, or parts of these roles, among institutions at different institutional levels. This chapter brings in an additional dimension to the analysis by showing how the execution of governing functions are allocated among institutions at different levels of government, and the politics of that allocation. The specific tasks that relate to these functions may be self-imposed or imposed by higher levels of government and constitutional rules. For instance, cities and regions frequently seek to mobilize resources through other sources than taxes in order to strengthen their economy. Subnational governments are also increasingly involved in developing international networks and to help local companies explore overseas markets in order to strengthen the local tax base (Pierre, 2011a; van der Heiden, 2010).

It is important to note the difference between the de jure and de facto division of jurisdiction and institutional capabilities on different levels of the political system. We will first discuss the formal arrangements before we look at how these arrangements tend to "drift" in contemporary states, with informal arrangements complementing or even supplanting formal structural features of governance.

Decision-Making. As mentioned earlier, we consider decision-making essential to governance. While it is not superior to other governance functions, our approach is rather that decision-making is present in the execution of all other functions. In the context of inter-governmental relationships, this perspective on decision-making helps us uncover explanations to problems and issues related to governance and administration, such as disjunctures between policy and funding or poor implementation of central government programs at the local and regional levels. Decisions at higher institutional levels define to a large extent the resources that are available to regions and cities, and indeed many decisions made by central government are implemented – and sometimes, as we will see, funded – by subnational government.

The inter-governmental aspect of decision-making has two significant dimensions, one which is related to jurisdiction and one which relates more to democratic theory. The vertical organization of jurisdiction could be organized in two basic models. One model links policy sectors strictly to institutional levels, so that for instance central government has complete jurisdiction over foreign policy and tax policy, whereas regions control issues related to infrastructure and economic development while local government is in charge of social welfare and day-care centers. In this arrangement, jurisdiction rarely becomes an issue.

The other model is to have institutions at two or more levels involved in the same policy sector but with different roles and competences. An example would be health care in Sweden, where central government sets policy goals and provides most of the funding while regional government provides advanced medical care and local government is in charge of primary medical care. In this model, jurisdiction over the same policy sector is shared among all institutional levels. Here, jurisdiction is more likely to be contested, not least because resources tend to allocated according to jurisdiction.

Such arrangements tend to be common except for foreign policy or macro-economic policy where central government retains exclusive control. In policy sectors which require some involvement of implementing agencies or institutions, as tends to be the case in most sectors, the predominant pattern is some form of shared jurisdiction. This arrangement helps bring in organizational resources from all levels at the same time as it may entail coordination problems and ambiguity and conflict over cost sharing among institutional levels. Education in most countries involves all levels of government and complex arrangements of cost allocation and control of the curriculum among those levels, and also with significant involvement of nongovernmental actors. In functionalist terms, such cases of shared jurisdiction often means that the responsibility for executing different governance functions rests with actors on different levels, so that, for instance, central government makes key decisions on a particular public service, local government is in charge of the implementation of those decisions and regional institutions are responsible for evaluating the performance of cities in delivering the service.

Different governance systems provide an array of mechanisms for coping with concurrent jurisdiction in policy. In addition to formal decisions made through constitutional means, bargaining among different levels of government, especially in federal systems, addresses issues such as distribution of financial burdens and benefits (Posner, 2007). Also, in federal systems premiers conferences are used to make decisions about more significant political and policy differences across levels (Cameron and Simeon, 2002). The grant system can also be used to induce compliance from lower level governments in federal or unitary regimes.

The second dimension of decision-making looks at the social embeddedness of the local state and the features of the local demos. A key reason why nation-states have developed a complex system of institutions at different levels with different jurisdictions and degrees of autonomy is that the population in different locales tend to have different needs and demands and make different priorities on how to allocate public resources. Nation-states vary considerably with regard to the autonomy they accord subnational government. Apart from fluctuations along the decentralization–centralization dimension, the constitutional distribution of authority among different institutional levels has remained surprisingly stable over the decades if not centuries.

Dividing the larger polity into a number of smaller systems with some autonomy in relationship to regional and federal government could thus be seen as a constitutional strategy to create smaller but more homogenous constituencies. In those smaller constituencies, decision-making and democratic discourse more broadly is less politicized and ideological compared to national politics. The homogeneity of the local demos suggests that decision-making is not shaped by ideological conflict but is driven more by a concern for the well-being of the local community as a whole than to reflect ideological cleavages and debate among contending policy alternatives (Hill, 1974). Further, this division can be used to manage potential ethnic or regional conflicts by allowing enhanced levels of self-government, especially for minority groups.

This somewhat rosy, de Tocquevillean account of local decision-making obviously overlooks the existence of divisive issues and entrenched interests in urban politics (John, 2001; Pierre, 2011a), but even so it does tell us something about the different political and sociological preconditions for decision-making at different institutional levels. de Tocqueville would probably also have frowned at the extensive amalgamation of local authorities in many countries in response to demographic developments, urbanization, and rising costs in delivering public services in remote and densely populated areas. The Scandinavian welfare states in particular experience significant problems in sustaining welfare-state service across their territory. We see similar developments also in Japan, France, and Germany where both amalgamation and institutionalized arrangements of inter-local cooperation are becoming increasingly important (Jacobs, 2004; Wollmann, 2010). Even in Norway, a country that for long has refrained from merging their often very small local authorities, such mergers are now on the agenda. The important point here is that democratic concerns no longer monopolize the debate on what should be the proper size of local or regional government. Economic factors now matter just as much, if not only more so.

Here, the comparative aspect of urban governance is essential. In some countries, for instance the United States, local government tends to be fragmented and with limited jurisdiction (see Keating, 1991; Wright, 1974). The likelihood of divisive issues and politicized conflict is smaller in such a context compared to several countries in Europe with bigger and more resourceful local governments who also has a wider jurisdiction. That said, more fragmented local governments may create specialized single-purpose governments to handle tasks that have effects that extend across borders, e.g. transportation.

Goal-Selection. Objectives for collective action are defined at all institutional levels. The issue here is the relationship between goals defined at different institutional levels. Subnational institutions, according to constitutional rules, can only define goals in specific policy areas and can only define goals that are consistent with goals defined by higher-level institutions. Furthermore, rules also define the areas within which institutions at different levels are allowed to articulate goals. Typically, foreign policy is to be exercised exclusively by central government but there are also several other policy fields where central government needs to be in control, depending on policy objectives and policy design. Policies that emphasize goals such as equal standard, for instance in education or social welfare, require that central government can redistribute resources among cities and regions. More decentralized governance arrangements, on the other hand, cater to goals that involve diversity and the adaptation of policy and public service to local or regional needs.

Thus, it is essential to consider the linkage between constitutional design and policy goals. Institutional arrangements have just as big an influence on what goals central government can, and cannot, pursue as do constitutional rules (Weaver and Rockman, 1993). True, in the longer term, governments are likely to seek to adapt constitutional rules and political practice to the policy style of the political regime but such revisions are very slow processes. It is such discrepancy between political practice and constitutional norms which account for the constitutional drift we will be discussing later in this chapter.

The definition of jurisdiction among the central, regional, and local levels depends on a number of factors, most importantly whether the state is federal or unitary. In federal countries, the gravity of the system is at the state. The key role of central government is to represent the union internationally and to pass legislation that affects all states. However, states have significant latitude on policy, often including major areas such as education, health care, and infrastructure. Local government tend to be subordinate primarily to the state government.[1] Unitary states, by comparison, display a more linear hierarchy where lower institutional levels are subordinate to higher levels. Goal-selection in these systems is, or should be, a process where lower-level institutional goals are nested within those goals defined at higher institutional levels.

Resource Mobilization. As is the case with goal definition, the mobilization of resources can take place at all institutional levels. The extent to which it actually does include all levels is defined by constitutional rules. The universe of countries displays an extensive variety in terms of different types of taxes and at which level of the political system they are levied. That said, in the context of inter-governmental relationships, we need to make a few important observations.

First, resources mobilized at one institutional level are not necessarily spent at that level. Grants, subsidies, and other financial transfers have for long been important instruments for central government to steer regional and local governments. In most countries, the taxes collected at the local and regional levels account for only a minor part of the government budget at these levels. In the European states but also elsewhere, subnational governments allocate a substantive fraction of their budgets to implementing nation-state programs and policies. In theory, central government compensates regions and cities for fulfilling these tasks (but see later). Another example of the diffusion of financial resources would be programs aiming at redistributing resources among different regions within a country, e.g. to support lagging regions.

---

[1]   In the United States, "Dillon's Rule" famously states that local governments "are the creatures of the state, mere political subdivisions, of the state" (see Gurr and King, 1987:64).

Secondly, and further from the previous point, decisions about how to spend resources mobilized at one institutional level may sometimes be made at other institutional levels. Financial resources are the grease of the institutional system of most states. Resources mobilized nationally are to a significant degree dispersed across the country, to regional and local governments in exchange for delivering services decided by central institutions. Such transfers can also include more general subsidies to subnational government. Furthermore, the EU frequently uses subsidies or conditional grants to cities and region in order to induce them to engage in various activities or programs.

Both of these points substantiate the politics of resource mobilization and public spending in inter-governmental relationships. Institutions and actors at all levels have incentives to maximize their spending while at the same keeping their own tax levels low and ensuring that funding is provided by other institutional levels. The result in many cases has been a divorce of public services and policies from the financial resources intended to fund those programs. Thus, the financial dimension of inter-governmental relationships is intrinsically political and we will return to these aspects later.

Implementation. Most policies require institutional exchange for their implementation. Agencies at the central government level placed in charge with implementation, which in many national contexts is the standard procedure of implementation, often depend on the active involvement by regional or local institutions. This means that regional and local government implement central government policies at the same time as they conduct their own policy processes. These regional or local policy processes should logically be embedded in and resonate with national policy goals.

The inter-governmental dimension of implementation is thus essential to consider, both in the functionalist analysis of implementation at a systems level and in the context of understanding local and regional government. For central government, relying on subnational government for policy implementation means bringing in street-level professionals with close proximity to policy targets while at the same time creating a principal-agent problem. From the point of view of cities and regions, contributing to the national systemic function of implementation is to be conducted alongside the institutions' own policy-making and implementation.

In virtually all intergovernmental systems, there is some delegation from higher level governments to lower levels. This delegation immediately raises questions of agency, as the subnational units may attempt to shirk or to sabotage the programs coming from the higher level within the system. And again bargaining becomes central to shaping the final programs being delivered, as for example in the case of waivers granted the American states from federal social programs (Geen, Waters Boots, and Tumlin, 1999; Pierson, 1995).

As noted above, decentralization (and especially decentralization of implementation) has been a common style of reform during the late 20th and early 21st centuries. The assumption is that local governments will understand better the wishes of their citizens and provide services that can therefore be more effective. That said, however, decentralization has rarely lived up to the expectations of its advocates (Faguet, 2014; Smoke, 2003). Subnational governments often lack the resources to deliver services effectively. Further, smaller and more closely-knit communities appear more likely to utilize corruption as a means of allocating resources (Andrews, 2012). While moving services down to localities has substantial appeal, care is required if that reform strategy is to be truly successful.

Feedback and Evaluation. Given the extensive involvement of subnational government in implementation, the involvement of cities and regions in providing feedback becomes essential to future policy decisions. As mentioned earlier, different types of political systems behave rather differently in these respects. In unitary states, central government is less constrained to interfere with subnational government, despite the nominal autonomy they enjoy in many such systems, to ensure that adequate data on performance is fed back into the policy process. In federal systems, states have more constitutional leverage to oppose such interventions.

In both cases, feedback and evaluation become more uncertain as a result of these processes being executed by institutions and actors at different levels. This is partly because of institutional interests, but it can also be related to the relationship between central, regional, and local policy. In policy areas such as education or health which tend to include all institutional levels in different capacities, evaluating the impact of central government programs and resources becomes extremely difficult because of problems in controlling for regional and local political initiatives in those policy sectors.

Norms and Realities of Inter-governmental Relationships

The five governance functions we study in this book – goal-selection, resource mobilization, decision-making, implementation, and feedback, evaluation, and learning – are all critical to the functioning of the political system. As a whole, the political system ensures that these functions are executed so that the system can provide governance. Insufficiency on any of the governance functions will manifest itself in a variety of ways, ranging from poor policy design to more full-scale governance failure (Jessop, 2000; see also Chapter 7).

However, as we have seen, dividing the execution of these functions among actors and institutions at different levels of the system opens up for behavior which causes tensions among those levels and which ultimately is dysfunctional to the system as a whole (Ostrom, 1990). Allocating functions – either as a whole or in part – among different institutional levels potentially creates a collective action problem where actors at all levels have incentives to maximize service while at the same time minimizing their share of the costs for those services. Also, as all functions contain elements of decision–making, there is an apparent risk that by diffusing the execution of functions across several different levels, decisions will create inconsistencies or contradictions in governance.

To take this analysis further, we need to distinguish between two different stylized models of interaction between institutions at different levels. In the classic intergovernmental relationship model, there is an emphasis on hierarchy and constitutional mandates. Power in this perspective tends to flow from the top to the mid- and lower levels of the institutional system. In this institutional order, the relationship between institutions does not necessarily lead to a collective action problem. The hierarchical design of the system ensures that lower levels do not dump resource mobilization on higher-level institutions. Thus, this is not a level playing field and the actors are not sovereign.

The other basic model of institutional relationships is multilevel governance (Bache and Flinders, 2004; Hooghe and Marks, 2003; Piattoni, 2010; Pierre and Stoker, 2000). This model has emerged in the wake of increasing social complexity, globalization, and cutbacks in public budgets. Multilevel governance is a more contextualized framework than inter-governmental relationships. It assumes, firstly, that although hierarchy in the institutional system still defines formal roles and relationships, the de facto nature of institutional relations is more one of negotiation and bargaining than of command and control. The relaxed rigor of hierarchy also means that exchanges among institutions at different levels takes place without following formal, top-down lines of communication. These emerging institutional relations are to some extent driven by not only the consolidation of transnational structures like the EU but also international protocols and accords that require subnational involvement for their implementation, e.g. the Kyoto Protocol or Agenda 21 (Le Galès and Lequesne, 1998; Torfing et al., 2012).

Secondly, multilevel governance refers less to institutional relationships but more to exchanges between systems of governance at different levels of the political systems. For instance, cities and regions that forge broad societal alliances within their respective jurisdictions in order to compensate for decreasing subsidies from central government tend to become less sensitive for policy signals from the center. Institutions at all levels today are seeking collaboration with societal partners in order to broaden the financial and organizational support for their public service. The relationships between different institutional levels are strongly influenced by these horizontal processes of resource mobilization. Indeed, decentralization has been implemented in many countries specifically to encourage the involvement of societal actors in the process of governing. Although such reform removes some financial responsibilities from the political and administrative center, it also makes subnational government less dependent – and therefore also less inclined to obey – on central government.

Thus, multilevel governance presents an account of institutional relations which is far more contextualized – some would say messy – than the one provided by the intergovernmental relationships model. Deil Wright (1974) once noted that some observers tend to portray intergovernmental relationships as a layer cake with neat boundaries between different levels of the system. The reality, he suggested, was more one of a marble cake where levels connect with each other in irregular patterns. This arrangement is not caused solely by constitutional drift or by actors' transgressing their formal mandates. It is also in part explained by overlapping jurisdictions where the same policy sector is in part executed at the central, regional, and local levels of government. With some simplification, we could say that jurisdictions are defined functionally at the central level, functionally and territorially at the regional level, and primarily territorially at the local government level. The marble cake analogy is simply an acknowledgment of this complexity.

If conventional intergovernmental relationships need not necessarily lead to collective action problems, it is also clear that in multilevel governance, we move closer to situations that approximate the "tragedy of the commons." This is mainly because arrangements which define intergovernmental relationships such as hierarchy and formal authority matter less in multilevel governance. Instead, bargaining and public entrepreneurialism seem to matter more in the contextualized multilevel governance. True, hierarchy and authority are still present, but they mean less in shaping institutional behavior compared to the conventional intergovernmental relationships.

Furthermore, multilevel governance is a more complex decision-making context compared to intergovernmental relationships. This is true both for decision-making as such and for decision-making as a component in other functions of governance. Multilevel governance brings in the international context into domestic governance. As cities and regions situate themselves in international arenas, decision-making tends to become more opaque and left to executive discretion (van der Heiden, 2010). This development can also be seen in other governance functions such as resource mobilization and implementation. Multilevel governance emphasizes executive autonomy, negotiations, and networking, and functions that are tied to formal institutions tend to be executed in much more contextualized settings, as we will see later. Let us now turn to a closer analysis of governing functions in a multilevel context.

The Functions of Governing in a Multilevel Governance Context

The distinction between intergovernmental relationships and multilevel governance is not a dichotomy, nor is there a temporal sequence between the two arrangements. Policy sectors and individual policy issues addressed in a predominantly intergovernmental relationships paradigm may well be negotiated and nonhierarchical in nature. For instance, local governments have for a long time had significant influence on national policy choice and design; a pattern which would not conform to the intergovernmental relationship model (Gustafsson,

1987; Rhodes, 1986). Also in many countries previously detailed legislation has been replaced by more framework-like legislation that gives local and regional government extensive autonomy in giving public service its final design. Such legislation is particularly common in countries with a long history of local autonomy like the Scandinavian countries.

Applying a functionalist perspective on inter-governmental relationships and multilevel governance and the functions exercised at different institutional levels shows why these relationships are not a zero-sum game (Bell and Hindmoor, 2009; Pierre and Peters, 2000). When the previous, rather tight hierarchical patterns of control and submission are relaxed, actors at all levels find both opportunities and incentives to engage societal actors in their respective jurisdictions. These new patterns of collaboration and resource sharing further reduce the dependency of lower-level institutions on support from the central level of government. Thus a development from intergovernmental relationships toward multilevel governance means the execution of governance functions tend to be pushed down through the organization to the front-level, executive levels. As noted, this movement of functions may also be associated with increased corruption.

Subnational internationalization and the consolidation of international regimes have reinforced these tendencies toward decreasing subnational government dependency toward central government institutions. Cities' and regions' resource mobilization strategies have changed significantly alongside the emergence of multilevel governance, as has the inclination among these institutions to unconditionally obey directives from central government. The central government's response, as we will discuss below, has been an increasing usage of unfunded mandates and load shedding.

Decision-Making. As already mentioned, goal-selection and decision-making in a multilevel governance context is less linear and rational compared to intergovernmental relationships. In multilevel governance, means and ends are almost interchangeable; given the contingencies on actors and institutions at different levels, it is extremely difficult for a city or a region to pursue a detailed strategy of action. Decision-making is also shaped by these contingencies. The context of decision-making – venues, participants, issues, etc. – is less institutionalized compared to conventional models of institutional relations. Indeed, these relationships may look somewhat like the multiple streams model of decision-making with the confluence of several factors necessary for a decision. As a result, decision-making frequently takes the form of the garbage model of decision-making where meetings, participants, problems, and solutions are connected to each other in unpredictable and rarely rational or logical ways.

Decisions remain however essential to provide justification for action. This applies of course particularly to the public participants in governance where at least a nominal accountability must be sustained. However, multilevel governance as a largely deinstitutionalized and nonhierarchical model of relating governance arrangements at different institutional levels is far from an ideal scenario for ensuring responsiveness and accountability.

Goal-Selection. Perhaps, the biggest difference between conventional intergovernmental relationships and multilevel governance is found in the ways in which the system sets goals and objectives. In intergovernmental relationships, as we saw, goal-selection is a fairly straight-forward, top-down process. Collective goals are also set at each individual institutional level, but the model assumes that lower-level goal-selection is embedded in goals formulated at higher institutional levels.

Especially, when there are marked social and cultural differences among subnational governments that embeddedness cannot be assumed, and there can be clear goal differences among units. For example, the government of the province of Quebec in Canada has significantly different goals in social policy than does the government in Ottawa, especially then the Conservatives are in power, as does the government of Scotland in the (presumably) unitary United Kingdom.

In multilevel governance, this hierarchy of goal-selection is relaxed. More importantly, the policy-making process is less rational and ordered compared to what we see in intergovernmental relationships. For example, the distinction between means and ends is often muddled. Regions or cities insert themselves into transnational networks and develop ideas about specific projects within those arrangements. In those networks, cities and regions sometimes agree on goals which go beyond goals and targets set by national governments, for instance in climate change issues (Bulkeley and Betsill, 2005). Similarly, central government may have set clear goals but they will have to be related to, or negotiated with, the objectives defined transnational and subnational systems of institutions. As a result, goal-selection as a governing function evolves much more interactively than is the case in conventional intergovernmental relationships (Torfing et al., 2012). Indeed, goal-selection, resource mobilization, decision-making, and implementation frequently involve more or less simultaneously; access to resources requires some sort of strategy, and goals and decisions are implemented along with the continued inflow of resources. The contingencies that are typical to multilevel governance means that there is little chance of rational and sequential decision-making. There is instead more similarity with the multiple streams model of decision-making (see Chapter 3).

Resource Mobilization. In the conventional intergovernmental relationship model, resources were mobilized at all levels of the system although the backbone of the subnational government budgets was provided as subsidies from central government. Given the strength of hierarchy, central government – after some dialogue with subnational government – had the privilege of changing the relationship between institutional levels whenever it saw such changes fit. In Australia, for instance, income taxes were moved from the states to the federal government to help fund the effort in World War II. The right to levy income tax has not yet been given back to the states.

Multilevel governance has developed alongside important policy changes in most countries, toward cutting back public expenditure and encouraging competition among cities and regions (see, for instance, Pierre, 2011a, 2013 and the relevant literature cited therein). Together these changes have provided powerful incentives for subnational government to explore alternative sources of revenue. Collaborative governance and service delivery was one strategy to cope with the new situation; seeking international partnerships was another.

However, central government has further added to the problems facing subnational government by imposing public services without providing financial compensation for the delivery of those services. A survey among city governments in Japan, Sweden, and the United States shows that 94 percent of Japanese city managers, 99.5 percent of the Swedish city managers, and about 80 percent of US city managers have had experiences with such unfunded mandates (Pierre, 2013). Thus, subnational governments in these different national contexts all testify to a severely strained financial situation and, paradoxically, growing financial dependency on central government although for the most part there is not much assistance to find there.

In terms of resource mobilization strategies, the turn toward a smaller state offering reduced financial support to subnational government has had a fundamental impact on those strategies (Posner, 2007). Cities and regions, not least in the United States, have seen their finances erode, as is manifested in a number of cities and towns going into Chapter 11 in order to avoid bankruptcy. While the situation is much less dramatic in Sweden, or indeed most of Western Europe, it is also clear that a state of nature where essentially all city managers report that they have to implement unfunded mandates testifies to the constitutional drift of intergovernmental relationships.

Implementation. Given that many multilevel governance decisions evolve through a garbage can model of decision-making, implementation often occur alongside, or even preceding formal decisions. After public management reform, local and regional authorities in many countries have developed significant operative capability. In the result-oriented governance style which is typical to multilevel governance, operatives have discretion and latitude on a wide range of issues. Civil servants, not elected officials, are deeply involved in national and transnational networks and, given their autonomy, can therefore pick up and implement ideas long before formal decisions are made.

Furthermore, as we touched upon earlier, a defining feature of subnational government is the integration of politics and administration. At the national scene, constitutional rules define the political and administrative spheres as well as the interactions between them. Regional and local government tend to see politicians and bureaucrats work side by side throughout the policy process (Röiseland et al., 2015). This means that it becomes difficult to separate decision-making (the sphere of politicians) from implementation (the administrative sphere).

Feedback and Evaluation. We mentioned earlier that in the conventional intergovernmental relationships model, there are institutional interests at regional and local level which may distort and inject bias into feedback and evaluation. While those interests are to some degree constrained by the presence of formal authority in that model, the contextualized multilevel governance provides similar incentives to give feedback which reflects institutional interests, only in this arrangement formal hierarchy does not deter or punish such behavior to the same extent. Also, in order for feedback and evaluation to fulfill its key function of informing future policy decisions, there has to be a fairly rigorous process in place. With multilevel governance decisions often resembling the garbage can model of choice, it is difficult to see how the information provided through feedback and evaluation can provide a base for future policy choice.

* * *

If thus multilevel governance compared to conventional intergovernmental relationships presents a more contextual, almost ad hoc account of how, and by whom, governing functions are performed, what does that mean in terms of the quality of governance at a systemic level? The informality and focus on results and performance which are typical to multilevel governance easily leads to a democratic deficit since elected officials cannot be held to proper account (Peters and Pierre, 2004). Similarly, collaborative governance which builds on pooling public and private resources tends to entail complex processes of accountability.

Another way of describing these problems would be to see them as the foundations of governance failure (see Chapter 7). The functionalist model of governance outlined in this book stipulates that in order for such governance to qualify as democratic, all five key functions need to be delivered in such a way that they uphold fundamental normative requirements of democracy. Multilevel governance is an institutional arrangement which probably capitalizes better on political and administrative entrepreneurialism than does the intergovernmental relationships model. At the same time, however, the reduced significance of hierarchy and authority encourages shirking, load shedding, and a displacement of tasks and resources.

Institutional Arrangements, Governing Functions, and Collective Action

The preceding analysis substantiates the problems and challenges that emerge as the result of constitutional drift. Constitutional arrangements – "the official version" of how governing should be conducted – accord actors and institutions roles which in different ways contribute to governance. The functionalist approach to governance outlined in this book defines necessary requirements for democratic governance. In that respect, there is some kinship between constitutional norms and the functions of governing; both depart from fundamental normative ideas of what constitutes democratic governance.

The dilemma facing constitutional architects is that while they control institutional design, they do not control the actors operating the system or the interests that drive institutions' behavior. Constitutional and institutional design departs from a belief that rules and norms embedded in institutions shape actors' behavior. This belief is a fundamental aspect of governance and several scholars have observed this tension between systemic goals and actors' objectives. Those objectives of individual actors may be a function of the institutions of which they are members. To March and Olsen (1989, 1995), actors are embedded in the norms and symbols reproduced by institutions. Social norms implicitly dictate compliance with the institution. That said, the norms and values which the institution represents do change over time in ways which may not always accord with constitutional rules.

Another approach to these issues is offered by rational choice and collective actions scholars such as Elinor Ostrom (1990) and George Tsebelis (1990). Ostrom famously argued that rational actors can agree on a Pareto-optimal sustainable regime which ensures collective goals. To Tsebelis, on the other hand, the primary interest is to what extent institutions facilitate or obstruct utilitarian behavior among the actors (see, e.g. Tsebelis and Garrett, 2001). In both cases, however, the criterion for assessment is not related to systemic performance or capabilities but to the degree of which institutional arrangements incentivize actors and the distribution of power among institutions.

Our main question, by contrast, is exactly the opposite; we ask to what extent rationalistic behavior among actors is consistent with the norms sustaining the functions of governing, or, to put it slightly differently, to what degree do the incentives of consequence-driven actors prevent systemic objectives and performance? While we are making no assumptions about what drives or motivates political actors, we suggest that constitutional and normative drift enables, sometimes even prescribes, behavior which is basically inconsistent with the norms and rules laid down in constitutional frameworks. Constitutional drift is not necessarily a bad thing and may indeed serve to reinforce basic values of democracy – Sweden introduced female suffrage, removed property requirements for voting, introduced parliamentary government, and marginalized the King without changing the constitution – but it does violate the logic which guided the design of the original institutional system.[2]

These issues speak directly to the analysis of intergovernmental relationships and multilevel governance. The emergence of multilevel governance has had a profound impact on the institutional systems of most western democracies. In Europe, the continuing integration of the EU has entailed complex governance arrangements linking local and regional government to EU institutions. In most countries, cutbacks in subsidies to local governments, load shedding, notions of inter-local and inter-regional competition, and unfunded mandates have added to this complexity. At the same time, these developments have fostered self-reliance and new strategies of collaborative governance and resource mobilization among cities and regions. Thus, the institutional map of many western democracies has seen a number of profound changes, so much so that there is reason to question the validity of conventional institutional roles as defined in the constitution.

Most importantly, multilevel governance has propelled a development where collective action problems have come to characterize the relationship among institutional levels. It is today easier for political elites to escape financial responsibilities for the programs the launch and to shed the financial burden to lower institutional levels. Similarly, transnational regimes – either deeply institutionalized as is the case with the EU or more loosely defined as international accords in the environmental policy field – with weak authority incentivize individual governments to avoid or defer the implementation of international norms. In both multilevel governance and in poorly institutionalized international regimes, we find that these collective actions problems are related to the decline or contextualization of political authority.

Concluding Discussion

Much of the literature on local and regional government heralds the proximity between citizens and government and the attention to the public interest rather than ideological confrontation that is often

---

[2] When the constitution eventually was revised in 1974, revision meant primarily a codification of changes that had evolved since the former constitution was adopted in 1809.

associated particularly with local government. "Kingdoms and Republics are man-made, but Townships seem to spring from the hands of God," wrote de Tocqueville (quoted in Goldsmith, 1992) about local democracy in the United States almost 200 years ago. Most if not all urbanists still tend to portray local government in very positive terms. However, local government has also a darker history, as an arena for elitism, corruption, and backroom deals.

More recently, the rescaling of political authority, the development toward multilevel governance, and public management reform have increased attention to the performance of local and regional government. The functional differentiation of different institutional levels remains complex; if anything even more so today compared to the heyday of more formalized intergovernmental relationships. For the present analysis, perhaps the most important conclusion is that governing functions such as decision-making and goal-selection still remain largely tied to political institutions, and since multilevel governance accords those institutions less significance than they enjoyed in the intergovernmental relationships model, the likelihood of governance failure has now increased. True, governance exercised by self-organizing networks may display strong capabilities in selecting goals and making decisions but the capacity of such networks to cater to the wider public interest is limited (Davies, 2011; Héritier and Rhodes, 2011; Kjaer, 2004; Klijn and Skelcher, 2007).

The ways in which governing functions are differentiated across institutional levels of the state clearly matters for the capacity of the system as a whole to deliver governance. The conventional intergovernmental relationships rested on a set of ideas of balancing functional organization against territorial governance. While far from perfect, there was a general belief that mandates given to subnational government should be funded and that all levels of government, albeit providing different contributions, were integral to democratic governance. The contextualization of institutional relations that is typical to multilevel governance has entailed opportunities for strategic behavior so that costs and functions are now frequently divorced. We see a growing tendency towards collective action problems where higher-level institutions define mandates which are not funded.

6 | *Implementation, Administration, and Governance*

Administration is the forgotten aspect of the state in the governance literature. The emergence of new forms of governance shifted scholarly attention from the internal processes of government to its interaction with societal partners. Indeed, for some scholars, the fundamental idea of governance is that the internal processes of government become less important than the involvement of nongovernmental actors. Further, to the extent that government itself was still of any interest, it related far more to the changing role of elected officials than to the public bureaucracy.

Several observers have bemoaned the decline of interest in public administration in governing, arguing that public administration is an essential institutional component of democratic governance and therefore deserves its due attention in governance studies (see Frederickson, 2007; Peters, 2001a; Peters and Pierre, 1998; Suleiman, 2003). As this chapter will demonstrate, the public bureaucracy is an important actor in the execution of all governance functions; indeed, in some cases, the key actor. Although implementation is the usual function associated with the public bureaucracy, it is also involved in other aspects of governing.

The governance literature concerns itself overwhelmingly with issues related to responsiveness, steering, democracy, accountability, and collaboration. As we argued in the introductory chapter of this book, the emergence of "new" forms of governance drove many scholars to focus almost exclusively on societal partners or possibly on exchanges between elected officials and those partners. This became all the more ironic as the public bureaucracy by design is the primary executive interface between state and society. Instead, much of the governance literature focused on various forms of collaboration between public and private agents with particular attention to the purportedly novel role of societal actors in providing public governance.

If thus the governance "turn" in mainstream political science meant that the public administration fell from many political scientists' attention, the market-inspired public management reform that was conducted under the heading of the New Public Management (NPM) gained significantly more interest. There are now numerous accounts of the introduction of NPM and there is little need for us to rehearse that literature here (Hood, 1991; Pollitt and Bouckaert, 2011; Savoie, 1994). NPM was a program aiming at a fundamental transformation of the structure and modus operandi of the public administration by bringing in the market into the public sector and redefine not just administrative but also political roles to make the bureaucracy cheaper, more efficient, and more customer-friendly. This reform meant both that the execution of the conventional role of the bureaucracy changed and to some extent that the functional requirements on the bureaucracy changed.

While NPM has been the dominant strand of administrative reform during the past several decades, there has been a second strand of reform that has emphasized greater participation by both employees and citizens in making decisions (see Peters, 2001a). Further, ideas such as the "New Public Governance" have emphasized the importance of public administration and the role of administrative leadership in supplying governance to the public. Thus, although NPM has been the dominant approach to reform of public administration and defining the role of administration in governance, there are alternatives that depend less on markets.

Since recent administrative reforms have impacted both the structure and the modus operandi of the public administration, an analysis of public administration in a functionalist perspective is thus a good test of the framework's capacity to deal with change. National administrative systems around the world have undergone profound change when implementing the variety of administrative reforms. The bureaucracy's interactions with politicians and clients have been redefined accordingly and internal processes of management and resource allocation have also been adapted to the new organizational norms and objectives. Our key question here is to what extent these changes in roles and procedures have impacted the functional contributions to governance conventionally provided by the public administration.

This chapter will pursue the argument that different idealized models of public administration and public management over time define different tasks for government, different steering mechanisms, different

institutional arrangements and, as a result, different state–society relations. For a very long time, public administration and public management have been taught as a province of government where there is no
role for political agency. In American academia, this perspective is
institutionalized in a disciplinary distinction between political science
and public administration (Bertelli and Lynn, 2006). This rather
extreme conception of public administration has complicated
a proper understanding of the politics–administration exchanges and
more importantly the role of the public bureaucracy in democratic
governance. Our point here is that although the constitutional blue-
prints and institutional arrangements in many, if not most, countries
suggest that the Weberian or Wilsonian policy–administration dichotomy continues to be the constitutional norm, the reality of policy-
making and administration strongly suggests otherwise. Woodrow
Wilson was a strong advocate of maintaining an institutional separation of "the expression of the will of the state," on the one hand, and
"the execution of that will," on the other. In Wilson's model, the public
administration was charged with the latter role (see Kettl, 2002).

The fundamental problem, from a constitutional point of view, is
that both political policy-makers and senior civil servants have strong
and mutual institutional incentives to engage each other for advice and
input on policy or implementation. NPM meant a rearticulation of the
politics–administration dichotomy, although now it was referred to as
the separation of policy and operations. Even so, however, policy-
makers remain deeply dependent on policy advice from the expertise
which is harbored in the bureaucracy. This contingency has become
even stronger over time along with the cutbacks in policy capacity in
government departments (Painter and Pierre, 2005). Likewise, in more
participatory conceptions of administrative reform political decision-
makers may be ignored, with their roles being replaced at least in part
by clients and organized interests.

The chapter will also substantiate a key theme of the book – to
emphasize functionalism as a framework for governance analysis and
to demonstrate the capacity of that framework to conceptualize
change. As this chapter will argue, essentially all aspects of public
administration – the structure and management of the bureaucracy;
the relationship with the political level of government and also with
the clients and citizens; and the role of the public administration in
state–society relationships more widely – have undergone fundamental

changes over the past few decades. It is difficult to find any other branch of government that has experienced a similar transformation of roles and function as has the public administration. Since several of these developments relate to the relationship between the governance functions and the state, the wider ramifications of this reform are not confined to the public administration but, indirectly, shape governance more broadly, too.

Although we can easily identify the role of public administration in all the functional requirements of governance, the primary function of public administration is implementation. Indeed, many of the contributions that public administration makes to the other governance functions will feed directly into the implementation of programs. For example, much of the decision-making taking place in the bureaucracy is developing specific rules for implementing programs based on the more general legislation enacted by the legislature (Kerwin, 2011).

We first study in some detail the governance functions of conventional public administration. The chapter then turns to NPM reforms and other styles of reform, to investigate the impact of this reform on the governance functions of the bureaucracy. We argue that NPM was driven by norms and ideas to a much higher degree than by adapting the bureaucracy to changes in public policy and therefore meant that policy and administration were "decoupled." The last section of the chapter will review issues related to the contribution of the public administration to governance more broadly as there are now several contending views and models put forth on what should be the role of the bureaucracy in governance.

The Governance Functions of Public Administration

The standard textbook account of the governing functions of the public administration is that its role – and basically only role – is the implementation of public policy. While implementation is central, a more in-depth analysis of the public administration's contributions to governing will however suggest that the bureaucracy is an essential actor throughout all stages of the governance process. Equally important, the public bureaucracy makes significant contributions to all the governance functions that we study in this book.

Decision-Making. Decision-making is a governance function where conventional models of governance see essentially no role for the bureaucracy. Instead, goal-selection and decision-making remain the province of elected officials. Democratic government hinges on power and responsibility being exercised by the same officials, and since decision-making could be seen as the most obvious manifestation of political power, it is essential that decision-makers can be held to direct electoral account. In the traditional model, therefore, public account-ability was through elected officials rather than directly with the bureaucracy. And even in authoritarian regimes, bureaucracies are subservient to their political masters – perhaps, even more so than in democratic regimes (Ezrow and Frantz, 2011).

However, democratic government would not work without a public bureaucracy (Suleiman, 2003), hence the impasse between insisting on political monopoly in decision-making, on the one hand, and acknowl-edging that the bureaucracy harbors both organizational capabilities and expertise which are essential to the implementation of policy, on the other. The solution to this impasse has been that politicians and bureaucrats, albeit sometimes being in an "uneasy relationship" (Aberbach et al., 1981), find a modus vivendi of working together with recognition of the requirements of democratic government and also the legitimacy of administrative involvement in policy-making (Niemann, 2013; Peters, 1987).

However, as is true for all functions of governance, decision-making takes places in context. Decision-making is an encompassing function covering a variety of different types of decisions. Indeed, differentiating between different types of decisions, for instance between selecting goals and making operative decisions, has been at the forefront of public management reform. This reform has emphasized goal-selection as the only essential decisions to be made by elected officials; decision-making which addresses more specific aspects of policy, or secondary legislation, could be left to senior civil servants (Page 2001, 2012). That said, street-level bureaucrats also make vast numbers of decisions that interpret the law and have real consequences for indivi-dual citizens.

Thus, if we differentiate between different types of decisions with regard to their scope or significance, we find that the bureaucracy is in fact quite involved in decision-making, albeit operating in the shadow of elected officials. But one role of bureaucrats is to provide advice and expertise; there is also merit in E. E. Schattschneider's (1960:68) observation that "the definition of the alternatives is the supreme instrument of power." The relationship between experts and elected officials is a major topic in itself and for the present context we note that although civil servants may not participate in overarching decision–making, their expertise still helps shape the decision outcomes.

Goal-Selection. As we have argued earlier, selecting policy goals is a key role for elected officials. As Woodrow Wilson and other constitutional experts have pointed out, this is a fundamental aspect of democracy as goal-selection is an important political activity and it is politicians, not bureaucrats, who are accountable to the electorate. That said, organizations within the public bureaucracy do press for certain goals that they believe to be important within their own policy domains. They may do this sotto voce, but they still do it (Goodsell, 2011). For example, environmental organizations are generally committed to values of protecting the environment and often come in conflict with other organizations in government committed to economic development, or energy exploitation.

Again, however, goal-selection, as was true for decision-making, always takes place in context. In order for politicians to be able to make informed priorities, they need information and advice from the civil servants, both in the government department and in the agencies. Understanding the complexities of many current issues and assessing the consequences of different choices require specialized expertise. Such expertise can be acquired from a variety of different sources: government departments' staff; the bureaucracy; international institutions (e.g. the EU, the World Bank UN subsidiaries, etc.); subnational government; or from consultants and think tanks. Along with the decreasing policy capacity in many countries (Painter and Pierre, 2005), there is a growing reliance among policy-makers on these different sources of expertise, and with that increasing difficulties in securing advice which is not biased in favor of the provider of that advice. The bureaucracy certainly has institutional self-interests in providing advice to politicians which is not damaging the bureaucracy itself. At the same time, there is a strong professional ethos among civil servants in most countries to serve loyally the government of the day.

How these interactions between policy-makers and civil servants evolve depends obviously on a number of contextual factors, not least the place of the bureaucracy in the political system (Knill, 1999).

The capacity for the bureaucracy to shape policy goals may also depend upon the degree of politicization of a policy area, with those that appear technical and of little interest to the average citizens being dominated at times by the bureaucracy. For the present analysis, the point we want to make is that although the bureaucracy is often to be passive in the goal-selection of policy, there is much to suggest that its expertise is a critical resource to governing in this context, too. Goal-selection entails making often difficult decisions and priorities. Democratic theory argues that these normative decisions should be made by elected officials. Even so, decision-makers will depend on the expertise and advice provided by civil servants and bureaucrats.

Resource Mobilization. We previously argued that elected officials play a critical role in deciding from which societal constituencies resources should be extracted to sustain policy and governance. The key contribution of the public administration is to ensure a high degree of efficiency in that extraction. For developing countries in particular, the state's capacity to extract taxes from its citizens is often seen as a key element of the state-building process (Persson, 2008). And for those countries, the extraction may require more from public personnel, given the reliance on income such as customs and excises, and public corporations.

The role of the public bureaucracy in resource mobilization is however important in all countries. The most obvious role of the bureaucracy in this context is tax collection, a task which has been an essential bureaucratic assignment ever since state building began. Tax collection is usually divided among different institutional levels, and financial resources are reallocated among those levels through grants and subsidies. Securing that taxes are paid is essential to any state; indeed, as we argue in the next chapter, state failure can frequently be attributed to a lack of capacity among state institutions to fund the core activities of the state.

In addition to tax collection, the public administration is also deeply involved in designing specific aspects of the tax system through secondary legislation (Page, 2012). As is the case in most sectors of public policy, programs get their final design during the implementation stage. Tax policy and tax collection are highly dynamic areas of public policy and it would be ineffective to have politicians rule on minor adjustments within the tax system. Thus the tax bureaucracy is constantly conducting adjustments of the tax system, partly as secondary legislation and partly in order to adapt the system to changes in society. There is also increasing international cooperation in the field of tax collection, conducted primarily at the administrative level. In order for this sector to be effective, it is essential that the public administration has a fair amount of discretion in relationship to the political level.

And, again, the public bureaucracy itself is an important reservoir of considerable resources in terms of personnel, organizational capabilities, expertise, and networks. These resources are at the disposal of the political leadership and can be employed to a wide range of tasks. Governments who see their chief role as regulators can accomplish those goals simply by relying on the in-house resources of the public bureaucracy.

The growing interest in "new" forms of collaborative governance and shared responsibilities in service delivery gave this discussion a partially new meaning. While resource mobilization in conventional government was mainly a technical issue of extraction of society, an essential component of these new forms of collaboration was that they should draw on resources pooled from both the public and private side of society. This type of resource mobilization differs in all important ways from conventional resource mobilization as it is contextualized, negotiable, and often contingent on tit-for-tat exchanges of resources rather than a transfer of private funds to the public treasury. Thus, the public bureaucracy will have to rely upon a different set of skills than those employed when merely taxing the public.

Collaborative governance has also to some extent redefined the concept of resources, from financial resources toward more immaterial properties such as knowledge, networks, organizational capabilities, and access to strategic actors. Since several countries have experienced a decline in policy capacity over the last ten to fifteen years, securing such immaterial resources has probably become increasingly important, not only in collaborative governance arrangements but also for the preparation of policy.

Implementation. The key functions of the public administration in conventional accounts of its activities are policy implementation and service delivery. As mentioned earlier, politics and administration should not be seen as distinctly separate processes but rather as integrated elements of the same process. Just as bureaucrats play a role in policy-making, politicians keep a close watch on the implementation of policy. From Pressman and Wildavsky's (1974) seminal study on the implementation of federal programs in the San Francisco Bay area onward, there is now a host of literature substantiating the complexities involved in implementation (see Hill and Hupe, 2015). Some of these complexities are endogenous to the bureaucratic process, while others are mainly related to the degree of correspondence between the policy program and the societal problems that those programs are addressing.

The role of the public administration in implementation is not confined to a mechanical execution of policies and programs. The implementation process is replete with decision-making. This is where programs are given their final design, a process that includes a large number of detailed decisions often conducted in collaboration with professional organizations or civil society (Elmore, 1979; Hill, 2003). Furthermore, the public bureaucracy may shape public policy during implementation and therefore require a fair amount of control of the detailed aspects of design and enforcement.

Implementation is obviously an essential governance function. Even so, however, we see a similar tendency with regard to this function as we saw earlier; governments increasingly rely on societal actors in the execution of governing functions (Lehmkuhl and Heritier, 2008). Needless to say that there is a wide range of societal involvement in policy implementation. At one extreme, there is the implementation of legislation conducted with a minimum of societal collaboration, whereas at the other end of the continuum, we see the bureaucracy transferring significant parts of the responsibility of policy implementation to NGOs, the market, or individual citizens.

Feedback, Evaluation, and Learning. The rapidly growing interest in implementation during the 1970s and 1980s also drove attention to issues related to policy evaluation and the capacity of government to utilize feedback in policy design. As pointed out earlier, the capacity of the state to evaluate and utilize observations on its performance to improve policy is essential to good governing. Given its centrality in implementation, the bureaucracy is a key actor in evaluation as well, although the political level may provide directives on what specific aspects of the public service that are to be evaluated.

Learning as a conversion of experience and policy outcomes into future policy design is usually considered to be more a political role than an administrative task. However, learning is contingent on the active and benevolent involvement of the bureaucracy. Indeed, the bureaucracy should be seen as the major source of memory in the public sector, while politicians are more birds of passage. Thus, feedback, evaluation, and learning is a governance function that draws on close interaction between the political and administrative levels of the system.

Here, too, we can see that NPM reform has had a significant impact, not least in according the bureaucracy increasing responsibility as a decision-maker on how to design performance measurement. Performance measurement and management are defining features of NPM (Bouckaert and Halligan, 2007). It is safe to say that policy-makers have never had as much data on the performance of the public bureaucracy as they have today. That said, focusing on performance and allowing performance measurement to play such an important role in future resource allocation have also had some more problematic consequences for public administration (Radin, 2006). There is today growing critique against performance measurement for incentivizing behavior in the public service that is driven more by achieving high performance scores than necessarily addressing societal problems.

Administrative Reform and Governance

As already observed, the major public sector reforms of the past several decades have been the market-oriented reforms associated with NPM. These reforms broke up public monopolies, introduced a strict focus on results, relaxed political control, and empowered managers (Pollitt and Bouckaert, 2011). It is clear that NPM has increased efficiency and provided clients (or customers) with a choice in service provision. At the same time, this reform has introduced the market in areas of public service where it is debatable whether it has a proper role to play, such as has been the case in law enforcement or where the integrity of the client is a paramount consideration (Bozeman, 2007; Christiansen, 1998; Gregory, 2011; Pierre and Painter, 2010; Pierre, 2011).

As we relate NPM reform to our set of governance functions, the basic question we ask is to what extent this reform has enhanced the capacity of public administration to contribute to these functions. NPM reform changed in profound ways the modus operandi of the public administration and its exchanges both with elected officials and with clients. This reform effort differed from most previous administrative reform in that it was driven more by norms – applying neoliberalism to the public bureaucracy – than by specific problems in the public administration. Thus, reform was decoupled from the problems it was supposed to address. Previous reform of public administration, what could be called Old Public Management (OPM) (see later), entailed a process of identifying the key problems in the bureaucracy and implementing a program to solve or ameliorate those problems.

We will now look more closely at the causes and consequences of the decoupling in administrative reform. We argue that there are aspects of NPM reform that have reduced the capacity of the public bureaucracy to contribute to the execution of the governing functions. To some extent, the emphasis on implementation contained within NPM reduced the capacity of the public bureaucracy to participate effectively in the other governance functions to which it might contribute. The decoupling of administrative problems and reform represents a significant departure from previous practices in administrative reform where the design of administrative structures and practices has tended to be driven by the need to solve distinct and well-defined public problems. To the extent that there were ideologies about governance, these were primarily concerned with finding functional solutions to policy problems rather than being concerned with ideological issues.

As well as altering significantly the manner in which the public sector functioned internally, the adoption of the NPM fed back into the policy process, thus supporting and even expanding the neoliberal political project and market-oriented changes within the public sector. The assumption that market values were both necessary and sufficient for shaping patterns of administration was easily extended to shaping the substance of the actions of the public sector. And, given the ideological nature of the claims, there was little apparent need for evidence to support these transformations of the public sector.

This linkage between institutions, processes, and substance within the public sector is hardly a new phenomenon. The literature in institutional theory shows how institutions rearticulate and reinforce fundamental policy values (Kratz, 2015). The combination of an ideational program of administrative reform and institutional policy feedback has, however, led to an extraordinary disjuncture between policy problems and the process of designing institutional arrangements to address those problems. This pattern helps explain several significant current issues where the root problem is a deficit of regulatory capacity within the public sector. Since the focus is on ideas more than practice, regulatory programs frequently fail to address the root cause of the problem.

The Traditional Relationship. The traditional relationship between public administration and public policy was that the administrative system was designed and then reformed in order to facilitate the delivery of public services. Governments have been in the business of reforming and reorganizing since they were first created, and the assumption of those changes had been to make government perform its tasks better. There is also an extensive academic literature on reform and reorganization that documents and analyzes these developments over the decades (Light, 1997; Pollitt, 1988; Szanton, 1981).

In this traditional conception of making government "work better," the chief objective of the bureaucracy was to implement public policies as designed by the legislature and to do so as effectively and efficiently as possible. Although there was some sense of using ideas from business to inform the manner in which government was to perform its tasks, much of the logic was to create efficient processes that would ensure probity and legality along with service delivery. Thus, the inherited pattern of reform and reorganization was peculiarly public and was directed to providing public services rather than doing so according to any particular template. In other words, the public administration was conceptualized as contributing to governance in ways that would go beyond implementation.

Another way of conceptualizing these relationships between administration and public policy is that public administration was conceptualized in an instrumental manner. Administration was to be a relatively neutral actor designed to put policy into effect and also to offer advice to policy-makers on improving policy. To the extent that there was an underlying theory motivating the reform and reorganization of the public sector, it was the need to inject greater rationality into the processes of governing. The standard critique of governing had been that the dominance of political logic and the complex organizational interactions involved in budgeting and other policy-making processes produced incremental outcomes. Further, the dominance of political logics tended to dominate over rational concerns in making policy, so that governments often adopt less than optimal policies and do so in a less than optimal manner.

With all the fascination with the NPM, we sometimes forget there was an "Old Public Management (OPM)." The changes that were implemented in the public sector, beginning at least in the 1930s, did begin to address the need to improve the management of public sector and to emphasize improving the capacity to deliver a growing range of services to the public (see Arnold, 1998). Again, these reforms emphasized the need to make the public sector perform better, but to do so in the context of public administration and the essential public nature of governing. This was a pragmatic trouble-shooting approach to administrative reform, acknowledging that efficient, responsive, and accountable public administration was essential to governing and governance.

In the United States, for example, the President's Committee on Administrative Management (the Brownlow Committee) considered a range of administrative problems in the United States resulting from the New Deal and the impending war. Many of the recommendations and ideas of this committee came to be described famously by Herbert Simon (1947) as the "proverbs of administration," but in their day they represented an attempt to provide public administrators with "scientific" guidance in how to perform their tasks better and to make government organizations perform better.

In addition to the various proverbs of administration that came out of Brownlow, there was one idea clearly borrowed from the private sector; the President should be the CEO of this large firm called government. This idea was, however, in many ways, the antithesis of the managerialism of NPM that has tended to denigrate political leadership. In this view, there was a definite need to enhance the capacities of the President to give direction to government and therefore to the country. To create this capacity, the personal staffing of the President was to be expanded and better organized – a centralizing reorganization also in contrast to the decentralizing style of more recent managerial reforms.

Although perhaps not as clearly articulated as principles of management as in the United States, other countries also engaged in exercises attempting to implement "the Old Public Management." For example, the Glassco Commission in Canada (Corbett, 1964) was a comprehensive evaluation of the machinery of government in Canada.[1] While it focused primarily on the structures of government and on some aspects of the policy process, this Commission did consider some aspects of management. It lacked any systematic philosophy about management and governing (McLeod, 1963), but still provided directions for improving the performance of the public sector. Indeed, this commission report appears to have coined the phrase "Let the managers manage" that became a mantra for the NPM (Osborne and Gaebler, 1992).

The Lambert Commission in Canada some years after Glassco built on the logic of the earlier Royal Commission. Although the Lambert Commission was nominally about financial planning, it also had a major emphasis on public management. For example, this commission also picked up the logic of letting the managers manage, but extended that to "make the managers manage," and especially to make them manage in the public interest.

Countries with rapidly growing welfare states in the 1960s and 1970s also had an interest in improving budgeting, management, and evaluation. Large amounts of public resources went into welfare-state programs and there was not least a political need to improve efficiency and to know where that money went. The Swedish civil service observed with keen interest the new ideas in these areas that emerged in the United States. A number of senior civil servants attended conferences on budgeting and evaluation in the United States and integrated new concepts into the Swedish system (Pierre, 2013; Sundström, 2003).

This pragmatic approach to administrative reform could be seen in different specific strands of reform such as management, evaluation, and budgeting. Like many of the other reforms discussed here, Management by Objectives was borrowed from private sector management, specifically the work of Peter Drucker. The rather simple idea of this approach is to identify the goals of the organization though participatory mechanisms and then assess the extent to which the goals are attained. The Nixon administration instituted this mechanism, following other performance-based mechanisms such as Planning Programming Budgeting System (PPBS) (Rose, 1976; see later). The experience with management by objective (MBO) was less than

---

[1] An even older example of these structural reforms in the public sector was the Haldane Commission in the United Kingdom (1918).

positive, given the difficulties in defining the complex objectives existing within the public sector. That said, the participatory element of MBO was a precursor to some of the more participatory reforms that were implemented during the Clinton Administration in the United States.

Although to some extent directly connected to the policy process, evaluation research was also integrated into public administration and was conceptualized as means of improving implementation of policy as well as the policies themselves (see Vedung, 2006; Freeman and Rossi, 1995). Although we consider evaluation a core governing function, it is in many ways surprising that evaluation as an integrated element of the policy process is such a recent phenomenon. The conception of evaluation research was, whether performed within the administration itself or by outsiders, that it would provide important insights into policy and would do so considering the longer term impacts of intervention by the public sector. That style of assessment is in marked contrast to the short-term assessments more common in performance management. These shorter term assessments provide some useful information for accountability purposes (Shah, 2007), but are not capable of addressing more fundamental issues about policy.

It must be pointed out that some of the policy analysis and evaluation of programs that was done *ex ante* at the time, and which continues to be conducted, has some of the ideological motivation about which we are concerned in contemporary administration. In particular, the widespread use of cost-benefit analysis and its allies imposed an "economism" on policy analysis that did not necessarily help governments perform their tasks well (see Self, 1975). It, like many contemporary approaches to management, assumed that market efficiency was the primary if not sole criterion for assessing policies, rather than talking a more rounded view of the role of policy and of public administration.

The public budget was another major target of reforms prior to the NPM. The traditional budget has several features that may make it a good instrument for controlling finances and the bureaucracy, but which may produce less than rational processes for allocating public resources. Most notably, the line-item nature of budgeting did not consider the need for flexibility in managing funds. Further, the allocation of funds to organizations tends to underestimate the extent to which delivering almost any area of public services involves a range of organizations. Finally, in a period of rapid inflation, the annual budget process may find it difficult to cope with changes in the costs of producing services.

Two reforms were particularly important in addressing the perceived deficiencies of traditional budgeting methods. The PPBS or program budgeting was an innovation imported from the private sector during the Kennedy and Johnson Administrations in the United States (see West, 2011) and was soon picked up in several countries in Europe, too (Heclo and Wildavsky, 1974; Sundström, 2003). PPBS emphasized the multi-organizational nature of programs and the need to consider the best utilization of public funds. This analysis involved longer term analysis of the consequences of investments in programs and detailed analysis of the alternative patterns of allocation.

On the other side of the Atlantic, the Treasury in the United Kingdom was able to implement the Public Expenditure Survey Committee (PESC) as a means of coping with inflation and changing patterns of production for public services (see Heclo and Wildavsky, 1974). The central concept in PESC was "volume budgeting," or making *policy* decisions about the volume of public services to deliver and then providing the funds necessary to produce the services despite high levels of inflation. Clearly, in this conception of how to budget, the financial decisions were seen to be in the service of policy, rather than vice versa as has been to some extent true in NPM.

This reform in management, evaluation, and budgeting – what we call OPM – was thus clearly based in an analysis of specific problems confronting government and the public administration. This meant that reform, to smaller or greater extent, contributed to increasing effectiveness and efficiency. More importantly, since reform departed from the conventional model of administration, it could also give a contribution to the capacity of the bureaucracy to contribute to the core functions of governing such as resource mobilization and feedback, evaluation and learning.

We have devoted some space and energy to trace the antecedents of NPM reform mainly in order to investigate to what extent the managerial concepts and ideas that were brought into the public sector also entailed a reassessment of the conventional governance functions of the public administration. We find very few traces indeed of such considerations. In fact, the organizational ramifications of NPM have in many ways enhanced the centrality of the public administration in governance. Its role in selecting goals may be less accentuated, given that this is to be the main role of politicians. As regards the other governance functions, however, it would appear as if the public bureaucracy is now a more important agent than it was prior to reform.

Thus, if public administration is to assist policy-makers in decision-making by providing information about its performance in program delivery, its role in implementation is either to deliver that function itself or to oversee contract management; and evaluation and feedback have placed the bureaucracy at the center of the flow of information. This development is probably more by default than by design and might appear paradoxical, given the massive critique against bureaucratic rigidity that preceded reform. But NPM's emphasis on operative autonomy and professionalization does reinforce the centrality of the public administration in the political system.

NPM also disseminates decision-making across the political system to a much greater extent than was previously the case. Not only conventional, decision-making institutions such as government departments are assigned that function. It also rests with executive agencies, with managers, and, indeed, with the market and individual customers and clients. Much of the fragmentation that has followed in the wake of reform is an illustration of this disaggregation of decision-making in the politico-administrative system. Moreover, as we will discuss in detail later in this chapter, there have also been ideas forming, to a large extent as a reaction to NPM, about how to increase the responsiveness and democratic nature of the public administration by empowering citizens vis-à-vis the bureaucracy. These ideas would diffuse decision-making even further among actors and institutions.

NPM as a Shift in Practice. If OPM was mainly concerned with increasing organizational capacity and efficiency within the existing framework of administration, NPM meant a clear break with many of the ideas that had shaped that framework. Also, while OPM was consistent with the conventional discourse of administration, NPM drew on a new, neoliberal discourse of the state and administration. Unlike OPM, which was driven by specific problems in the public administration – low efficiency, lack of client orientation, rigidities, inertia, and so on – and where the strategies implemented to address those problems corroborated pre-existing organizational features, NPM reform was clearly driven by ideas (Suleiman, 2003). The predominant ideational roots of NPM were public choice theory and a neoliberal theory of the state.

Public choice theory – "the economics of nonmarket decision making" (Mueller, 1979:1) – could be seen as an application of neoclassical economic theory on the state and the public sector. Public choice evolved from a group of economists known as The Blacksburg Group, featuring prominent economists such as James Buchanan, Gordon Tullock, and William Niskanen. Their basic idea was that many of the pathologies that could be found in the public sector were related to a lack of market mechanisms, both within the state and between the state and its customers. Competition had fostered efficiency in the market and would achieve similar goals in the public sector, too. Thus, the theory does not recognize any other value of the public sector than those that can be derived from economic theory, such as cost-efficiency, customer satisfaction, and efficiency in allocation of resources (Buchanan, 1975; Mueller, 1979).

The fundamental idea sustaining public choice theory was that the public sector could, and should, operate under similar criteria and objectives as those that characterize for-profit organizations. Indeed, a core reason why the public sector was performing so poorly according to market criteria was those features which set the public sector apart from market organizations; the political control, the emphasis on due process and legality, and the absence of competition.

With the implementation of these ideas, the Blacksburg economists were convinced that the size of the public sector would decrease significantly. As government reorients its role toward a regulatory state and with public service either privatized or delivered by contractors, taxes could be cut and large numbers of bureaucrats sent home. Further, those portions of the public sector that remained public would be (it was assumed) more efficient and more effective.

The Blacksburg group had followers both in the academy and among practitioners. Murray Horn in New Zealand was one of the first to translate public choice theory into political action. With the election of Mrs. Thatcher in the United Kingdom and Ronald Reagan in the United States around 1980 and the subsequent neoliberal turn, public choice quickly came into vogue as a foundation for administrative reform in a neoliberal spirit (Madrick, 2009; Savoie, 1994). With those two large economies embarking on an extensive program of financial deregulation, a large number of countries followed suit to keep a level playing field. Later, as the Organization for Economic Co-operation and Development

(OECD) picked up the ideas of public management and insisted that its member states implement management reform, the global avalanche of NPM reform had begun.

Unlike most previous attempts at modernizing the public bureaucracy, NPM departed from a radically new way of looking at the public sector. It drew on a new set of intellectual ideas sustained by a changing discourse of administration and an aggressive political campaign against traditional bureaucracies (Peters, 2001b; Savoie, 1994). The ideational and deductive nature of NPM meant that it was brought in as a solution to problems which may or may not have been extremely significant. As an idea of administration, it was not causally related to the often complex problems troubling the bureaucracy. NPM promised to cut costs significantly by privatizing or contracting out services; to turn frustrated clients into satisfied customers by providing them with a choice among competing suppliers of services; and to significantly increase the cost-efficiency of the public service by bringing in market mechanisms into public service delivery.

Thus, NPM added a layer of organizational objectives without explicitly addressing the question of the compatibility between those new goals and the conventional norms of public administration (see Olsen, 2008). The tensions between, on the one hand, cost-efficiency and conventional norms of administrations such as legality, transparency, due process, and legal security, on the other, were not discussed and little advice on how they should both be accommodated in administrative practice was provided. As a result, the gains recorded by NPM reform according to its criteria frequently came at the expense of the administration's capacity to uphold conventional values and norms.

Another way of describing the implementation of NPM was that policy outcomes became less significant than the efficiency of the provision of those outcomes. The empowerment of middle-level managers and the goal-selecting role of elected officials meant that the administrative system became less sensitive to political directives. The OPM version of efficiency, based on procedure, was redefined into cost-efficiency based on performance. There was a shift from a rationality defined by administrative goals (what Weber called *Zweckrationalität*) toward rationality in terms of values (or *Wertrationalität* in Weber's terminology), predominantly managerial and economic values.

That having been said, however, there are also elements of NPM that served, or could have served, to increase the policy responsiveness of the bureaucracy. The structural dimension of NPM, particularly the creation of single-issue executive agencies, was implemented in part to institutionally separate policy from operations, but also to create structures with a mandate to implement a single policy and thus to be in a position to do it well. However, with the separation of policy and operations and the goal-selecting role of elected politicians, the political mandate given to agencies became rather vague. Performance measurement and management has provided an *ex post* instrument to correct the actions of agencies, but responsiveness to political directives has remained a problem in the steering of the agencies. In many cases, political control has taken the form of steering by organizing where policy defines the institutional system to manage a policy sector and delegates the details of policy design and implementation to those institutions.

Policy Consequences. If the operative elements of the civil service thus have been fairly secluded from political control, it appears as if there have been significant policy consequences of the institutional aspects of NPM. The idea that bureaucracies shape, to a larger or smaller extent, public policy is hardly novel – indeed, much of the neo-institutional "turn" in the 1980 and 1990s drew on this research – but this issue has gained much less attention in the context of NPM reform.

NPM enables policy feedback from the bureaucracy both through its institutional design and by its flow of communication and information. Performance management created a new interface between the political leadership and the operative elements of the bureaucracy which has provided agencies with a channel to help shape policy. By design, performance management provides feedback about those aspects of policy outcomes that can be measured and thus tend to direct policy and operations to those aspects of policy that are amenable to measurement while ignoring other policy areas (see Radin, 2006).

Secondly, steering by organizing allows institutional reform like agencies to feed back into policy design, not least since it leaves the final decisions on design to the agents of implementation (Jacobsson, Pierre, and Sundström, 2015). Together, steering by organizing and management by objectives shift much of policy design and significant parts of decision-making from the political to the operative level of the system. Again, as an ideas-driven strategy of reform, this is an arrangement which feeds both policy and ideas back into the policy process, only now in a context with a significant principal-agent problem as politicians have only set the policy goals and decided on the organizational aspects of policy.

It is difficult to say if there was autonomous effect of reform on policy. The basic argument we wish to make here is that NPM was based on fundamentally new ideas about the public sector and that what appears to be a rather limited success of NPM in some countries can be attributed to the fact that those new ideas did not correspond with entrenched norms and values of public administration. In addition, we suggest that once in place, NPM as an administrative practice, again based in ideas rather than problems, fed back into policy thus reinforcing the larger neoliberal project. At that time, NPM had become what Macdonald calls the Swiss army knife of governance and administrative reform (Macdonald, 2008), capable of solving any problem. Again, as an ideational project, there were few issues or problems which NPM was believed to be an inappropriate instrument to solve those problems.

A more significant point in the context of governance is that neoliberalism and NPM redefined the primacy of agency, from the state to the market. The principal logic shaping behaviors in this transformed system of governing has become the economic foundation of decisions rather than the public nature of the choices. This transformation has had a major impact on both policy and administration.

We have chosen to provide a rather detailed account of the development of administrative reform in order to show, firstly, that reform did not begin with NPM and, secondly, that much previous reform was path dependent with pre-existing norms of administration whereas NPM signaled new objectives, methods, and even discourse of administration. This is why previous reform represented less of a challenge to the capacity of the public bureaucracy to contribute to governance functions than has been the case with NPM reform.

Governance with Different Ideology

NPM was one of two powerful drivers of transformation of the public service in the 1990s and early 2000s. The other, and chronologically speaking later, reform effort has aimed at reasserting the role of the administration in governance. As was the case with NPM, there is a strong element of ideas, rather than specific problems driving the reform and further there is little path dependency in terms of the prescriptions for change. The NPM came under attack early in its hegemony for ignoring issues of responsiveness and accountability (Pollitt and Bouckaert, 2011). The governance reform advocates did not take aim at NPM, however, but rather at the conventional bureaucracy. Despite extensive reform, critics argued, the public administration remains detached from democratic governance, lacking both responsiveness to elected officials and accountability to its clients.

The key purpose of this reform was thus not to enhance efficiency but to enhance democracy. Much of this was the opposite of what NPM wanted to achieve; increasing political control, responsiveness, and transparency and accountability not through the market but through political leadership of the public service. Thus, over time three philosophies of the public administration and administrative reform evolved. One was the path dependent, incremental reform of the conventional bureaucracy. The second was ideas-driven NPM reform, and the third model emphasized reform which deviates from NPM but also to a large extent from the conventional model of administration. This third model has been outlined by the Denhardts in what they call "the new public service" (Denhardt and Denhardt, 2002) and by Peter Aucoin as "new political governance." The Denhardts in particular search for a more transparent, responsive administration reaffirming citizenship and accountability while rejecting both conventional models of administration and NPM.

This reform too has the effect of decoupling problems and solutions. Reform with the objective of democratizing the public administration has been implemented primarily at the local level. Engaging clients, stakeholders, users, and not least public sector employees can be achieved more easily and pragmatically at the local level compared to other institutional levels. Interestingly, this is also the level where NPM reform has been most visible and local authorities have occasionally found themselves torn between these different philosophies of administrative reform.

Strengthening democracy and popular involvement in the bureaucracy and public affairs more broadly has meant that policy has evolved less from analysis but more from negotiations with different social groups. Stakeholder arrangements or user boards thus elevate those immediately concerned with a public service to influential positions and public policy is the outcome of bargaining both among these groups and with the state. Thus policy and policy instruments are likely to reflect the interests of participating interests, while the relationship between policy and the societal problems it is supposed to address becomes a less salient feature of programs.

There are exceptions to this pattern, of course. First, bringing in stakeholders, customers, and users is sometimes criticized for interfering with both the politico-administrative relationship and also with the administrative line organization. Also, the power given to these groups has to come from somewhere – usually the traditional public servants – and they are not likely to surrender such authority without opposition. There is also an argument that democratizing the bureaucracy in this way poses a threat to due process and legality (see Pierre, 2009 and the literature cited therein) and that this campaign, while noble in terms of its objectives, may compromise the institutional integrity of the public administration.

The wider policy consequences of the democratization of the bureaucracy are to some extent related to that loss of institutional integrity within the political system. As governance changes ideology toward a more inclusive, populist mode of governing, the distinction between policy-makers and policy targets becomes blurred and as negotiations and bargaining replace more conventional forms of control and regulation, there is a very real risk that the efficiency of that regulation decreases.

Decoupling, Recoupling, and Multilevel Governance

The previous chapter argued that conventional intergovernmental relationships are gradually being replaced by a more negotiated and contextually defined order. Cutbacks in public budgets, public management reform, and globalization have driven a nationalization of subnational government, as we saw earlier. We use the multilevel governance framework to understand the causes and consequences of those developments.

We mentioned earlier the international dimension of administrative reform. This aspect of reform is crucial to an understanding of the decoupling of problems and solutions and the degree to which the solutions implemented contribute to the functions of governing.

The problems found in national bureaucracies tend to be more culture-specific than is often assumed. And, although there may be some basic similarities in the nature of those problems, for instance low efficiency or lack of coordination, the solutions that would effectively address those problems in one national context might not work in a different context. International dissemination of reform concepts, however, departs from a tacit assumption that solutions are universally effective.

There are a variety of international organizations involved in the dissemination of administrative reform models and ideas. The World Bank launched an extensive campaign during the 1990s aimed at creating "good governance" in countries receiving foreign aid (Andrews, 2008; Doornbos, 2001, 2004; see also Rothstein, 2012). Much of the campaign was less concerned with governance in a democratic sense but more focused on the deregulation of domestic markets in the recipient countries. The International Monetary fund (IMF) in particular has become the target of fierce criticism for insisting on "conditionality," i.e. specific domestic administrative reform, as a prerequisite for assisting countries in financial distress (see Feldstein, 1998; Stiglitz, 2003). Also, the OECD, through its "public management" section (PUMA), has been a strong advocate of public management reform among its member states.

The EU has overall maintained a rather low profile in terms of promoting specific administrative reform ideas. Part of the reason for this is the diversity of administrative traditions among the EU member states, where Napoleonic, Anglo-Saxon, continental European, and Scandinavian administrative traditions co-exist (see Painter and Peters, 2010). A rather soft version of a common model of administration, the European Administrative Space, has been advanced but it has not reshaped the administrative systems of the member states (Trondal and Peters, 2003).

In some ways, the introduction of these purportedly universal reform models could be seen as a functional decoupling and territorial recoupling. There is multilevel governance involved in this process; the relations between individual states and transnational institutions linking national institutions to the global level are typically negotiated and contextualized. These processes tend to increase the functional decoupling between problem and solution.

It is also important to note that the decentralization and devolution associated with the NPM, and to some extent with governance approaches to administration, is coming under revision. There have been attempts to restore the center of government and to restore the "primacy of politics" (see Dahlström, Peters, and Pierre, 2013). In governance terms, this will imply attempts to impose a more strategic and integrated vision of policy and attempts to direct the administration of policy as well as policy formulation. These attempts at control may lead to politicization of administration, but they are intended to produce clearer policy control through democratic means.

Concluding Discussion: Rethinking the Governing Functions of Public Administration

We began this chapter by noticing that public administration has been the forgotten structure of government in the governance debate. Instead, the bureaucracy became perhaps the main arena of market-based reform. This is not to say that the public administration was not affected by the emergence of new modes of governance, but we do argue that the impact of NPM reform has been much more profound and comprehensive than governance reform. This latter reform, too, challenged the conventional bureaucracy albeit from a different perspective than NPM reform. Governance reform of the bureaucracy has taken aim at the perceived lack of responsiveness and democracy in the public administration.

In functionalist terms, collaborative governance and shared responsibility for public service delivery ties the execution of resource mobilization to other functions of governing such as goal-selection and perhaps even to decision-making. Indeed, this argument applies to the broader NPM reform project with its normative denial of public sector specificity. If organizational structure, management, and relationships with political leaders – "policy" – and "customers" are defined in the market vernacular, this will inevitably have a bearing on the public administration's execution of governing functions, too.

Both NPM and governance reform, albeit in different ways, reproduce a discourse focused on outcomes as the key criterion of action and thus downplays the specificity or "publicness" of public institutions and actors. Extensive NPM reform or governance arrangements, which accord political agency and institutions a minimal role, or a role with only limited societal visibility, are likely to raise questions among the citizens about which elements of governance are public and which are private and, as a result, about the significance of this difference. There is currently extensive debate on the degree to which government is perceived primarily because of its elected leadership or because of the services it delivers. Both types of legitimacy relate closely to the "publicness" of the public administration and other branches of government. Ultimately, the legitimacy of public institutions hinges on citizens' capacity to identify and assess public action and to differentiate such action from the market.

The governing functions which we study in this book stipulate a set of core requirements for governing and are directly derived from democratic theory. This chapter shows the contribution of the public bureaucracy to all the functions we study. The public administration, by virtue of its role not just in implementing policy and providing feedback to the political leadership but also in its capacity as the key daily connection between citizens and the state, is integral to democratic governance. This means that reform of the bureaucracy, regardless of whether it seeks to increase effectiveness and efficiency or open up new channels of citizens input and accountability, basically means altering the structure or modus operandi of a keystone of democracy. Several observers of recent reform have cautioned that extensive reform may compromise the role of the democratic role of the public administration. Ezra Suleiman (2003:18) argues that in implementing NPM reforms, "democratic societies have been following a path that leads to undermining, or even destroying, one of the central institutions on which a democratic polity depends."

As we look closer on the impact of NPM on the capacity of the public administration to deliver on the governance functions, we find that decision-making has to some extent been displaced and removed from the political leadership and instead been assigned to operative managers although the elected leadership still sets long-terms goals and objectives. As we have shown, decision-making as a function of governance is present in the other functions, and the public administration contributes to the execution of all those functions. This role is justified mainly by the public administration's nature of a reservoir of expertise and resources. Interestingly, NPM reform has not curtailed this role but rather the opposite. With elected officials left to define long-term goals and leave all operative work to the bureaucracy, the centrality of the administration in governance has rather increased than decreased. The interesting pattern in an NPM-reformed bureaucracy is that unlike a conventional bureaucracy, goal-selection and decision-making are now provided by two different cohorts in the organization where politicians define goals and managers are charged with making operative decisions.

Resource mobilization, too, has been largely redesigned. By introducing quasi-markets in the public sector, resource allocation within the public sectors is increasingly tied to performance and competitiveness in relationship to other service providers and contractors. Government agencies still receive the bulk of their resources from government procurements, but there are growing expectations that agencies mobilize their own resources. In a wider societal perspective, governments now mobilize resources from a wider variety of sources than they did just a few decades ago, primarily by charging fees for the provision of different types of services in areas such as regulation, education, and health care. Thus, resource mobilization both within the public sector and from the surrounding society is becoming more and more complex; with the increasing diversity of revenue sources, the role of the public bureaucracy in resource mobilization is accentuated.

The public administration remains deeply involved in implementation and evaluation although NPM reform has to some extent altered the nature of that involvement. Public agencies today probably spend at least as much time overseeing contractors as they deliver public service as they deliver service themselves. Performance measurement and management have become major administrative tasks for government. Most governments have created administrative structures – what Hall (2011) calls management bureaucracies – charged with monitoring the provision of public services by public institutions or private contractors. Bringing in the market to deliver public services has increased efficiency and cut costs at the same time as it has raised questions about a possible loss of legality and "publicness" (Bozeman, 2007).

Thus, NPM reform has had significant consequences for the public administration's capacity to contribute to the governance functions. The impact of reform could be assessed in terms of institutional and normative change. With regard to institutional change, reform has altered both the relationship between the public administration and the political leadership and that between the bureaucracy and its clients. In terms of normative change, NPM reform has brought in a market discourse into the public bureaucracy and put a premium on individualism and market-like efficiency at the expense of values and norms usually associated with public administration such as legal security, due process, and equal treatment (Bozeman, 2007; Suleiman, 2003).

Together, these institutional and normative transformations of the public administration have changed the modus operandi of the bureaucracy as it delivers governance functions. The governance roles of public administration have become subordinate to managerial objectives. Bureaucracies obviously still make decisions; goals are set; resources are mobilized; and policies are implemented and evaluated. What has changed is the definition of political and administrative roles, the norms and incentives guiding agency within the bureaucracy, and the evaluative criteria for administrative behavior. These changes, in turn, influence the public administration's capacity to provide governance. The public administration has proven capable of extensive change in terms of organization and process, but these changes have to some extent come at the expense of the capacity of the bureaucracy to contribute to governance.

We have recently observed how the core executive in many western democracies are reclaiming some of the powers and organizational levers that NPM reform delegated to executive agencies in order to address growing problems with fragmentation of the system and to strengthen responsiveness and accountability (Dahlström, Peters, and Pierre, 2011). This reform has helped reintegrate public administration with governance; the bureaucracy is now more responsive to signals from the political leadership, and accountability has been at least somewhat restored.

7 | Governance Failure, Functional Failure, and State Failure

Citizens and their political leaders often have high hopes for the capacity of governments and their partners to supply effective governance. Political campaigns are filled with promises and with hope for reaching the "broad, sunlit uplands" of effective, efficient, and humane public governance.[1] All too often, however, those hopes are not achieved and the public must cope with poor governance and continuing disappointment concerning their possible future. Some, like Bob Jessop, take a somewhat dystopian view on these issues and suggest that governance failure should only be expected since "failure is a central feature of all social relations" (Jessop, 2000:30). In the extreme, states and governance fail entirely and the public must confront years if not decades of poor governance, and perhaps not governance at all (John, 2010).

This chapter will concentrate attention on the rather depressing topic of failure. In part, the reason we have governments is that markets fail and societies fail and therefore there is a need for some form of collective rule-making to overcome those failings. There is a well-developed literature in economics and public policy analysis on market failure (Weimer and Vining, 2011), and the sociological literature on societal breakdowns of all sorts is indicative of the failure of societies (Mooney, Knox, and Schacht, 2011). Likewise, there is a literature on how governments fail (see Scharpf, 1988; Wolf, 1987; Jänicke, 1990; Dollery and Wallis, 1997), and indeed some of the impetus for the initial development of the government approach in political science was the perception that governments were failing to provide the collective steering necessary for society and economy.

In comparative politics and in international relations there has been an emphasis on failed states – governments without governance (see for

---

[1] This phrase was used by Winston Churchill to describe the future after victory in World War II.

instance Acemoglu and Robinson, 2012). These are states that are incapable of providing basic security to their citizens, as in cases such as Somalia that have continuing civil wars, and they also serve as havens for terrorist activities (Piazza, 2008). Failed states can, however, also be conceptualized from other policy perspectives, as when seemingly capable and effective countries cannot provide basic public services such as education, health, and infrastructure for their citizens.

In governance terms in failed states, other actors may replace the state in providing those essential services (including security) as mining companies have in some areas of Africa.[2] These governance arrangements may also be conceptualized as "enabling states," meaning that given the limited capacity of these states for implementation and resource mobilization, perhaps all they can do it to generate governance goals and then promote actions to achieve those goals, through moral suasion more than through the direct provision of public services. Differing levels of social integration within the societies may generate more or less positive outcomes even when the state structures themselves are incapable (Cheeseman and Tendi, 2010).

Also, new constellations of governance may emerge to compensate for state failure (Jessop, 2000). Such new governance arrangements may have the capacity to cut through the complex issues that precipitated the state failure by mobilizing new resources or to commit previously recalcitrant societal actors to the pursuit of collective objectives. Indeed, just as Scharpf (1994) argued that delegation to networks meant that these actors where governing in the "shadow of hierarchy," so too do governments govern in the shadow of markets and social actors (Peters, 2012a).

Rather than just focusing entirely on failed states, we will take a rather broad perspective on governance failures (see Peters, 2014). Given that we have adopted a broad perspective on governance and the involvement of a range of actors in governance, we must also examine a range of possible failures in governance and consider the complex interactions among states, societies, and markets that can be involved in effective, and ineffective, governance. The political tendency has been to assume that failures in governance are the fault of the public sector, but in reality other actors may contribute as much or more to

---

[2] Historically, much of India had been supplied governance by the British East India Company, and much of Canada by the Hudson's Bay Company.

the failure of governance and some apportionment of blame is important.

We need to be aware of the differences between governance failure, functional failure, and state failure. The first two types of failure will be discussed in detail in this chapter. State failure can be the result of major domestic or international conflict. Countries defeated in war may see their state structures collapsing and key functions associated with governing no longer being provided. This may also be the outcome of major domestic upheaval where government structures are seen as intimately related to *l'ancien regime* and therefore ignored or dismantled. The growing literature on state failure also includes a range of political economy causes of state failure such as extractive institutions and corruption (Acemoglu and Robinson, 2012).

Although there are obvious close connections between state failure, governance failure, and functional failure, there are also examples where failure in one of these respects will not automatically cause other types of failure. This has partly to do with the degree of government centrality in governance and partly with the fact that success and failure is not a dichotomous but rather a continuous variable (Peters, 2014).

A fundamental argument in the governance literature is that the role of the state in governance varies significantly across jurisdictional borders, across time, and even among different policy sectors (see Chapter 1). As mentioned earlier, failure (or even absence) of the state in providing governance is sometimes resolved by other societal actors providing governance. Thus, state failure will only lead to governance failure in those contexts where government dominates governance. In many of the small, 19th-century, one-company industrial towns in Europe and the United States, the corporation would provide a range of services which elsewhere were provided by the government (see footnote 2). Similarly, in many developing countries, networks bringing together civil society, churches, and NGOs provide governance and service delivery in areas where the state fails to do so. In these cases, state failure would not in and of itself have a detrimental impact on governance.

Further, we intend to take a more nuanced approach to governance and "failed states" than has been common in the literature. In particular, we will assume that failure is not a simple dichotomy but rather there are varying degrees of failure. Further, much of the literature on failed states has focused on the inability of those states to provide security for their citizens and the impact of those failures on international terrorism. Those failures are certainly important but there are other dimensions of failure that may have negative consequences for citizens. We will also use our functionalist framework to differentiate between failure in the delivery of different governing functions. For example, the failures of resource mobilization (meaning primarily taxation) in the US federal government have not only reduced services for current citizens but also imperilled the longer term financial well-being of citizens.

Thus, governance failure is a matter of degree as well as of type, it may refer to different functions of governing and it may arise from a number of sources. While that makes governance failure more difficult to measure and to identify, it also enhances the capacity of our framework to address broader issues in comparative politics, and especially in comparative policy analysis. We can now locate political systems (and more broadly governance systems) along several dimensions of success and failure (see Bovens, 't Hart and Peters, 2001) and understand better how governance does succeed or fail in different political and social settings.

Some aspects of governance failure may be strictly political, meaning the capacity to maintain political order and respond to popular demands (see Huntington, 1968). This conception of the political dimension of governance failure involves both an element of control and an element of participation. As Huntington argued, one of the principal developmental challenges for states is to be able to institutionalize sufficient responsive capacities to be able to channel participation, while still maintaining some authoritative control. While criticized as conservative and perhaps even repressive, this conception of political success and failure does point to the linkage between responsiveness and legitimate authority in governance. More recently, Acemoglu and Robinson (2012) argued that inclusive institutions are capable of providing effective governance and economic prosperity while extractive institutions cannot. In terms of our governance model above, any failure of inclusiveness may be conceptualized as a failure of one aspect of goal-selection.

The second dimension of governance success and failure is the substantive delivery of public services. This dimension also has a responsive aspect, given that there should be some linkage between the demands of the public and the services provided. But this dimension also has a substantial policy-making and administrative dimension as well. States may respond to demands of their citizens with laws, but if the governance apparatus – implementation and resource mobilization in the terms of our model – is not sufficient to deliver those services then the legislation is essentially non-existent. Alternatively, policies and programs may be so poorly designed that they do not produce the intended results. Thus, as we have been arguing throughout, effective governance depends upon the capacity to marshal resources and to develop effective delivery systems for public programs.

Further, the effective delivery of public services is becoming as much or perhaps even more significant for legitimating governments as are the participatory aspects of governing. At least in many developed democracies there is clear evidence of declining participation through conventional mechanisms such as voting and membership in political parties (Keane, 2009). Output legitimation is important for the European Union in particular, but is also significant in legitimating individual states (Gilley, 2009; Scharpf, 2009). The countries of Western Europe, for example, have been legitimated through the success of the mixed economy welfare state, and many Asian countries have been legitimated through the rapid economic growth they have achieved.

On both of these dimensions of governance success and failure, there is an underlying continuum rather than a simple dichotomy (see Sartori, 1991). For example, totalitarian regimes may suppress almost all feedback and independent evaluation, but democratic governments also tend to ignore evaluations that do not support their own policy preferences. Rothstein argues that nondemocratic regimes are often more efficient in enhancing citizens' well-being than are democratic governments (Rothstein, 2014), a pattern which would suggest that there is an inverse relationship between the two dimensions of governance success and failure. Similarly, all governments at times may choose not to respond directly to popular preferences, perhaps from strong preferences and perhaps because they are indeed better informed about the policy questions being considered. If successful, this seemingly undemocratic response may allow them to claim credit for policy successes, but also places them at risk for substantial political blame (Hood, 2011; Weaver, 1986).

Market Failure

We will begin the analysis of governance failures by examining failures in markets, as this literature has been the foundation for understanding other patterns of failure in political and social institutions. Market failure has been a standard argument to justify the role of government in allocating resources (Musgrave and Musgrave, 1989; Wolf, 1987), and the categories that have been used to understand this failure have been used analogously to understand failures in the public sector (Jänicke, 1990). While this analysis of market failure is based on an idealized, neoclassical model of the market, it nonetheless provides an important starting point to think about the failure of social processes, including governance.

Public Goods. Perhaps the strongest argument for the failure of markets and the consequent need for governance is the need to provide public goods. These are goods which, once created, the producers cannot exclude potential consumers and therefore they cannot be priced or marketed effectively. Standard examples would be clean air and national defense. These goods therefore must be supplied by government, or through governance structures, and must be paid for through taxation.

Externalities. A second common type of market failure is described as externalities, meaning that the full cost of production of a product is not contained in the market price, and hence some of that cost is externalized to actors not involved in the production or consumption of the product. The classic example here is pollution that imposes substantial social costs in health and lost amenities that are not included in the market prices of the goods. The obvious answer in this case has been for government to regulate the pollution, or force the producer to internalize the costs through effluent charges and analogous mechanisms.

Imperfect Information. The third criterion justifying government interventions into the market is the absence of perfect information, especially by consumers. Producers may have little incentive to provide consumers full information about products, especially if those products are defective or dangerous. Therefore, governments must regulate the market to protect consumers either through mandating more information be provided (Thomas, 2014) or through prohibiting shoddy products from being in the market (product safety regulations).

Natural Monopolies and Increasing Returns. The public sector may also have to intervene in order to manage natural monopolies. Although there is a general bias against monopolies in market theories, some products, e.g. water, are most efficiently provided through monopolies that provide increasing returns to scale. It would make little sense to have multiple companies each laying its own water pipes within the same city. Therefore, governments will either provide the commodity itself or regulate the industry that is granted the monopoly franchise. The market, as Jänicke (1990:32) points out, "has a constant tendency to abolish itself" and the state therefore needs to enforce regulations to ensure continued competition in the market.

Distributional Inequities. Finally, the market tends to produce inequitable outcomes for citizens. To some extent, capitalist societies may accept those unequal outcomes as a natural, and even desirable, outcome of market forces. But extreme inequalities have become politically unacceptable in most democracies and the state intervenes though taxation and social programs to rectify the inequities. It should be noted, however, that the willingness of governments to make such interventions has declined as a consequence of the neoliberal movement in governments, and levels of inequality have been increasing, especially in Anglo-American democracies (see Stiglitz, 2012).

In summary, although markets are often extolled (especially by right-wing politicians) as the best source of allocation available for modern societies, in fact they have significant imperfections that require intervention from government and its allies in governance. These governance interventions allow goods that could not be produced readily, or as efficiently, through competitive markets to be produced and also compensate the losers in the market allocation, at least to providing a social safety net. Although these interventions are generally considered desirable and even essential in contemporary political systems, they are themselves not perfect and may create their own social and economic problems, as discussed later.

Governance Failures

The five categories of market failure above have clear analogues in the public sector and in the practice of governance. In some cases, the failures are very similar to those in the market, while in others they may be the exact opposite of those in the market. In addition to those governance failures that are directly analogous to market failures, there are others that also should be considered when thinking about the potential for governance failure, and hence choices about the selection of modes of intervention into society.

Private Goods. Just as the market has difficulties in allocating public goods, governance systems may encounter difficulties in the provision of private goods, and these goods may create significant governance failure. These private goods may be of two types. One is that government organizations, and individual bureaucrats and politicians, may attempt to create private goods for themselves through rent-seeking activities (Brown, Earle, and Gehlbach, 2009; Niskanen, 1971). That is, public sector actors appropriate public revenues and other public goods for themselves, or use their offices for personal gain. The extreme example of this rent-seeking by actors in the public sector is corruption (Helm, 2010; Rothstein, 2012).

The second source of governance failure through the creation of private goods is that the state and its allies may be captured by particular interests and produce goods that benefit those interests rather than the public more generally. This capture of the state and its organizations for private gain has been described in the United States famously by Lowi (1979) and is a standard critique of regimes in less-developed countries. But this pattern may not be confined to those regimes but may also extend to clientelism in Southern Europe and to the domination of cartel parties in much of Western Europe (Katz and Mair, 2009; Streeck and Schmitter, 1986). In all these cases, the pursuit of the public interest becomes subsumed to the use of public power for private purposes.

Internalities. Charles Wolf (1987) discussed "internalities" of public sector intervention as the direct analogue of externalities in the market. Government decision-making and policy choices often contain elements that deviate from allocative efficiency and hence impose costs on society. In governance arrangements, the allocative system is shaped largely through the relative political power of different groups, and when that power is imbalanced, inefficient choices are made. These usually conform to the upper-class bias identified by Schattschneider (1960; see also Schlozman, Verba, and Brady, 2012) but also may reflect differential power of regional and ethnic groups in allocation. This argument begs the question, however, of whether allocative efficiency is the primary quality by which we should assess governance.

Imperfect Information. Markets often do not provide consumers adequate information to make effective choices about the products they may purchase. The public sector may also risk failures because of difficulties with information processing. In contrast to the market, however, information processing in the public sector is embedded in an organizational structure with recognized process and actors. Although this does not in any way preclude the occurrence of flaws and errors in the information processing, organizational learning would suggest that the quality of information processes improves over time. The obvious problem is of course if there are organizational or other incentives for actors to control and withhold information (see earlier). In addition, governments often confront problems of "groupthink" ('t Hart, 1980; 't Hart, Stern and Sundelius, 1997), meaning that the ideological or partisan commitments of the actors involved may lead them to close prematurely the range of policy options being considered.

Unnatural Markets. Just as markets may fail because of the desirability of providing some types of goods and services through monopolies, so too can governance perform inadequately when it fails to recognize the limits of markets to provide certain goods (Gingrich, 2011). The emphasis on market provision of public services in neoliberalism, and within the NPM, has produced privatization of some public programs that might not be good candidates for market provision, and also the use of market mechanisms, e.g. vouchers, for the delivery of services when again the assumption that a market can be viable within the policy area is at best questionable.

Governments also may create their own monopolies of services that can be argued to produce higher costs and lower quality than might be present in a more competitive market. This has long been argued to be the case for public education, with voucher programs of various sorts being proposed as remedies. Even in well-established government programs, such as postal services, the monopoly has been broken and alternative sources of transmitting mail (both virtual and physical) have undermined the public service.

Other Governance Failures. In addition to the governance failures that may be analogous to market failures, there are several other issues that arise within governance itself that produce failures. These tend to be characteristic of political action, but they may also afflict the social actors who cooperate with public sector actors. Indeed, in governance settings the interactions of the two sets of actors – public and private –

may exacerbate the problems rather than ameliorate them as is often assumed by the advocates of interactive forms of governance.

Perceptions of time and the relative time schedules of actors can produce other governance failures. Politicians often have a short-time perspective, given that they must face reelection within a limited period. This in turn means that their policy preferences are for short-term results, even if the problem in question requires a longer time for effective solution. That said, administrators also may want quick results, given that they are now motivated by performance indicators that are at the most annual, and also their organizations depend upon annual appropriations. Finally, the social actors also may have relatively short-time horizons, given that they want to demonstrate success for their own members, and perhaps to their international partners.[3]

The disjuncture of costs and benefits within the public sector also often produces suboptimal outcomes within the public sector. James Q. Wilson (1980) has classified policies in terms of the concentration of costs and benefits. In terms of governance failure, the difficult cases may be those that have concentrated benefits and diffuse costs, and vice versa. The former case is characteristic of policies dominated by interest groups who are capable of gaining benefits with the costs being less visible to the broader public who pay for them. Agriculture policy is a clear example, with consumers bearing the costs of subsidies not only in taxes but also in higher food prices.

It is more difficult politically to produce situations of concentrated costs and diffuse benefits. Most public programs that have diffuse benefits, such as defense and regulation, are funded from general taxation, so that there is a correspondence between benefits and costs. The benefits of programs that have diffuse impacts on the population may be difficult to identify for the ordinary citizens and hence building a political coalition to support them is difficult. Depositor insurance may come close to being this type of program, with charges on banks paying for insurance that benefits all depositors.[4]

---

[3] The private sector may also have relatively short time horizons, as businesses and their management are increasingly evaluated by quarterly profits rather than by their long-term profits and growth.

[4] This will depend in part on whether banks can pass along the costs of the program to depositors in the form of higher fees or lower interest rates.

Governance Functions and Failure

Are all the functions identified in Chapter 2 as elements of governance equally critical for performance and for good governance? While all of these functions are important for governing, they may make different contributions to governing and may have differential impacts for different types of policies and for different types of political systems. Few governance systems are total failures, but similarly few are total successes, and therefore we need to consider the various patterns of success and failure in governance in order to understand governance in more comparative perspective.

As well as thinking about each of these functions, and its possible contributions of success and failure independently, we should also consider their interactions. For example, if a governance system has difficulty in selecting among competing goals and in making those goals coherent, that in turn may make implementation more problematic as the implementors may be forced to select among competing and inconsistent goals (Lane, 1983), and evaluators may find it difficult to determine whether goals really have been reached (Vedung, 2006). Similarly, failures to extract sufficient resources from the environment will diminish the capacity of the governance system in any numbers of ways. Indeed, we will be arguing that each of the functions we discuss in this book is critical to successful governance to the extent that failure in one function is sufficient to arrest the process of governing. It is little help if a government excels in making informed decisions if it lacks the resources or implementation capacity to put its plans into operation. Similarly, if the selection of goals fails to define relevant, attainable goals, performing all other functions flawlessly will not make up for the failure in goal setting.

Failures of Decision-Making. Making formal decisions, whether those decisions concern public policy, governance arrangements, or institutional design, is the critical stage in the governing process. As mentioned earlier, this is where commitments are put to the test and where priorities are translated into action. Given the centrality of decision-making in governance, this is also the stage which is perhaps most prone to failure. These failures relate both to the extent to which substantive decisions are made and to the discriminatory and steering nature of those decisions. Even the weakest and most fragile governments do make decisions; the issue is rather the degree to which those decisions have a distinct substantive meaning.

Decision-making failure are often related either to complex decision-making rules, making it exceedingly difficult to produce majoritarian support for proposals, or by constellation of actors obstructing decision-making; filibuster would be the most obvious example of such behavior. Sometimes, however, purpose action can make up for institutional or procedural complexities. A case in point would be the long line of parliamentary weak, and therefore short-lived, Italian governments during much of the early postwar period. In this deeply divided parliamentary system with frequent government turnover, providing governance, particularly making substantive decisions, was a major challenge (di Palma, 1977). Di Palma observed how the political parties would attempt to circumvent the parliamentary gridlock and instability to produce decisions which provided at least some policy direction and governance.

Similar situations of sustained parliamentary gridlock and institutional paralysis have been recorded in many other national contexts. We mentioned earlier the political turmoil in the US Congress, which in 2013 drove the federal government to the point of budgetary deadlock and inability to cover running costs in the public service. While this situation is a good illustration of failures in resource mobilization, it also highlights the problems in decision-making and the impact of multiple veto players on the capacity to govern (Ganghof, 2003). In particular, in this case, the deadlock had dire consequences of failure to deliver that governance function. Formal decision-making is not just important in a governance perspective; it is also an essential part of organizational life and leadership. Public institutional systems such as bureaucracies or subnational governments are designed specifically to produce decisions on legal, administrative, or budgetary matters.

The important observation here is that governance failure related to decision-making is not just a dichotomous matter of whether or not decisions are being made; it is just as much a matter of the quality of those decisions. Political systems under stress may make decisions which do not reflect the needs of the system or the preferences of its elite but are more compromises among contending views and constituencies inside the system. Most political scientists are familiar with Bachrach and Baratz' (1962) seminal distinction between decisions and non-decisions, but there could also be added a third category of decisions which are mainly symbolic and hollow of priorities or directives.

More broadly, by focusing on the quality of decisions, we should consider the role of expertise and policy capacity in the public decision-making process. Decisions that are built on a process where expertise has not been invited or its views have been ignored are more likely to lead to imperfect governance decisions compared to those emerging from more comprehensive processes. Thus, the relationship between politicians and bureaucrats and the capacity of the system to learn hold important parts of the puzzle of how to relate governance failure to decision-making.

Furthermore, different models of governance tend to display different types of decision-making failures. If we compare the étatiste and network models of governance, we find that both models engender risks for governance failure related to decision-making. In the étatiste governance model, decisions are made with very little consideration of how the surrounding society is likely to respond to those decisions. The points of contact between state and society are few and tend to be characterized by communication in one direction only (see Pierre and Peters, 2005). As a result, decisions in this governance model tend to be much more reflective of the state's preferences and analysis of societal problems than of the society's and citizens' preferences. That creates a risk that governance decisions will not be efficient or even relevant to specific issues or problems.

In network governance, decisions are deeply embedded in society, or perhaps more correctly in segments of society. Governance decisions are likely to address specific problems, but they will do so drawing on the preferences of the members of the network and therefore often fail in articulating the wider public interest. Furthermore, different types of networks differ significantly in their decision-making capacity. Inclusive networks excel in mobilizing constituencies but will have problems making decisions which go beyond values defined by the least common denominator in the network. Exclusive networks, on the other hand, have a more homogenous cadre of members than open networks but that also means that they represent an even smaller segment of society and that therefore their capacity to make good governance decisions is equally constrained.

All of this means that decision-making, which we see as the most significant of the governance functions discussed in this book, holds an important part of the answer to the question of why governance failure occurs. Crucially, this account of governance failure has significance irrespective of institutional arrangements or even the wealth of the country. Decision-making capacity is related to a large number of factors related to institutions and actors and the relationship between these two (see Chapter 3). Again, governance failure may be the result not so much of the absence of decisions as of poor decisions.

Failures of Goal-Selection. Governments and their publics are rarely short of things that they want to do, and therefore selecting goals may not appear to be a particularly important source of governance failure. That capacity to set goals, however, may depend upon the nature of the political systems, their linkages with social actors, and degree of social division within the society. These factors may affect the capacity to establish *collective* goals, and to create coherence among the goals that individual components of the governance system may want to implement. As Buchanan and Tullock (1962) pointed out, establishing goals through imposition is relatively easy (in terms of the decision-making costs involved) but will involve extensive exclusion costs upon many segments of the society.

The capacity to set goals effectively may also depend upon the nature of the challenges facing the governance systems and the extent to which those challenges are agreed among the various actors within the governance system. For example, countries in the midst of major civil conflicts or with limited economic resources may be incapable of establishing realistic goals. Further, if there are intense social and political divisions within a country, then goal-selection and coherence may be almost unattainable. For example, the United States in the period following the 2010 Congressional elections was characterized by rather intractable policy differences and hence an incapacity to address the major challenge of the "fiscal cliff."

The multiplicity of possible goals in governing, and the political contention over those goals, may produce outcomes that will contribute to subsequent failures in governance. In democratic regimes, multiple goals may lead to compromise and in turn to rather diffuse and vague goals as expressed through legislation. In hybrid forms of governance, there is the additional problem of integrating different goals, and different types of goals, into a coherent program. As argued earlier, private interests are not likely to advance goals and policy objectives that are reflective of the public interest but more an articulation of their own interests. Again, goals may be formulated eventually but possibly at the expense of clarity and coherence.

Failures in goal-selection may also occur through the opposite dynamics, with inadequate consultation and limited involvement of social actors. While this hierarchical form of governance is usually characteristic of authoritarian regimes, it may also occur within democratic regimes, especially those that have powerful and professionalized bureaucracies. Those organizations, or perhaps even well-placed individuals within them, may be able to shape policies with limited involvement of political and social forces. In some instances that insulated form of decision-making may include some extremely talented individuals, but its lack of connection with the surrounding realities may produce inadequate governance choices.

Further, policy choices may be driven by ideologies and policy choices that may not reflect the political or substantive realities of the problems being addressed (see Castles, 1998). In either case, the program resulting from this style of policy-making may be difficult to implement and may not produce the desired outcomes. The actors responsible may, however, be more concerned with the capacity to extract (Acemoglu and Robinson, 2012) than they are with the quality of governance being produced.

While social actors often are conceptualized as major positive contributors to governance, they can also create problems for creating coherent sets of policy goals. Especially, when those groups perceive themselves to be in opposition to the government, and the government considers the groups to be outsiders attempting to undermine the existing political order, then conflict and incoherence may be the logical outcome. This pattern appears characteristic of some developing regimes in which civil society groups are perceived as being more representative of the international community than of national political interests (White, 1994).[5] Indeed, civil society organizations are often seen as components of some global governance ambition rather than as components of national governance (Scholte, 2004), especially by Conservative regimes that seek greater control over their citizens.[6]

---

[5] There may be some element of validity in those claims given that many civil society groups receive substantial funding from international sources and may tied to organizations, e.g. Amnesty International, that may not be friendly to the existing regime.

[6] This may include the opposition of the Republican Party in the United States to the United Nations Convention of the Rights of the Disabled.

Failures of Resource Mobilization. If governments know clearly what they want to do, they still must mobilize the resources to make those policies work successfully. Governments in most developed countries assume that they can extract what they need from the economy and society, with the principal questions being whether the political costs are worth it, and what would the possible economic effects be of taking more money for the public sector. Even in those countries, the assumption that resources are there for the asking may be excessively optimistic, and the politics of revenue raising is far from painless for politicians or for those being taxed.

In the more developed systems, there are several crucial constraints on the capacity of governments to extract revenue. One is the willingness of the public to pay their taxes. Tax evasion is not distributed evenly across countries but is also not uncommon even in the most law-abiding countries (Cowell, 1990). In the countries of Southern Europe, there is significant evasion that makes it difficult for governments to raise adequate revenue, or at least deny governments the most effective forms of revenue collection. Greece, for example, is only capable of raising less than 20 percent of its total government revenue from income taxation (personal and corporate), while the average for OECD countries is almost 40 percent. Therefore, Greece has had had difficulties in raising enough revenue for its expenditure commitments and has had to rely on less buoyant taxes like expenditure taxes.

The other major constraint on revenue generation in the developed democracies has been ideological. At least in the more liberal democracies, the parties of the political right tend to resist taxation, and in the case of some, elements of the Republican Party in the United States tend to resist taxation quite vehemently. This resistance may be part of an explicit strategy of "starving the beast" in order to undermine effective governance, but even in the milder forms this resistance to taxation may prevent the public sector, and its allies, from achieving the level of effectiveness, and efficiency, that might be possible.[7]

The resource mobilization constraints for less-developed countries are substantially more pressing (Persson, 2008; Radian, 1980) than are those for more developed countries. Obviously, these countries are

---

[7] The point here is that low-cost governance may not be the most efficient governance. For example, if inadequate investment in public transportation means that the system will be running with antiquated equipment that is not energy efficient and is prone to breakdowns, then this will not be an efficient service.

poorer and therefore have less money for governments to tax. At the most basic level, some sectors of the economy in these regimes may not be monetized, and hence it is difficult for governments to tax. Barter and other forms of nonmonetary exchange may constitute up to half percent of the economic activity in some countries but there is no effective tax "handle" for government. Even when the economy is monetized, much of the economic activity is in small enterprises and individual traders so that it is more difficult for governments to collect income than if that activity were occurring in larger firms with proper accounting.

For both developed and less-developed systems, there are other problems for resource mobilization. Governments do not need only money to be successful; they must also mobilize human and organizational resources. The capacity of the public sector to attract the "best and brightest" to work in its ranks varies markedly across governance systems. In some European and Asian systems, working for the state carries extremely high prestige, while in countries such as the United States, it is considered tantamount to failure (see Derlien and Peters, 2008). Clearly, everything else being equal, the capacity to attract high-quality employees will enhance governance capacity. In governance terms, however, the capacity to utilize the talents of individuals within the social partners will also enhance the overall governance capacity of the system, so that even with relatively less-skilled public servants, the governance apparatus as a whole may function effectively.

In governance terms, resource mobilization also involves the capacity to cooperate with nongovernmental actors and how to utilize their resources, along with the resources available from the public sector itself, in order to address policy and governance issues (see Torfing et al., 2012). Thus, within the terms of the governance scenario, failure might even be defined as the incapacity to mobilize actors from the private sector, and as a consequence of that being forced into an excessive reliance on the public sector and its own resources. The public sector may be capable of delivering the services but would do so in an excessively expensive and intrusive manner.[8]

---

[8] The "new governance" literature has emphasized the desirability, as well as the actuality, of moving away from formal command and control regulation and direct provision of all public services in favor of softer forms of service provision (see Salamon, 2001; Héritier and Rhodes, 2008; Mörth, 2004).

The hybrid nature of many contemporary governance arrangements often involves mutual co-optation of the actors involved (Duran, 1998). State actors need the political legitimacy of some social actors with whom they work, as well as the human and material resources commanded by these groups. The social actors need access to formal institutions for governing, as well as the material resources commanded by the state. In an increasing number of situations, one cannot expect to govern effectively without the assistance, or at least the acquiescence, of the other.

Failures of Implementation. Of all the aspects of the governance process, the implementation stage has been the most subject to discussions of failure, and perhaps also more subject to actual failures. Indeed, the original research on implementation (Pressman and Wildavsky, 1974) began with an analysis of why programs are difficult to implement in the manner desired by their "formators" (Lane, 1983). Even as the implementation literature has continued to evolve (Winter, 2012), the specter of failure has continued to haunt the analysis of how public programs are put into effect, and real governments and their allies also continue to encounter genuine difficulties in making programs function as intended.

Failures of implementation may arise from a number of sources.[9] As already noted, poorly drafted legislation may be virtually impossible to implement successfully. For example, laws may have vague goals that cannot be translated into effective action, or which may engender conflicts over the interpretation of those vague prescriptions. Further, even well-drafted legislation may not understand fully the causal sequences involved in the policy area and hence may produce "fatal remedies" for the problem being addressed (Sieber, 1981). Legislators may also underestimate the resources (including time) necessary for effective implementation and hence forestall effective implementation.

Further, the various organizations, public and non-public, involved with implementing public policies may have their own ideas about what constitutes appropriate policy in their area, and may therefore attempt to thwart the intentions of the framers of the policies. That opposition is rarely overt, but does involve finding ways of slowing implementation and questioning the foundations of the policy (Brehm

---

[9] For a somewhat dated but still useful survey of the sources of failure in implementation, see Hood (1976b). See also Pülzl and Treib (2006).

and Gates, 1997).[10] And given that most implementation is conducted in a multi-organizational environment (O'Toole, 2012), inadequate coordination and cooperation among those organizations may produce failure, whether those can be seen as lacunae, duplication, or merely conflicts.

Finally, we must remember that implementation success may be a function of the economy and society into which the programs are being inserted. Governance requires some level of governability in the society, and specifically within the policy area being addressed.[11] This concept of governability has been applied most often to specific policy areas (see Kooiman et al., 2008), but societies as a whole may be more or less governable and more or less receptive of interventions from the state and its allies. Failed states are often not failed solely because of their own inadequacies, although those may be manifest, but also because the society within which they are attempting to govern is itself fragmented, weak, and contentious.[12]

Some of the factors that affect the governance capacity of states may also affect the governability of their societies. For example, the need for resources that is crucial for the public sector may also be true for social actors, and likewise some degree of social consensus on appropriate goals for governance may make the task of implementing those goals that much easier. And the availability of civil society organizations that can function as effective partners for government in governing also influences the capacity for governing, as well as the style of governing that may be undertaken.

---

[10] While potentially a problem for legislators and executives attempting to have their won conceptions of good policy implemented, the commitment of organizations to their goals may also contribute to their success (see Goodsell, 2011). This commitment, in turn, argues for more of a "backward mapping" style of implementation in which the ideas and commitments of the implementers are considered in the design of the programs.

[11] To some extent the concern with governance in the academic literature began with problems of perceived ungovernability in society, especially advanced democracies that had significant policy commitments but apparently diminishing capacities to reach the goals they had set for themselves. See Huntington, Crozier, and Watanuki (1975) and Rose (1979).

[12] Even societies that appear to have well-developed and well-resourced governance systems may not be as successful as might be expected because of the divisions within their societies, and perhaps some rejection of governance. See Tilly (1986).

To some extent, the implementation literature adopted what is now commonly referred to as a governance, or hybrid governance, perspective long before that nomenclature became popular. The original Pressman and Wildavsky analysis pointed to the numerous actors involved in the process, although their analysis concentrated on the multiple actors within the public sector, operating at all three levels of American government. For example, Hjern and Porter (1981; see also Peters, 2013) discussed the importance of understanding implementation structures involving multiple organizations and hence being subject to inter-organizational sources of failure. In Wolf's conceptualization of nonmarket failures, these are "derived externalities" resulting from inadequate coordination and collaboration among the actors, especially in the process of implementation.

What differentiates the contemporary conception of hybrid governance and implementation from the earlier conceptions of implementation is that the contemporary conception is more positive about the interactions involved in governance. Indeed, much of the contemporary discussion of hybrid governance tends to advocate that form of governance, as well as the reliance on non-state actors to the exclusion of state actors. However, as we have argued elsewhere (Pierre and Peters, 2000), that literature tends to underestimate the continuing importance of state actors, an underestimation that is perhaps especially evident in components of the process such as implementation that have long involved non-state actors.

Failures of Evaluation and Feedback. The final source of failure in governance arises when governance actors are unaware of their own actions or fail to assess in an objective manner their own performance. This stage of the process should be the most important for preventing governance failure, or at least in providing rapid corrections to those failures. At a minimum, if this component of the governance process works successfully, then decision-makers will know that they are failing and would begin to address the failures. Those expectations of responsiveness from actors in the governance process often are not fulfilled, and therefore constitute a major source of failure.

This responsiveness to failure must be considered in a strictly policy manner and as a part of the political process. On the one hand, we may expect political leaders and public administrators to monitor the objective consequences of policies and to adapt those policies to reflect success and failure in reaching policy goals. On the other hand, politicians must also attend to the responses of their constituents to the policies being implemented and attempt to respond to negative feedback from the voters in order to preserve their own seats. The difficulty in responding, in policy terms, may be that these objective and subjective evaluations of policy may differ, and the political responses and the substantive responses may be different.

To some extent, the failure of governments to respond effectively to their own actions is understandable. First, the policy-making process itself is sufficiently difficult in many circumstances that there may be an unwillingness of the policy-makers to reopen discussions, even in response to less than positive policy outcomes. Most policy-making is indeed remaking policies that have been made in the past (Hogwood and Peters, 1983; for a similar argument from a different perspective, see Carter, 2012) but returning to those debates soon after the adoption of a program will not be easy politically. Further, there is some liability of newness for programs so that if they are newly formed, they may be more readily terminated, regardless of their level of success (see Boin, Kuipers, and Steenbergen, 2010).

In addition to the political issues that may suppress attempts at evaluation, the commitments that public sector organizations, and their allies in the private sector, have to existing programs as well as to general approaches to policy, may inhibit their willingness to engage in extensive evaluation efforts. The organizations may simply not want to know if their favorite programs are not successful, or could be improved. To that commitment of organizations to particular styles of policy, we can add inertia and the search for stability as further reasons why organizations may not seek out evaluation (see Hanusch, 1983).

Just as individual organizations may not want to know about their failures, or even their successes, so too are governments often unwilling to evaluate their own actions on an objective basis. There has been a significant emphasis in many governments on "evidence based policy making," meaning using not only evidence from other settings but also evidence of their own actions (Bogenschneider and Corbett, 2010; but see Marston and Watts, 2003). But if the governance apparatus (again perhaps social actors as well as government itself) is dominated by ideology, then evidence may not be particularly welcome. And even if that evidence might be utilized were it available it would not be sought out, and evaluation would not be institutionalized as it has been in many political systems.

The continuing reforms of government beginning in the late 1980s have also tended to pose challenges to evaluation, at least evaluation involving more extensive and intensive analysis of policies and their consequences. Evaluation is expensive and time consuming (Vedung, 2006) and does not provide quick and simple answers for policy problems. The emphasis on efficiency associated with the NPM has tended to downplay the importance of those more extensive analyses in favor of short-term performance measures. While those measures may be useful in some ways for accountability purposes, assessing the extent to which goals have been attained, they do so without careful examination of the dynamics of the policies, and often without the consideration of alternative approaches.

As noted earlier, at the extreme governance, arrangements can be conceptualized as being a cybernetic system in which there are close linkages between the outputs of the governance process and the next round of action (Galnoor, 1982; Peters, 2012a). This style of governing would require continuous monitoring of the activities of governments, and the capacity to assess rather efficiently the actions of governments and their partners. That may, in turn, require substantial agreement on the means and ends of governance and also substantial analytic capacity within the public bureaucracy. Further, if this style of governing were to be truly effective, it would also require some reflective capacity (Schön, 1983) so that those making decisions would not just be responding to short-term circumstances, but also consider possibilities for learning from their actions.

In governance terms, the interactions between social actors and the public sector itself may be able to facilitate accountability and feedback. One of the virtues of interactive styles of governing is that actors in the public sector remain in frequent contact with actors in society who tend to be the targets of public policies, or at least are themselves in close contact with the clients or targets of programs. In these interactive arrangements, feedback may be built into the system. That said, the social actors themselves may have the same types of ideological blinders as do governments, or they may be too closely linked with certain groups to be able to assess governance actions objectively.

The evaluation and learning aspects of governance are important in policy and administrative terms, but those concerns may be subsidiary to a more fundamental political concern about accountability.

Evaluation and learning are about how to make policies better, but the more significant political (and governance) question is, are those policies the ones designed by the legitimate political authorities and are they being delivered in appropriate, legal, and effective manners. In democratic systems, there may be an additional criterion that the policies and their mode of implementation should conform to the wishes of the public, as inchoate as those wishes may appear at times.

As noted earlier concerning implementation, hybrid approaches to governance are often excessively optimistic about the capacity of these complex arrangements to supply governance. Accountability, however, may be especially difficult to supply effectively through hybrid arrangements. The very hybridity of these arrangements may be the root problem in providing public accountability for actions. The logic of accountability is that the responsibility for success and failure of programs can be identified, and the actors involved sanctioned if necessary.[13] The complexity inherent in hybrid forms of accountability therefore limits the capacity to provide clear answers to questions of responsibility.

It could be argued that the search for clear and unambiguous answers about responsibility for success and failure in public governance is a fool's errand, even in less-complex, hierarchical policy-making systems (Page, 2010). There are numerous actors involved even in more traditional state-centric governance arrangements, and there are also numerous other sources of potential governance failure that the learning and evaluation elements of this final stage of the policy process are more fruitful points of emphasis. That said, however, accountability is a sufficiently important element of the political process that mechanisms must be identified to enforce accountability over bureaucracies and other actors within government. And in hybrid forms of governance, that necessity also extends to the social actors involved in making and implementing policies.

In summary, neither all governance systems nor all organizations within those governance systems are effective in learning from their actions and in correcting any policy failures that are detected. In some

---

[13] Thinking about accountability totally as crime and punishment tends to devalue the importance of learning and improvement. As accountability regimens move toward performance measures, the capacity to monitor may be increased, but the danger becomes that the process will become merely technical without any consideration of the political foundations for accountability.

cases, this is willful neglect of information and the possibilities of learning, but in more cases, it reflects the effects of the numerous barriers that exist to effective learning in the public sector. Likewise, not all governance systems are effective at holding the actors involved in making and implementing policies responsible for their actions.[14]

In both policy and democratic terms, these may be crucial failures not only because they both limit the capacity of governance systems to improve the quality of their programs but also because they limit their capacity to improve the processes of governance themselves. Also, these two dimensions of failure can be closely linked, with the failure to evaluate and learn making effective accountability impossible. Likewise, the absence of a ready consumer of evaluation information, in the form of accountability institutions, may lessen the interest of potential evaluators in investing in the type of work needed (see Peters, 2012b).

Summary and Conclusion

Governance is certainly not an easy task. It involves multiple actors, public and private, interacting in a number of different ways. It also involves attempting to control societies and economies that may not be particularly amenable to being controlled. Thus, it is not surprising that there are governance failures (but see McConnell, 2010). Some of these failures are glaring and some are rather subtle, but they all represent the inability to establish and reach collective goals, and also the failure to learn from mistakes that inevitably are made. It is important when thinking of governance failure not just to think of dramatic instances of failed states but also to consider the more subtle but nonetheless significant failures.

The length and complexity of the governance process provides a number of points at which failure may occur. Also, there is no single cause for failure. In many cases, failure is the result of institutions, and the design of governance arrangements. In others, it may be the fault of politics, and the difficulties in reaching agreement in deeply divided political systems, and especially the difficulty of reaching agreements

---

[14] See Howlett, Ramesh, and Wu (2015) for a review of the literature on policy failure.

that are more than the lowest-common denominator (see Scharpf, 1988). And failure may be the result of individual factors, and failures of leadership in governing (Helms, 2012). For whatever reasons governance may fail, it is important to understand the logic behind those failures and to find the ways possible for enhancing the quality of governance and improving the lives of ordinary citizens.

8 | The Change of Governance and the Governance of Change

One standard critique of governance theory, and of other functionalist approaches in the social sciences, is that they find it difficult to cope with change. The logic of this critique has been that functionalist approaches depend upon a stable set of structures that will fulfill the functions posited to be essential for governance or for society more generally. Further, to the extent that they do include change in their analysis, functionalist approaches tend to be teleological, with an assumption that all systems will evolve in a certain direction. This social and political evolution often involves some notion of modernity or development, as was the case of the structural-functional models popular in comparative politics in the 1960s and 1970s.

The same, and perhaps even more severe, argument concerning change has been applied to systems approaches to politics that share some characteristics with functional models. The homeostatic nature of systems theory means that there is a tendency to resist change (Finkle and Gable, 1973) and to return to equilibrium if the stability of the system is upset. Despite the apparent resistance to change implied in these theoretical approaches, we are arguing that change is possible, and that with appropriate political action can be made to happen. But saying that change occurs is not sufficient, and we need to understand the nature of those changes.

We will be arguing that governance as we have conceptualized it contains a much stronger dynamic element than is usually assumed, and it can indeed cope with change and even drive change within the public sector itself and within the society. This dynamism of our model is in part a function of the responsiveness of the governance system to external demands. This democratic premise about change is important, but there are also options for change from within governance institutions itself. In comparative terms, the more étatiste governance systems may be more capable of producing change because they have, or are willing to exercise, greater control over social and economic processes.

This chapter will look at two aspects of change as related to governance. The first is how governance systems respond to their external environments, or to their own internal calculations, and change. This view of governance then is largely responsive as these systems for making decisions attempt to match their policies and performance with the changing environment. For contemporary governance, the pervasive effects of globalization and continuing fiscal austerity (Kickert and Randma-Liiv, 2015) are but two of the factors requiring adaptation. The other version of change is more how to govern that change, and how to act in ways that produce effective change either with or without inputs from the external environment. In this latter case, the governance system may have its own preferences transformed as a result of political change, or changes in the understanding of social dynamics.

The governance of change emphasis in this chapter makes more apparent that there is a close linkage between the literature on governance and the study of public policy in political science. We have been discussing the governance process somewhat as we would the policy process (Jones, 1984), although we have emphasized more the systemic nature and consequences of action that is related to change. Further, governance – very much like Lasswell's (1936) definition of politics – is about who gets what. And public policies are the means through which governance systems attempt to determine who gets what.

Thus, we will be looking at change occurring at two levels. The first is at a more macro-level in which the institutions and patterns of governance are altered. Our earlier discussions of governance in comparative politics has identified a number of aspects of governance, e.g. the manner in which policies are implemented, that create patterns of governing within different systems. For example, if implementation changes from being state-centric and bureaucratic to more network-based, then the patterns of governance will have changed and we should expect different interactions in the process of governing as well as perhaps different policy outcomes. Likewise, the ideal-type models discussed in Chapter 4 may be altered significantly by these gradual transformations.

The second level of change is defined by governance systems utilizing their resources–power, money, law, and so on, to alter their surrounding environment. This level of change is closely analogous to the utilization, and analysis, of public policies and their impacts of economy and society. Governments (and their allies) have a range of policy instruments that they can employ to attempt changing that environment (Hood and Margetts, 2007; Lascoumbes and Le Gales, 2007). This is an ongoing governance activity that can occur with or without any fundamental change in the underlying governance apparatus, although it may have feedbacks into those governance arrangements. For example, changing the mix of policy instruments used to achieve goals may alter the internal power distributions of actors within government, and between government and social actors (Howlett and Rayner, 2007).

The above statement about managing change may appear excessively state-centric since it does not include the possibility of societal actors driving or supporting many aspects of change. Those changes range from large-scale social upheavals such as the Arab Spring through social changes generated by the development of social media to ongoing processes of economic innovation (Gerbaudo, 2013). The extent to which governance actors attempt to control these changes is a matter of political ideology as well as capacity. More *dirigiste* systems may seek to control many aspects of economy and society that others would consider either impossible or unwise to attempt to govern.

This chapter first reviews the complex issues that are associated with a functionalist theory of governance in the context of responding to change and changes in governance. We then discuss in more detail different aspects of these two aspects of the governance and change. These discussions demonstrate that this model of governance is indeed capable of providing insights into change, and that governance theory need not be simply a static description of relationships among actors.

Conceptualizing Change in Governance

Those two basic varieties of change begin to unpack the complexity of change in governance, but we should also consider the types of change that may be involved. These types of change may occur either in the governance system itself or in the specific interventions made by those structures and actors.

Innovation. The most fundamental type of change is innovation. Genuine innovations in governance may be relatively rare events, but certainly do occur (Torfing and Triantafillou, 2015). At the extreme, they occur with changes in constitutions, or altering of other fundamental structural arrangements, or they may occur more gradually through processes such as layering and displacement (Streeck and Thelen, 2005). Even the constitutional change may occur through more gradual means – the American constitution in 2015 is very different in interpretation than it was in 1789, or even 1889.

Innovation may also occur at the second level, as individual governance systems have creative moments that produce novel forms of addressing policy problems (Light, 2002). Even here there may be relatively few truly innovative developments (see Hogwood and Peters, 1983) as most policy change builds on established patterns and may involve simple alterations of existing patterns of intervention. Politically, however, these more modest interventions may need to be "sold" as innovations in order to create sufficient mobilization behind them to shift the entrenched power of clients and bureaucrats defending the status quo.

The public sector does make policy innovations, and sometimes very important ones. At times these innovations develop from the ideas and political will of individuals, as in the case of individuals such as Robert Moses and the Port of New York (Ballon and Jackson, 2007), or David Lilienthal and the TVA (Colignon, 1997). Other scholars are now arguing that innovation is more likely to occur in collaborative arrangements in which multiple actors present ideas and discuss the range of possible reforms (Sørensen and Torfing, 2013). The assumption, supported by some evidence, is that bringing together a range of stakeholders in a policy area may be able to generate effective and innovative responses to challenges in the environment.

It may well be that both of these conceptions of innovation are correct, if in respect to different aspects of governance and policy. It appears as if individuals are better at conceptualizing large-scale changes in the governance arrangements of a political system, while the collaborative processes may be more successful at developing more specific policy changes. Further, innovations involving multiple actors and interests will generally be better addressed with more involvement of those stakeholders,[1] while more technical versions of innovation may be best addressed through top-down processes.

---

[1] One could argue, however, that involvement of stakeholders will inhibit innovation as each actor will attempt to defend their own interests. This collaborative process therefore will tend to produce innovations by the lowest common denominator. Alternatively, innovation and decision-making in homogenous and consensual groups can lead to groupthink with detrimental outcomes ('t Hart, 1980; 't Hart, Stern and Sundelius, 1997).

Diffusion. The second form of governance change will be diffusion, with governing systems learning from other systems. Some of this learning may occur within multilevel governance systems in which one level of government (and its partners) learns from another. This usually involves higher levels within the multilevel system learning from lower levels, given that innovations is generally easier at lower levels.[2] This has certainly been the case in federal systems that permit their subnational components substantial policy autonomy and hence substantial opportunity to innovate.[3]

And again we may need to differentiate this conception of change in order to consider changes in policy from fundamental changes in governance, and to consider how these two dimensions of response interact. The economic crisis beginning in 2008 provides one clear case of these two varieties of change. The crisis produced some immediate policy responses but it also provoked some fundamental changes in patterns of governance. For example, in the United States, there were immediate policy responses such as the bailout of some banks and automobile manufacturers, but this more interventionist style of governing the economy became enshrined in law (Dodd-Frank), in structures (the Consumer Financial Protection Bureau), as well as in a generally more active style of coping with the economy.[4]

Finally, change may involve termination. This level of change is difficult to conceptualize for overall governance arrangements, except perhaps as interregnums following a revolution or other complete change of governance systems. Failed states may come close to representing the termination of governance, but even here the functionalist conception of governance would require us to consider the role of firms, warlords, clans, or other unconventional forms of governing as

---

[2] Everything else being equal the smaller scale and generally greater homogeneity with smaller units reduces conflict and makes innovation easier. That said, however, the closer personal and institutional ties among individuals and groups may also make change more threatening to the established social orders within the localities.

[3] In the famous words of Mr. Justice Brandeis, "the states are the laboratory of democracy."

[4] What may be particularly important in governance terms is that these changes were initiated by a Republican president but then expanded and institutionalized by a Democratic president. This active form of governing is certainly not without its critics but seemingly has become more a component of the usual governance regimes in the US.

fulfilling the fundamental tasks of governing. The way in which governance would occur would not be desirable, democratic, or even effective, but governance of some sort would be occurring.

Termination of governance systems as a whole may be difficult or impossible, but termination of governance interventions into society and economy may also be relatively rare (see Bauer et al., 2012). Of course, the degree of difficulty of termination is to some extent a product of the conceptualization used. For example, when various European countries ended their period of colonial rule in Africa and Asia, they terminated their colonial administrations. But they replaced those administrations with various aid and development organizations. Was the function of dealing with those African and Asian nations terminated, or only changed to one for promoting development of the former colonies?

Leaving the definitional questions aside for the moment, under almost any definition, policy terminations are difficult (but see Geva-May, 2004). Once the public sector, again often with its allies from the private sector, intervene, they tend to alter the dynamics of economic and social activity in ways that may require continuing interventions. At the extreme, programs such as pensions that create stocks of benefits in the public sector and alter individual saving behavior can be reversed only with significant social hardship. Even programs that are more flows, providing benefits year on year – for example the CAP program in the European Union – create expectations and alter behavior with enduring consequences.

Mechanisms for Change. We now have some idea of the various types of change that may be occurring in governance. Some of these involve changes within the governance apparatus itself, while others involve implementing and managing policy changes using governance devices. In the discussion of our model of governance (Chapter 2), and in the discussion of governance as a framework for comparative politics (Chapter 4), we began the discussion of change, albeit more implicitly than explicitly. We can, however, use that earlier analysis of governance to consider what mechanisms can be useful for implementing changes of either type.

One central element of our comparative analysis of governance presented above was the importance of openness in the governance system to external information and pressures. That responsiveness is central to change, as governance actors attempt to match their outputs with changing demands from their environment. Even among democratic regimes, there are marked differences in the openness of the systems of political pressures from the environment. For example, those systems that have close connections with social actors, whether through neo-corporatist or network arrangements (Bogason and Musso, 2006), will be more capable of responding to society than will governance systems that are more autonomous from society.[5]

The openness of governance systems to inputs from their environment points to the importance of *learning* as a mechanism for promoting change. There is an extensive literature on how organizations – in both the public and the private sectors – learn (Cohen and Sprull, 1996; Schön, 1983), as well as the mechanisms through which they can enhance their learning capacity. The underlying assumption of this literature is that organizations and governance systems will perform better if they can learn, with the object of the lessons to be learned being either the consequences of their own actions or information coming from other sources. This emphasis on learning is also evident within governments themselves, with the sometimes excessive concern with "evidence-based policy" (Botterill and Hindmoor, 2012).

The primary emphasis on learning in the public sector has been on learning from others about how to make better policy. This process has been discussed in a variety of ways – diffusion (Berry and Berry, 1999), policy transfer (Dolowitz and Marsh, 2000), lesson-drawing (Rose, 1993) – all of which are concerned with the capacity of the public sector to understand what policies have been adopted and implemented (one assumes successfully) in other jurisdictions, and then transplant it into another jurisdiction. Too often this transplantation is undertaken too blithely, without understanding the social and cultural elements that may undergird the success of that policy in a particular setting and hence make transplantation impractical. Still, these attempts at learning do open governance to its environment in a search for superior solutions to public problems.

Evidence-based policy-making to some extent represents the apotheosis of the utilization of learning models for public policy, but also demonstrates very clearly the dangers of adopting policies without

---

[5] The concept of state autonomy is discussed most commonly now in terms of the capacity of the state to act within the international financial marketplace. We are, however, thinking of autonomy in the more traditional sense of autonomy of the state from society (Katzenstein, 1987; Nettl, 1968).

adequate understandings of the policy environment into which a particular policy is being inserted. This danger is apparent because a good deal of evidence-based policy is not built on successful policy initiatives in other jurisdictions but rather attempts to bring the findings of science, and other sources of expertise, directly into the policy process (see Black, 2001, Sanderson, 2002).

To some extent, governments have always sought to utilize expertise. In comparative terms, this has varied across time and across governance systems. For example, expertise has tended to be more important in developmental states that are seeking to use their governing powers to alter the economy and society – examples would be 19th-century France and 20th-century Singapore and Japan (Johnson, 1982). Likewise, crisis – economic, military, or climate-related – tends to invoke the need for expertise in governing. But some governance systems, the Netherlands and the Scandinavian countries perhaps, tend to focus more attention on expertise and learning (Calder, 1988).

The learning models, and again particularly evidence-based policymaking, also raise fundamental questions about democracy, and the linkages with nongovernmental actors involved in governance. At the extreme, evidence-based policy appears to want to bypass normal policy processes and to assume that the scientific facts speak for themselves (Botterill and Hindmoor, 2012). The experts involved in these processes may become frustrated with the length of time and the contention involved in governance processes, while political decision-makers may need to integrate the ideas of the experts into the existing political and policy frameworks. These conflicts were identified previously as the danger of technocracy (Meynaud, 1968) but may be more real in contemporary governance than in the past.

As well as reacting to changes in their environment, governance actors will also differ in their willingness to learn from its own actions. As already noted (p. 151), governance actors differ in the extent to which they evaluate their actions and attempt to learn from them. Some of the differences that are hypothesized to exist in learning capacity are a function of the level of self-confidence of the political elite and its institutionalization as an elite with relatively common Self-confidence is in many ways a positive attribute for governance, but so too is learning and adaptation.

While positing that the openness of the central governance institutions to pressures from the environment is crucial for understanding change, it is also important to understand the nature of the environment itself. In the stereotypical globalized world, all governance systems are to some extent subjected to relatively common pressures for economic and social adjustment, Further, with globalized media and rapid diffusion of the ideas that become those "in good currency" to some extent, all governance systems are facing almost identical forces from the outside. For governance the important question may be how they choose to respond, and how well they can respond, to these types of forces rather than if they will respond.

There are certainly some common forces pressing on countries and other governance systems for response, but there are also differential forces. Further, the same forces pressing in from the environment will be interpreted differently in different settings and may be more or less powerful stimuli for responses in governance. The obvious case is that changes in the international economic system may be more threatening for less-developed governance systems, or for very open affluent economies, but will not play such a significant role for the more affluent and more autarkic systems. And ideologies, such as the largely anti-market policy climate in France, may also inhibit the willingness and capacity for response.

Another element that is crucial for understanding change in governance is the capacity of the governance institutions to process information and to develop and implement programs for change (see Baumgartner and Jones, 2015). For much of the history of governing the principal problem facing governments was having adequate information needed for good decision-making.[6] Governments were often having to make decisions without sufficient, timely information and may have erred simply because of that. The "fog of war" is often used to describe these difficulties in making decisions in military situations, but there can be a "fog of peace" as well. Governance actors may attempt to gather sufficient information about their societies and economies to provide adequate guidance, but the measures and amount of information is often inadequate.[7]

---

[6] The word "statistics" originally referred to the information needed by the state to be able to govern. As the analysis of the data became more developed the mathematical models we now consider statistics emerged.

[7] Ford Maddox Ford (*No More Parades*) provides an amusing discussion of these problems in the form of two young British statisticians attempting to measure everything possible about their economy.

For contemporary governments, the governance problem may almost have reversed with such a huge amount of information and opinion available that the problem becomes separating what is truly useful from all the chaff that is on the Internet and also available from think-tanks and other institutions and individuals attempting to influence policy (Peters, 2013). These difficulties have been exacerbated by some changes within government itself that have de-emphasized the role of career public servants in policy advice (Eichbaum and Shaw, 2010). The absence of career public servants with extensive knowledge of their policy areas makes sorting through all the available information more difficult and almost certainly less fruitful.

In addition to the decline of the career public service, most governments have also de-emphasized the role of policy evaluation within government (Hatry, 2013). The evaluation function has to some extent been replaced by an emphasis on performance indicators and performance management, but these short-term measures do not provide for the deeper understanding of processes that may be required for effective governance. Performance management may say how well programs are being delivered but provides little information about the effectiveness of programs, or potential options for reforming the programs that evaluation can provide (Vedung, 2006).

Contemporary governments may have a surplus of information, but the indicators of important governance processes and outcomes remain difficult to measure (Erkilla, 2012). The availability of so much information which has limited, or at least questionable, validity may actually be worse for governance than the absence of information. Having the questionable information may make decision-makers assume that they actually do know something whereas in reality they are being seriously misguided. Indeed, given that many sources from the Internet are not edited or mediated, users risk relying upon poor quality, or totally inaccurate, information when attempting to govern.

Adapting to the Environment: Learning and Change

The above discussion of information and information processing and its relationship to governance change points to a complex interaction among these processes. Table 8.1 presents a simplified version of that relationship, albeit one that is directly related to governance as an approach to comparative politics. Different patterns of learning and

Table 8.1 *Relationship of Learning and Governance Change*

| | | Learning | |
		High	Low
Change	High	Cybernetic	Authoritative
	Low	Blocked	Hyperstable

change are associated with governance differences across countries, and this provides another set of insights into comparative governance dynamics.

Learning capacity, and actual learning, does not necessarily translate into change in governance (or public policies). As shown in Table 8.1, we can conceptualize levels of learning and levels of change as varying independently of each other. Further, the relationship between these two variables can be argued to be related to different governance styles. At one extreme, governance systems that are engaged in learning from their surroundings and which also respond to that information are labeled as cybernetic (see Peters, 2012c; Galnoor, 1982). While few governance systems could match the criteria for a completely cybernetic arrangement, the attempts to match information received and change moves governance in that direction.[8]

At the other extreme, some governance systems can be described as being hyperstable. These systems appear to pay little attention to the changes occurring in their environments, and they do not attempt to transform their own governance styles. Traditional regimes and those adopting a specifically isolationist perspective, e.g. Myanmar prior to its softening of military rule in 2011, appear to fit into this category. Governing in this manner may be a manner in which elites can preserve their positions, but in the process may only accumulate pressures that will lead to their eventual downfall.

The other two cells of this table represent perhaps more interesting, and more common, governance styles. The "blocked" governance

---

[8] This leaves aside the possibilities of false learning and overreaction (Maor, 2012) when governance actors either learn the wrong lessons or respond excessively to relatively minor changes in their environment. The latter may be especially common in foreign and defense policy when a perceived threat produces a very large reaction.

arrangements are those in which the actors involved are cognizant of changes in their environments but appear incapable of acting upon them. Whether because of self-satisfaction or more likely internal political blockages, they are not able to utilize the information they have at their disposal. The United States in its period of continuing political gridlock (Mann and Ornstein, 2012) appears to be a clear example of the blocked pattern of governance; there is adequate information and learning, but no capacity to act on that information.[9] Some less-developed political systems may also fit into this pattern, with adequate understanding of their environment but without the capacity to do anything significant to alter that environment.

Finally, an authoritative (often but not necessarily authoritarian) style of governance would produce change without necessarily being connected with the external environment. The authoritative regimes may be motivated by a particular ideology, or may simply consider that they have sufficient understanding internally to be able to govern effectively. For example, the Chinese regime under Mao may have considered that the thoughts of the chairman were sufficient to guide change within the system, with disastrous results (Dikotter, 2011). In these cases, and less extreme cases such as the United Kingdom under the Thatcher government, the evidence about the environment of political action may be difficult to escape but the regime persists in doing what it considers correct.

The above discussion has linked the learning capacity and learning activity of governance regimes with the amount of change being implemented. It has, however, been perhaps too optimistic about the role of learning and the use of information by governance actors. Just because a governance system attempts to use information, there is no certainty that the learning will be effective nor that the right decisions will be made with that information. Individuals and organizations all have filters that inhibit the use of information, especially new information, and that tend to produce ineffective responses (see 't Hart, Stern, and Sundelius, 1997) even when information is being processed.

---

[9] It may actually be worse than that. While the Obama administration has sought to implement an "evidence-based" regime, the Congress has tended to ignore almost all attempts to introduce evidence into the policy process (Haskins and Margolis, 2015).

Changing Governance: Anticipation and Foresight

This discussion of change in governance has to this point been concerned primarily with reaction to the external environment, but we should also consider more carefully the capacity of governance actors to anticipate needed changes. A planning and anticipatory style of governing have largely gone out of favor with governments in a period dominated by neoliberal ideologies, but the need to consider the future and to make policies for that future remains crucial. Indeed, when coping with significant "wicked problems" such as climate change, declining natural resources, and the like, the need to anticipate may be all the more important.

Paradoxically, that need to anticipate may be most important for the very governance systems that are least capable of anticipating their environments and their own capacities for action. More affluent countries with well-developed administrative systems and informational capacities are generally more capable of processing information and developing anticipatory strategies for change. On the other hand, the less-affluent regimes without the administrative and information resources are more at the mercy of events, but less capable of making and implementing relevant plans to cope with those events. They may still attempt to plan and to anticipate but will generally be less successful in doing so.[10]

The capacity to anticipate in governance may be associated with some capacity to innovate. Anticipation implies that actors in the governance system are capable of identifying problems as they emerge, or even before they emerge, while innovation represents the capacity to respond in creative (one hopes) ways to the problems that can be foreseen. At times, merely adjusting existing programs may be adequate for governing adequately, but for more extensive changes in the environment, more creative and innovative responses may be required. There may also be a "success curse" involved here, with countries that have been successful in governing, assuming that they can achieve success simply by doing what they have always done.

[10] For example, Ghana emphasizes planning, and has a large and talented National Planning Commission. But the information they are using, even basic information such as the census, is often years old and only in aggregate form so that the plans that are being made are unlikely to be successful.

But innovation may occur without anticipation of any new threats to the governance status quo. Just as actors in the private sector may continuously attempt to improve the performance of their firms or even households, so too may governance actors attempt to improve their performance. Changes in internal management of the public sector, in the form of performance management (Bouckaert and Halligan, 2007), also emphasize the need to improve the quality and efficiency of service delivery. While these managerial devices emphasized management in the delivery of services, they have been less concerned with policies and innovations in the substantive content of interventions.

Inter-generational policy-making represents one of the more important forms of anticipation. As well as anticipating the future, this longer term view on policy and governance requires the political capacity to make difficult decisions that may disadvantage current voters while advantaging their children and grandchildren. For this difficult style of inter-temporal policy-making to be viable, Alan Jacobs (2011; see also Schneider, 1991) has argued that a number of conditions are necessary within the governance system. Politically, the capacity to make anticipatory choices requires substantial political security given that most long-term choices involve possibly disadvantaging current citizens while advantaging those in some indefinite future.

Making these inter-temporal choices also requires some degree of institutional insulation from the immediate and institutional political pressures within the governance system. If leaders who want to make decisions that will disadvantage present-day interests in favor of longer term interests (including perhaps the public interest), it is easier if they can avoid immediate political pressures. The effects of an absence of insulation were seen in the case of pension policies in many southern European countries that favored current pensioners (and would be pensioners) and disfavored future generations and the fiscal probity of the entire government. This was, at least in the short term, good politics but politics with disastrous longer term consequences.

Change and the Capacity for Change. We can begin thinking about change in governance by thinking first about the capacity to change. This capacity is closely related to general capacities to govern (see Painter and Pierre, 2005) and reflects the generalized capacity of the state, along with its allies in society and market, to govern. This issue has been raised more commonly with respect to less-developed system (Brautigam, 1996; Geddes, 1994), but many of the same issues are relevant for more developed political and economic systems, albeit perhaps in different ways. Indeed, there can be a curse from success that makes it difficult for governance systems to adjust to changing conditions when their old ways of doing things have been so successful.[11]

The institutional capacities of the public sector are perhaps most important in understanding the capacity of governance to produce change. This internal capacity for producing change is most important for the public bureaucracy that must implement change within the society. Although the bureaucracy may be the most important actor, other parts of the governance apparatus are also significant players in designing and legitimating change. Legitimacy of the entire governance system will play a significant role in producing changes, given that social and economic actors are being asked to move away from established and perhaps comfortable patterns in their life and work.

In a governance framework, the relationship with social actors is also important for understanding the capacity for change. On the one hand, interactive forms of governance may involve social actors in the process of governing, at once co-opting them into the governance process and using their capacities to facilitate the process. On the other hand, however, the involvement of social actors in governance may make change more difficult as groups may develop virtual veto powers over any changes in policy or governance that might worsen their situations. Thus, the question for governing change is not so much whether social actors will be involved in governance but rather how they are involved.

The capacity for change in governance is also a function of the society, as well as the structures formally charged with governing. The governability of societies has been discussed since at least the time of the Trilaterial Commission's report that become associated with a notion that most welfare states were becoming ungovernable because of the mismatch between demands of the public and the capacity of governments to meet those expectations (Crozier, Huntington, and Watanuki, 1975; for a different perspective on governability of industrial societies see Dahrendorf, 1980). More recently

---

[11] In the famous words of Di Lampedusa, "if we want things to stay as they are, things will have to change."

the literature on the "decay" of the state has argued that governments (and their allies) have become increasingly dysfunctional and incapable of adapting (Fukuyama, 2015).

Policy Change and Governance Change. Throughout this chapter, and to some extent throughout the entire book, there has been some tension between understanding governance as overall systems of establishing and implementing goals and the role of governance systems in making public policy. While the primary emphasis of this book has been on governance in a rather broad sense, it is difficult to understand the dynamics of governance without linking that broader concept to the public policies being made through the governance arrangements (see Hacker, Levin, and Shapiro, 2004). Further, as we attempt to understand change in governance, changes in policies at a lower level of generality may contribute to, or actually require, changes in the governance system.

For example, continuing expansions of public sector commitments (either in the warfare or the welfare state) may produce significant transformations of the governance apparatus to cope with the increased level of activity. This expansion of governance apparatus may be especially apparent for the welfare state, in which programmatic expansion has often meant increased involvement of non-governmental actors.[12] This increased involvement will rather naturally generate a more interactive format for governance and with it increased difficulties in accountability.

Also, changes in the apparatus of governance may produce changes in policy. Salamon (1981) noted that reorganization in government generally did not improve the efficiency of the public sector but it did tend to change policy. The same may be true for most reforms in governance systems, except perhaps for the most radical changes. If we take the case above and run it in reverse, then attempts to generate more interactive forms of governance will tend to privilege different types of actors than would be true for more state-centric forms of governance and therefore likely change the composition of public policy.

The above discussion should make it clear that changes in the apparatus of governance and changes in policy will not necessarily covary.

---

[12] Some of the same change may occur in the warfare state also as increased involvement of military contractors produces a form of interactive governance, albeit one that is quite different from that found in welfare state programs (Markusen, 2003).

Table 8.2 *Governance Change and Policy Change*

		Governance Change	
		High	Low
Policy Change	High	Adapters	Tinkerers
	Low	Reformers	Conservatives

While the substance of each individual policy change or governance change would require careful consideration of the cases, we can get some sense of the relationships between degrees of change by beginning with a simple two-by-two table. Although the degrees of change can only be described loosely (see Sartori, 1991), beginning with these general classifications provides some insights into the ways in which policy and governance change interact.

We have been arguing that policy change and change in governance apparatus are possibly linked, but those two types of change are not necessarily linked. Table 8.2 shows the relationship between change in these two dimensions, again dichotomizing these two complex dimensions. Further, this analysis is static and change along one dimension may contribute to subsequent change in the other dimension. That interaction may, however, require substantial time to become apparent, with policy changes likely to have a significantly delayed impact on more fundamental governance processes.

The adapters category here contains governance systems that change both their governance arrangements and their policies on a relatively frequent basis. While this may appear to be an effective pattern of governance, and can be, it also can be potentially dysfunctional if change is too rapid, especially within the fundamental governance systems. That said, if the system can adapt some aspects of governance, e.g. the public bureaucracy, while maintaining the principal constitutional features (see Knill, 1999) as it also changes policy it may be able to produce highly effective governance. For example, the majoritarian style of governing discussed by Lijphart (1984) with its "winner take all" style of policy alteration may fit the logic of this category.

At the other extreme, there are conservative systems that do not alter neither their fundamental governance arrangements nor their policies. This lack of adaptation may be the result of either a conservative ideology or internal political or social blockages that inhibit adaptation. Or in the best of all worlds, this conservative stance may result from success, or at least perceived success, and the sense that change may actually be dysfunctional. This complacency may have been possible historically but it is difficult to think of even conservative regimes, such as Saudi Arabia or the Emirates, being able to maintain this much stability.

We have used the term "tinkerers" to describe governance systems that engage in policy change on a reasonably regular basis while maintaining the basic governance apparatus. The majority of industrialized democracies would seemingly fit into this category, with limited change of the governance system (except perhaps their public bureaucracies) but continuing policy change – "tireless tinkering" to adjust to the environment and changing political control. This pattern may actually represent the equilibrium position for most governance systems, with systems with less policy capacity and less legitimacy being moved away from this equilibrium more readily, in response to social pressures and political mobilization.

Finally, we have labeled as "reformers" those systems that maintain their policy stances while continuing to alter their governance apparatus. This is the least probable of all the four categories, although there are cases of countries with significant internal political cleavages attempting to find means of coping with those difficulties. For example, Belgium (Deschouwer, 2012) has gone through significant constitutional reform and has created a rather radical version of federalism, all while maintaining the commitment to a welfare state, and to the European Union, that is little changed. At the extreme, the several governance changes in Egypt following the fall of the Mubarak regime, all maintained the same policy regimen, albeit with very different conceptions about the nature of good governance (Smith, 2010).

In summary, policy and governance both may change independently but to the extent that they change together, or do not, they produce comparative political patterns. Or alternatively, these patterns reflect comparative political differences that in turn influence the capacity to govern in particular manners. The continuing interaction of governance systems and public policy, and their capacities to alter their status quo, represent fundamental foundations for comparative political and policy analysis.

Conclusions

In most contemporary governance systems, there are powerful forces resisting change. Entrenched political interests, entrenched public organizations, and the absence of persuasive alternatives to the status quo all tend to make maintaining existing governance patterns and existing patterns of public policy easier than producing change. But if change is difficult, it is not impossible, and this chapter has demonstrated some of the dynamics associated with changing public governance and policy.

Changes may come in a variety of forms, ranging from tinkering with relatively minor aspects of public policy to complete constitutional revisions. And changes may be innovative or merely ideas and practices diffused from other settings, or in the extreme they may be terminations of existing programs and organizations. Adopting anticipatory changes with genuine innovations is perhaps the most difficult form of change to create, but attempting to respond to changes in the immediate environment of governance systems is by no means a straightforward exercise either. The absence of adequate and timely information may make responsiveness difficult, and perhaps also just wrong. But understanding change emphasizes the capacity of governance models to illuminate comparative politics, and likewise the importance of comparison for understanding governance.

9 Conclusions

Governance, Functionalism, and Comparative Politics

The chief purpose of this academic enterprise has been to outline an analytical framework that will provide students of governance with a roadmap into the area of comparative politics. This map should help explain why governance looks different and performs differently in different national contexts. We believe that in doing so we have made contributions both to comparative politics and to governance theory. This approach has allowed us to show how governance theory and comparative politics can be integrated. In addition, by bringing comparative politics research into governance theory, we have been able to shed new light on issues that previous governance scholars may have observed but not pursued at any depth, for instance the multidimensionality of causes of governance failure or change in the configuration of governance arrangements.

Let us briefly recapitulate the main arguments developed in this book. We began (Chapter 1) by rearticulating the role of government in governance and suggested that recent governance research has spent much attention on understanding the involvement of societal actors in governance while ignoring the key actor – the state. While the involvement of social actors certainly is a defining feature of contemporary governance, that observation must not obscure the fact that government, by virtue of significant financial and regulatory powers, remains very much in control (Bell and Hindmoor, 2009). The governance roles accorded societal actors are for the most part roles delegated by government and executed under government scrutiny (Héritier and Rhodes, 2011; Scharpf, 1997).

We then proceeded (Chapters 2 and 3) to outline our theory of governance, drawing on functionalist theory and investigating the role of government and other actors in key governance functions – decision-making, goal-selection, resource mobilization, implementation, and feedback and evaluation. From there, we elaborated different models of governance with regard to differences in the centrality of the state (Chapter 4; see also Pierre and Peters, 2005) and investigated how, and by whom, the functions of governance are delivered in different governance scenarios. Since our main focus in this study is on the state, we then (Chapters 5 and 6) turned our attention inward, into the organization and management of government and the public sector. The two penultimate chapters (Chapters 7 and 8) analyze governance failure from a functionalist theoretical perspective and change in governance, respectively. These two analyses oscillate between an intra-state and state–society perspective. Thus, we have demonstrated the potential of approaching governance from a functionalist perspective; we have uncovered the endogenous ramifications of state–society collaboration toward governance outcomes; and we address critical issues that conventionally have been aimed at functionalism (see later).

In terms of the academic roots of our study, we are in some ways intellectually looking back in order to look forward. The complexities of governing are as old as government itself, and as we pointed out earlier in this book, many of the problems facing government in past decades such as overload and governability were in fact governance problems. We have found that revisiting some of the older literature in comparative politics has significantly aided our understanding of governance. Our colleagues of a few decades ago delivered insightful analyses on these and other pressing issues, but, with all due respect, since the more overarching questions about governance were not addressed at that time, they missed the bigger picture. And, to the extent that those bigger issues were addressed, they would typically be approached in deductive "grand theory" (Mills, 1959) design with very little leeway for the role of actors or contextualization.

This need to involve actors and agency is also why one of the key tasks for this book is to demonstrate how a modern version of functionalist theory can inform comparative politics research. The framework we outline in this book is, as mentioned earlier, unashamedly functionalist. We saw two major reasons for choosing the functionalist path into governance and comparative politics. First, although rarely explicated, functionalism is nearly always implied in governance theory. In order for a political system to deliver governance, some fundamental requirements must be met: goals must be defined; resources must be mobilized; there must be structures charged with the implementation of public policy, and so on. Most importantly, the system must have the capacity to make authoritative decisions. Throughout the book, we have emphasized decision-making as the core function of governance. Decisions are essential to all aspects of governance: they allocate resources; define paths of action; provide the electorate with records of government action which facilitate choice and accountability; and bring closure to issues which then can be dismissed from the political agenda. Decision-making is thus the defining moment of governance. Political systems that fail in that respect are likely to fail in most other aspects of governance as well.

Secondly, we argue that we have successfully overcome two of the standard criticisms against functionalist theory; its static nature and its inability to conceptualize or account for agency. These two weaknesses of functionalism are closely related and, interestingly, one helps to a large extent solve the other; by addressing the agency problem, we solve the rigidity problem. With regard to the purported static nature of functionalist theory, we believe this to be a fair criticism of the conventional versions of that theory. Much of that rigidity, however, was related to the deductive nature of the theory, stipulating functions while ignoring agency. Since a key point in governance theory is that agency – i.e. who delivers the fundamental aspects of governance – is a variable and not, as was previously stipulated, government and government alone, our functionalist model of governance is quite dynamic.

This dynamism and the role of multiple actors in governance raise the question of to what extent the actor who delivers a function also to some degree shapes the nature of that function and the degree to which it contributes to systemic efficiency or just to the expected utility of the agent. Let us now turn to that issue.

Governance, Agency, and Functionalism

One of the problems in previous functionalist theories was their poor capacity to conceptualize or account for agency. Studying a political system without considering the actors populating that system is like observing a skeleton and thinking that you are seeing a human body. It is, we submit, essentially impossible to understand political processes without studying in some detail agency. "Reforms, like decisions, do not 'just happen'," as Goldfinch and 't Hart (2003:236) point out; they are outcomes of struggles among actors embedded in institutional frameworks. There is thus a paradoxical twist to this line of reasoning in previous functionalism; if the performance of specified roles is critical to the overall performance of the system, surely we would want to know who is performing those roles. In governance research, a recurrent issue among different groups of scholars has been precisely whether it makes any qualitative difference which actor – government or societal actors – that deliver different governance functions (see later). We would also want to know how the actor's rationale of action correlates with systemic objectives. As we introduce agency in functionalist theory, we must therefore also consider these issues.

Given the growing diversity in agency in contemporary governance, functionalist theory is far more relevant and useful today than it was when it first emerged in the social sciences. The functionalist analyses of the 1960s and 1970s had little variation to account for in terms of who delivered functions critical to governance – and arguably very little need to accommodate such variation as government monopolized the execution of the functions of governance. In contemporary governance, however, explaining that variation – its causes; its manifestations across policy sectors and institutional levels; and its consequences for democracy – is at the heart of governance research.

We can now take this argument further by integrating governance, functionalism, and agency. Throughout this book, we have outlined the fundamental tasks and functions of governance; if the socio-political system (Kooiman, 1993) fails to conduct efficient decision-making, goal-selection, resource mobilization, implementation, and evaluation and feedback, governance is very likely to fail. In previous analyses of governing from a functionalist perspective, government was the key provider of these tasks with only very limited involvement by societal actors. In contemporary governance, by comparison, agency is not only a variable with extensive variation in terms of government presence, but it is also essential to an understanding of governance outcomes. Other agents are now joining government institutions and actors in the delivery of governance functions, making the composition of agency itself an important theme in governance research.

Perhaps most importantly, we now need to ask ourselves to what extent societal actors will fulfill the governance functions in a similar way that government institutions would provide those functions. For example, to what extent does it make a difference if a network or a hierarchy defines collective goals, makes collective decisions, mobilizes resources to attain collective goals, and implements collective goals? These are obviously issues that are central to governance theory and they have for some time been at the forefront of the governance debate (see, for instance, Bogason and Musso, 2006; Considine, 2002; Koppenjan, 2008; Klijn and Skelcher, 2007; March and Olsen, 1995; Pierre, 2000; Rhodes, 1997; Sørensen and Torfing, 2003, 2005, 2007). Much of the debate surrounding this aspect of governance has revolved around issues of democracy, transparency, and accountability, where critics of network governance argue that networks largely fail in these respects.

We should ask to what extent the very nature of the governance functions is altered as the composition of the agents delivering those functions changes. This problem speaks ultimately to our understanding of actor rationality. If we conceive of actors as guided by what March and Olsen (1989) call "the logic of consequentiality," i.e. a maximization of expected utility, we should not expect actors to consider the value of contributing to systemic efficiency unless that in some way or other would benefit the actor. If, on the other hand, we assume (as we discuss in Chapter 3) that actors' behavior is "bounded rational" (Simon, 1947) or even guided by "the logic of appropriateness" (March and Olsen, 1989), societal actors participating in the delivery of governance functions become more likely to consider not just their own benefit of their involvement but the larger systemic and societal returns of that involvement.

A more detailed analysis of these issues would obviously have to consider the heterogeneity of what we here refer to as "societal actors" which is a grab bag of NGOs, stakeholders, private businesses, etc. All this variety of actors are involved in governance and can, as demonstrated in Chapter 7, potentially compensate for problems in governance being supplied through the state.

The outcome of this analysis is not very easy to predict. Some would argue that societies where there is no collective logic but merely an aggregate of individual rationality may have severe consequences on the prospects of collective action (Barry and Hardin, 1982). That being the case, why do we not see political systems collapsing more often than we do? The answer to this question, many social scientists would argue, lies in the institutional arrangements underpinning government, governance, and democracy.

Stipulated and Emergent Governance Functions

The governance functions we analyze in this book are derived from the functionalist literature and aim at covering the core aspects of governance. As is always the case with such deductive reasoning, however, they run the risk of capturing society in snapshots. The capacity of functionalist theory and the functions stipulated by that theory to conceptualize change has been a theme throughout this book. The performance of stipulated functions is however only one aspect of the functionalist argument. We must now turn to a brief discussion on the relationship between those functions on the one hand and emergent functions on the other.

Emergent functions could be defined as spontaneous behavior either by the political system or its external environment to deliver tasks that are essential either to that system or to collective action in other forms. For instance, Jacob Torfing sees the emergence of network governance arrangements as "the functional response to the increasingly fragmented, complex and dynamic character of society" (Torfing, 2007:8; see also Esmark, 2009). Torfing thus assumes that actors in a policy sector or community have an inherent tendency toward collective action and that, in the absence of political institutions or failure of those institutions to deliver governance, such arrangements will emerge. Such behavior may be induced by social norms about obligations or self-interest embedded in such social norms (Hertting, 2007). There is nothing inherent in these emergent functions that suggests that they cater to systemic requirements in all respects, but they do offer support to a system that fails in delivering essential governance functions.

These types of functions emerge for a variety of reasons. Perhaps, the most obvious reason would be partial governance failure. The pattern described by Torfing (2007) could be the outcome not just of increasing societal complexity but also, and probably more likely, to failing capacity of government institutions to provide governance and coordination. There are few, if any, areas of society that are not subject to regulation and some presence of government institutions. Thus, if networks are a functional response to social complexity, it appears likely that that complexity first caused governance failure which, in turn, propelled the emergence of governance networks.

Another driver of emergent functions is a disjuncture between the functional organization of society and the structure and performance of government (Esmark, 2009). There is continuous tension between political institutions and societal organization. Institutions are not just inherently inert structures; there is from a democratic point of view some virtue in that inertia insofar as continuity is a prerequisite for institutional trust and legitimacy. Societies, on the other hand, are characterized by continuous change. Thus, there is not likely to be a perfect adaptation of state structures to societal organization: market regulation is impaired by the globalizing economy; government departments continue to be functionally organized while a growing number of issues cut across those jurisdictional borders; and constitutional rulings still explicate a hierarchy of domestic institutions while there is growing evidence of "rescaling" and multilevel governance (Brenner, 2004; Hooghe and Marks, 2003); and so on. This disjuncture between state organization and patterns of social and market behavior or what Ruggie (2008) and Pierce (1993) call "governance gaps" creates a need for alternative sources which provide structure and direction to collective action.

A third driver of emergent functions, finally, is related to the softer and more negotiated type of policy and regulation in a governance context. Conventional government's policies and regulation offered very little leeway and shirking opportunities for the policy targets. In a more negotiated form of policy-making and regulation, societal compliance is less unconditional and social constituencies (NGOs, neighborhood organizations, etc.) or corporate actors can choose not to subscribe to a negotiated arrangement.

Regardless of what drives the emergence of governance functions, this development speaks directly to some of the key questions we address. Unlike the stipulated, systemic governance functions, emergent functions are dynamic and represent a spontaneous adaptive process of the political system. The emergence of governance functions represents an adaptive element derived from state–society interactions which overcomes some of the critiques against functionalism. Furthermore, functional responses either to societal complexity or to state incapacity can take different forms which requires agency and some form of decision-making.

We believe that we have demonstrated the utility of functionalist approaches to governance, as well as the utility of governance as an approach to comparative politics. Although mass behavior, political parties, legislatures, and a host of other actors and dimensions are important for comparative politics, the fundamental question is can the system govern, and if so how will it govern? And that governance determines the even more fundamental question that Lasswell used to describe politics – "Who Gets What?".

States in Society: The Research Agenda Ahead

Throughout this book, we have discussed the degree to which different configurations of actors can deliver critical governance functions and the outcomes of those different governance arrangements. Across the governance literature, we can see three different perspectives on governance, two of which are rather common in the governance debate and one which is more rarely discussed.

The first perspective is the extreme state-centric view that societies are governed "by the state, the whole state and nothing but the state." This view is inherent in most constitutions, sometimes clearly stated and sometimes merely assumed; it is the official version of the tasks of government. The assumption that states are in control of their societies is in many ways a trademark of political science as an academic discipline; we study politics because this is where fundamental decisions about our societies are being made and implemented. It is an account of governance which for the sake of simplicity ignores a large number of societal forces inside and outside the state. Although this perspective provides an obviously very stylized account of governance, it nonetheless serves as an ideal type or a benchmark against which more realistic models of governance can be compared.

An alternative view is that governance is conducted differently in different national contexts, different policy sectors, and perhaps even different specific issues. The role of the state in this view varies considerably, both in terms of its overall centrality in the process of governing and in terms of which specific governance functions it performs. The purpose of this book has been to outline a set of models which present different accounts of the governance roles performed by government, networks, the market, or societal actors in concert with the state. We believe that these models provide analytical structures or frameworks for comparative research on governance arrangements. This perspective on governance is much closer to real-world governance than the previous version. This also means that it is more contextual and challenging and less susceptible to formal modelling.

A third, less common, perspective states that although the state is an indispensable component of society, its capacity to actually govern that society is severely constrained by factors which are either endogenous or exogenous to the state. Students of political economy have for a long time demonstrated the complex relationships between state and market, where the state by no means is invariably in charge but rather finds itself in complex patterns of dependency in relationship to the market. Similarly, the globalization and the dramatically increasing mobility of information, money, and people have forced the state to adapt to its environment rather than to proactively guide and steer society. Furthermore, numerous studies highlight the growing complexity of society, up to the point where the governability of society has become a very real issue. Last but not least, a significant reduction of the encroachment of society by the state is the result of policy choice, guided by a belief that it should not be the task of government to control and regulate every aspect of society. The state, in this perspective, lacks the capacity required to intervene, to steer, and to set goals which the surrounding society perceives as legitimate (Helmke and Levitsky, 2004).

In functionalist terms, these three different perspectives on governance reflect a decreasing centrality of the state, from a model of complete state dominance in the delivery of all governance functions via a more varied and contextual account where state and society interacts in the pursuit of collective goals to a governance arrangement where the state is portrayed as in charge of core public roles of governing but at the same time largely insignificant as a goal setter or decision-maker on matters of any major consequence for all of society.

As we integrate governance theory and comparative politics, we find that all three perspectives have some merit. The five alternative models of governance we have presented represent various mixtures of these three perspectives, and all these mixtures are able to govern within their particular social and economic contexts. Therefore, rather than thinking about governance research as a contest among these three alternatives, we should instead be more concerned with understanding the mixtures of the three perspectives and the manner in which they can interact, positively or negatively.

These interactions have been approached from a number of different vantage points. In political economy, there are any number of studies on the logic and consequences of political intervention in markets, and also on economic considerations in policy-making. Our key point here is that judging by the institutionalized state–market relationship in the more successful countries, that relationship is not competitive but collaborative. As the titles of Michael Porter's *The Competitive Advantage of Nations* (Porter, 1990) or Peter Katzenstein's *Small States in World Markets* (Katzenstein, 1985) suggest, countries that have succeeded in developing sustained economic growth have done so largely by devising efficient collaborative interactions between state and market. Several Asian countries have seemingly squared the circle of developing globally competitive economies while at the same time according the state a leading role in the economy (Johnson, 1982). There is nothing paradoxical about this pattern; a functional economy requires some degree of state presence, just as all governments are extremely dependent on a competitive economic base.

This argument also applies to collaborative strategies in state–society interactions more broadly. It is interesting to note how collaborative strategies in service delivery in many cases tend to develop into collaborative governance arrangements (Ansell and Gash, 2007; Donahue and Zeckhauser, 2011). As we have demonstrated throughout this book, these interactions can be organized in many different ways. The functionalist approach, we argue, is particularly useful in understanding the logic of these interactions since it helps us escape a narrow focus on institutions and offers a more open-ended analytical question about who actually does what.

The obvious objection to this argument is that the regulatory role of the state sometimes prevents it from catering to specific interests of market actors or other societal actors, and that the key role of the state is to articulate the general public interest and not primarily cater to parochial interests. There are also obvious questions about accountability surrounding these collaborative, interactive governance arrangements (Torfing et al., 2012). All of this suggests that government has to ensure some primus inter pares role in the state–society interaction, but also that the performance of that role is conducted in such a way that it does not prevent the synergies from the collaboration.

The research agenda that this simple typology presents is concerned both with how governments operate internally, i.e. how they pursue governance as a process of making decisions, as well as externally in terms of the degree to which government enjoys the societal legitimacy and consent in its role in governance. Our key point here is that these exogenous perceptions and expectations on the state is likely to be shaped in significant part by the quality of governance provided by the state, either by itself or in collaboration with societal partners. The empirical evidence is not that low-tax, laissez-faire governments are perceived as more trustworthy or legitimate by their citizens; it is in fact just the opposite. What might appear to be a nonlinear paradox between the degree of government presence in society, on the one hand, and the level of trust that governments in different countries enjoy, on the other, may well be resolved by observing what governments actually do; high taxes are rarely very popular but a comprehensive and universal welfare state has gained widespread societal acceptance and support where it has been put in place, just as low taxes may help political leaders score political points until the downsides of tax cuts in public services become visible to society.

This argument leads us to a need for closer examination of the critical functions of governing and the quality by which governments deliver those functions. Questions of governance are not only about who influences policy choices and governance, but what policies are pursued. As we pursue the study of governance, we must always be aware of the need to think about how these various models contribute to the capacity to solve problems faced by ordinary citizens, and to steering society more broadly.

References

Aberbach, J. D., R. D. Putnam and B. A. Rockman (1981), *Bureaucrats and Politicians in Western Democracies* (Cambridge, MA: Harvard University Press).

Aberle, D. F., A. K. Cohen, A. K. Davis, M. J. Levy, Jr. and F. X. Sutton (1950), "The Functional Prerequisites of Society", *Ethics* 60:100–1.

Acemoglu, D. and J. A. Robinson (2012), *Why Nations Fail: The Origins of Power, Prosperity and Poverty* (New York: Crown).

Acuña, C. (in press), *Instituciones y actores de la política y las políticas públicas en la Argentina* (Buenos Aires: OSDE).

Alam, M. S. (1989), "Anatomy of Corruption: An Approach to the Political Economy of Underdevelopment", *American Journal of Economics and Sociology* 48:441–56.

Alford, J. and J. O'Flynn (2012), *Rethinking Public Service Delivery: Managing with External Providers* (Basingstoke: Palgrave).

Allison, G. and P. Zelikow (1999), *Essence of Decision: Explaining the Cuban Missile Crisis* (2nd edn) (New York: Longman).

Almond, G. A. (1988), "The Return to the State", *American Political Science Review* 82:853–74.

Almond, G. A. and J. S. Coleman (1960) *The Politics of Developing Areas* (Princeton, NJ: Princeton University Press).

Almond, G. A. and J. S. Coleman (1957), *Politics in Developing Societies* (Princeton, NJ: Princeton University Press).

Almond, G. A. and G. B. Powell (1966), *Comparative Politics: A Developmental Approach* (Boston, MA: Little, Brown).

Ames, B. C. (2001), *Deadlock of Democracy in Brazil* (Ann Arbor, MI: University of Michigan Press).

Anderson, C. W. (1970), *The Political Economy of Modern Spain* (Madison, WI: University of Wisconsin Press).

Andrews, M. (2008), "The Good Governance Agenda; Beyond Indicators Without Theory", *Oxford Development Studies* 36:379–407.

Andrews, M. (2012), *The Limits of Institutional Reform in Development: Changing Rules for Realistic Solutions* (Cambridge: Cambridge University Press).

Ansell, C. and A. Gash (2007), "Collaborative Governance in Theory and Practice", *Journal of Public Administration and Theory* 18:543–71.

Arestis, P. and M. C. Sawyer (2004), *Neoliberal Economic Policy: Critical Essays* (Cheltenham: Edward Elgar).

Armstrong, J. A. (1973), *The European Administrative Elite* (Princeton, NJ: Princeton University Press).

Arnold, P. E. (1998), *Making the Managerial Presidency: Comprehensive Reorganization Planning, 1905–1996* (Lawrence, KS: University Press of Kansas).

Ashworth, R., G. Boyne and R. Delbridge (2009), "Escape from the Iron Cage: Organizational Change and Isomorphic Pressures in the Public Sector", *Journal of Public Administration Research and Theory* 19:165–87.

Aucoin, P. (2012), "New Public Governance in Westminster Systems: Impartial Public Administration and Management Performance at Risk", *Governance* 25:177–99.

Aucoin, P. and M. Jarvis (2005), *Modernizing Government Accountability: A Framework for Reform* (Ottawa: Canada School for Public Governance).

Axelrod, R. M. (1984), *The Evolution of Cooperation* (New York: Basic Books).

Bache, I. and M. Flinders (eds.) (2004), *multilevel Governance* (Oxford: Oxford University Press).

Bachrach, P. and M. S. Baratz (1962), "Two Faces of Power", *American Political Science Review* 56:947–52.

Bachrach, P. and M. S. Baratz (1963), "Decisions and Non-decisions: An Analytic Framework", *American Political Science Review* 57: 641–51.

Ballon, H. and K. T. Jackson (2007), *Robert Moses and the Modern City: The Transformation of New York* (New York: W. W. Norton).

Bardach, E. and R. Kagan (1982), *Going by the Book: The Problem of Regulatory Unreasonableness* (Philadelphia, PA: Temple University Press).

Barry, B. and G. Hardin (1982), *Rational Man, Irrational Society? An Introduction and Sourcebook* (London: Sage).

Bauer, M., A. Jordan, C. Green-Pedersen and A. Heritier (2012) *Dismantling Public Policy: Preferences, Strategies, Effects* (Oxford: Oxford University Press).

Baumgartner, F. R. and B. D. Jones (2009), *Agendas and Instability in American Politics* (2nd edn) (Chicago: University of Chicago Press).

Baumgartner, F. R. and B. D. Jones (2015), *The Politics of Information: Problem Definition and the Course of Public Policy in America* (Chicago: University of Chicago Press).

Béland, D. and R. H. Cox (2011), *Ideas and Politics in Social Science Research* (Oxford: Oxford University Press).

Bell, S. and A. Hindmoor (2009), *Rethinking Governance: The Centrality of the State in Modern Society* (Cambridge: Cambridge University Press).

Benn, M. (2002), "New Labour and Social Exclusion", *The Political Quarterly* 71:309–19.

Bennett, A. and A. L. George (2005), *Case Studies and Theory Development in the Social Sciences* (Cambridge, MA: MIT Press).

Berger, P. L. and T. Luckmann (1967), *The Social Construction of Reality* (New York: Random House).

Berry, F. S. and W. D. Berry (1999), "Innovation and Diffusion Models in Policy Research", in P. A. Sabatier (ed.), *Theories of the Policy Process* (Boulder, CO: Westview Press), 169–200.

Bertelli, A. M. and L. E. Lynn (2006), *Madison's Managers: Public Administration and the Constitution* (Baltimore, MD: Johns Hopkins University Press).

Birch, A. H. (1984), "Overload, Ungovernability and Delegitimation: The Theories and the British Case", *British Journal of Political Science* 14: 135–60.

Birkland, T. A. (1997), *After Disaster: Agenda Setting, Public Policy and Focusing Events* (Washington, DC: Georgetown University Press).

Birkland, T. A. and S. E. DeYoung (2013), "Focusing Events and Policy Windows", in E. Araral, S. Fritzen, M. Howlett, M. Ramesh and X. Wu (eds.), *Routledge Handbook of Public Policy* (London: Routledge), 175–88.

Black, N. (2001), "Evidence-Based Policy: Proceed with Care", *British Medical Journal* 323:275–9.

Blais, A. and S. Dion (1991), *The Budget-Maximizing Bureaucrat: Appraisals and Evidence* (Pittsburgh, PA: University of Pittsburgh Press).

Bogason, P. (2000), *Public Policy and Local Governance: Institutions in Post-Modern Society* (Cheltenham: Edward Elgar).

Bogason, P. and J. A. Musso (2006), "The Democratic Prospects of Network Governance", *American Review of Public Administration* 36:3–18.

Bogenschneider, K. and T. J. Corbett (2010), *Evidence-Based Policymaking* (New York: Routledge).

Boin, A. (2004), "Lessons from Crisis Research", *International Studies Review* 6:165–94.

Boin, A., P. 't Hart, E. Stern and B. Sundelius (2005), *The Politics of Crisis Management: Public Leadership under Pressure* (Cambridge: Cambridge University Press).

Boin, A., S. Kuipers and M. Steenbergen (2010), "The Life and Death of Public Organizations: A Question of Institutional Design", *Governance* 23:385–410.

Bolke, V., M. A. Brown and K. P. Clements (2009), "Hybrid Political Orders, Not Fragile States", *Peace Review* 21:13–21.

Botsman, P. (2001), *The Enabling State: People Before Bureaucracy* (Sydney: Pluto Press).

Botterill, L. C. and A. Hindmoor (2012), "Turtles All the Way Down: Bounded Rationality in an Evidence-Based Age", *Policy Studies* 33:367–79.

Bouckaert, G. and J. A. Halligan (2007), *Managing Performance: International Comparisons* (London: Routledge).

Bouckaert, G., B. G. Peters and K. Verhoest (2010), *The Coordination of Public Sector Organizations: Shifting Patterns of Public Management* (Basingstoke: Macmillan).

Bovens, M. A. P. and P. 't Hart (2001), *Understanding Policy Fiascos* (New Brunswick, NJ: Transaction Publishers).

Bovens, M. A. P., P. 't Hart and B. G. Peters (eds.) (2001), *Success and Failure of Public Governance: A Comparative Analysis* (Cheltenham: Edward Elgar).

Bozeman, B. (2007), *Public Values and Public Interest: Counterbalancing Economic Individualism* (Washington, DC: Georgetown University Press).

Braibanti, R. (1966), *Asian Bureaucratic Systems Emergent from the British Imperial Tradition* (Durham, NC: Duke University Press).

Brautigam, D. (1996), *State Capacity and Effective Governance* (New Brunswick, NJ: Transaction Books).

Brehm, J. O. and S. Gates (1997), *Working, Shirking and Sabotage: Bureaucratic Response to a Democratic Public* (Ann Arbor: University of Michigan Press).

Brenner, N. (2004), *New State Spaces: Urban Governance and the Rescaling of Statehood* (Oxford: Oxford University Press).

Bresser-Pereira, L. C. (2004), *Democracy and Public Management Reform* (Oxford: Oxford University Press).

Brettschneider, F., J. van Deth and E. Roller (2002), *Das Ende der politisierten Sozialstruktur* (Opladen: Leske & Budrich).

Briquet, J.-L. and F. Sawicki (2000), *Le clientelisme politique dans les sociétés contemporaines* (Paris: Presses Univeritaires de France).

Broschek, J. (2012), "Historical Institutionalism and the Varieties of Federalism in Germany and Canada", *Publius* 42:662–87.

Brown, J. D., J. S. Earle and S. Gelbach (2009), "Helping Hand and Grabbing Hand: State Bureaucracy and Privatization", *American Political Science Review* 103:264–83.

Brunsson, N. and B. Jacobsson (eds.) (2000), *A World of Standards* (Oxford: Oxford University Press).

Bryson, J. M. (2012), "Strategic Planning and Management", in B. G. Peters and J. Pierre (eds.), *The Handbook of Public Administration* (2nd edn) (London: Sage).

Buchanan, J. M. (1975), *The Limits of Liberty* (Chicago: University of Chicago Press).

Buchanan, J. M. and G. Tullock (1962), *The Calculus of Consent* (Ann Arbor, MI: University of Michigan Press).

Budge, I. (1998), "Great Britain: A Stable, But Fragile, Party System?", in P. Pennings and J.-E. Lane (eds.), *Comparing Party System Change* (London: Routledge), 116–26.

Budge, I., H.-D. Klingemann, A. Volkens, J. Bara and E. Tanenbaum (2001), *Mapping Policy Preferences: Estimates for Parties, Electors and Governments, 1945–1998* (Oxford: Oxford University Press).

Bulkeley, H. and M. Betsill (2005), "Rethinking Sustainable Cities: Multilevel Governance and the 'Urban' Politics of Climate Change", *Environmental Politics* 14:42–63.

Burstein, P. (1991), "Policy Domains: Organization, Culture and Policy Outcomes", *American Review of Sociology* 17:327–50.

Calder, K. E. (1988), *Crisis and Compensation: Public Policy and Political Stability in Japan* (Princeton, NJ: Princeton University Press).

Cameron, D. and R. Simeon (2002), "Intergovernmental Relations in Canada: The Emergence of Collaborative Federalism", *Publius* 32:49–71.

Camilleri, J. A. and J. Falk (1992), *The End of Sovereignty* (Cheltenham: Edward Elgar).

Carter, P. (2012), "Policy as Palimpset", *Policy and Politics* 40:423–43.

Castles, F. G. (1998), *Comparative Public Policy: The Politics of Postwar Transformation* (Cheltenham: Edward Elgar).

Chatriot, A. (2007), "Les apories de la représentation de la société civile", *Revue française de droit consttutionelle* 3 (no. 71):535–55.

Cheeseman, N. and B.-M. Tendi (2010), "Power-Sharing in Comparative Perspective: The Dynamics of Unity Government in Kenya and Zimbabwe", *Journal of Modern African Studies* 48:203–39.

Christiansen, P. M. (1998), "A Prescription Rejected: Market Solutions to Problems in the Public Sector", *Governance: An International Journal of Policy, Administration, and Institutions* 11:273–95.

Cobb, R. W. and C. C. Elder (1972), *Participation in American Politics: The Dynamics of Agenda-Building* (Boston, MA: Allyn and Bacon).

Cohen, M. D. and L. S. Sprull (1996), *Organizational Learning* (Thousand Oaks, CA: Sage).

Cohen, M. D., J. G. March and J. P. Olsen (1972), "A Garbage Can Model of Organizational Choice", *Administrative Science Quarterly* 17:1–25.

Cole, A. (2011), "Prefects in Search of a Role in a Europeanized France", *Journal of Public Policy* 31:385–407.

Colignon, R. A. (1997), *Power Plays: Critical Events in the Institutionalization of the Tennessee Valley Authority* (Albany, NY: State University of New York Press).

Collier, D. and J. E. Mahon (1993), "Conceptual 'Stretching' Revisited: Adapting Categories in Comparative Analysis", *American Political Science Review* 87:845–55.

Commission on Global Governance (1995), *Our Global Neighborhood* (Oxford: Oxford University Press).

Conley, R. S. (2003), *The President, Congress and Divided Government: A Postwar Assessment* (College Station: Texas A & M University Press).

Considine, M. (2002), "The End of the Line?: Accountable Governance in an Age of Networks, Partnerships and Joined-Up Government", *Governance* 15:21–40.

Corbett, D. C. (1964), "The Glassco Commission and the Machinery of Government", *Australian Journal of Public Administration* 23:263–7.

Cowell, F. A. (1990), *Cheating the Government: The Economics of Evasion* (Cambridge, MA: MIT Press).

Crozier, M. P. (2010), "Rethinking Systems: Configurations of Politics and Policy in Contemporary Governance", *Administration and Society* 42: 504–25.

Crozier, M. J., S. P. Huntington and J. Watanuki (1975), *The Crisis of Democracy: Report on the Governability of Democracies to the Trilaterial Commission* (New York: New York University Press).

Dahlström, C., J. Pierre and B. Guy Peters (eds.) (2011), *Steering from the Centre: Strengthening Political Control in Western Democracies* (Toronto: University of Toronto Press).

Dahrendorf, R. (1980), "Effectiveness and Legitimacy: On the 'Governability' of Democracies", *The Political Quarterly* 51:393–409.

Davies, J. S. (2011), *Challenging Governance Theory* (Bristol: Policy Press).

Denhardt, J. V. and R. B. Denhardt (2002), *The New Public Service: Serving, not Steering* (Armonk, NY: M. E. Sharpe).

Derlien, H.-U. and B. G. Peters (eds.) (2008), *The State at Work* (vols. 1 and 2) (Cheltenham: Edward Elgar).

Deschouwer, K. (2012), *Politics of Belgium* (Basingstoke: Macmillan).

De Swaan, A. (1973), *Coalition Theories and Cabinet Formations* (San Francisco, CA: Jossey-Bass).

Deutsch, K. W. (1966), *The Nerves of Government* (New York: The Free Press).

Dikotter, F. (2011), *Mao's Great Famine: The History of China's Most Devastating Failure* (New York: Walker Publishing).

Di Palma, G. (1977), *Surviving Without Governing: The Italian Parties in Parliament* (Berkeley, CA: University of California Press).

Dollery, B. E. and J. Wallis (1997), "Market Failure, Government Failure, Leadership and Public Policy", *Journal of Interdisciplinary Economics* 8: 113–26.

Dolowitz, D. and D. Marsh (2000), "Learning from Abroad: The Role of Policy Transfer in Contemporary Policy-Making", *Governance* 13:5–23.

Donahue, J. D. and R. G. Zeckhauser (2011), *Collaborative Governance: Private Roles for Public Goals in Turbulent Times* (Princeton, NJ: Princeton University Press).

Doornbos, M. (2001), "Good Governance: The Rise and Decline of a Policy Metaphor?", *Journal of Development Studies* 37:93–108.

Doornbos, M. (2004), "Good Governance: The Pliability of a Policy Concept", *Praxis* 8:272–88.

Downs, A. (1957), *An Economic Theory of Democracy* (New York: Harper and Row).

Dreyfus, F. (2013), "Far Beyond the 'Napoleonic Model': The Richness of French Administrative History", in J.-M. Eymeri-Douzans and G. Bouckaert (eds.), *La France et ses administrations* (Brussels: Bruylant).

Dror, Y. (1986), "Adjusting the Central Mind of Government to Adversity", *International Political Science Review* 7:11–25.

Dryzek, J. S. (1986), "The Progress of Political Science", *Journal of Politics* 48:301–20.

Dryzek, J. S. and P. Dunleavy (2009), *Theories of the Democratic State* (Basingstoke: Palgrave).

Dunn, W. N. (2003), *Public Policy Analysis* (3rd edn) (New York: Pearson).

Dunn, W. N. (2008), *Public Policy Analysis: An Introduction* (Upper Saddle River, NJ: Prentice-Hall).

Duran, P. (1998), *Pesner l'action sociale* (Paris: L. G. D. F).

Duverger, M. (1951), *Les partis politiques* (Paris: A. Colin).

Dyson, K. H. F. (1980), *The State Tradition in Western Europe: A Study of an Idea and an Institution* (Oxford: Oxford University Press).

Easton, D. (1965a), *A Framework for Political Analysis* (Englewood Cliffs, NJ: Prentice Hall).

Easton, D. (1965b), *A Systems Analysis of Political Life* (New York: Wiley).

Eckstein, H. (1963), "A Perspective on Comparative Politics, Past and Present", in H. Eckstein and D. Apter (eds.), *Comparative Politics* (New York: Free Press).

Eichbaum, C. and R. Shaw (2010), *Partisan Appointees and Public Servants: An International Analysis of the Role of the Political Adviser* (Cheltenham: Edward Elgar).

Elmore, R. F. (1979), "Backward Mapping: Implementation Research and Policy Decisions", *Political Science Quarterly* 94:601–16.

Erkkilä, T. (2012), *Government Transparency: Impacts and Unintended Consequences* (Basingstoke: Palgrave).

Erkkilä, T. and O. Piironen (2009), "Politics and Numbers: The Iron Cage of Governance Indices", in R. W. Cox III (ed.), *Ethics and Integrity in Public Administration: Concepts and Cases* (Armonk, NY: M.E. Sharpe), 125–45.

Esmark, A. (2009), "The Functional Differentiation of Governance: Public Governance Beyond Hierarchy, Markets and Networks", *Public Administration* 87:351–70.

Esping-Andersen, G. (1990), *The Three Worlds of Welfare Capitalism* (Princeton, NJ: Princeton University Press).

Evans, P. B., D. Rueschmeyer and T. Skocpol (eds.) (1985), *Bringing the State Back In* (Cambridge: Cambridge University Press).

Ezrow, N. W. and E. Frantz (2011), *Dictators and Dictatorships: Understanding Authoritarian Regimes and Their Leaders* (London: Bloomsbury).

Faguet, J.-P. (2014), "Decentralization and Governance", *World Development* 53:2–13.

Fairbanks, C. H. (1987), "Bureaucratic Politics in the Soviet Union and in the Ottoman Empire", *Comparative Strategy* 6:333–62.

Feiock, R. C. and C. Stream (2001), "Environmental Protection and Economic Development: A False Trade-Off?", *Public Administration Review* 61:313–21.

Feldstein, M. (1998), "Refocusing the IMF", *Foreign Affairs* 77:20–33.

Finer, S. E. (1997), *The History of Government from the Earliest Times* (Oxford: Oxford University Press).

Finer, S. E. (1999), *History of Government from the Earliest Times: Vol. 3, Empires, Monarchies and the Modern State* (Oxford: Oxford University Press).

Finkle, J. L. and R. W. Gable (1973), *Political Development and Social Change* (2nd edn) (New York: John Wiley).

Fiorina, M. P. (2002), "Parties and Partisanship: A 40 Year Retrospective", *Political Behavior* 24:93–115.

Fiorina, M. P. and S. J. Abrams (2008), "Political Polarization in the American Public", *Annual Review of Political Science* 11:563–88.

Fleming, E., D. Heinecke and B. Dollery (2007), "An Analytical Framework of Assessing the Internalities on Policy and Projects Using Examples from Papua New Guinea", *Impact Assessment and Project Appraisal* 25:199–207.

Foley, M. (2000), *The British Presidency: Tony Blair and the Politics of Public Leadership* (Manchester: Manchester University Press).

Frederickson, H. G. (2007), "Whatever Happened to Public Administration? Governance Governance Everywhere", in C. Pollitt, L. E. Lynn and E. Ferlie (eds.), *The Oxford Handbook of Public Management* (Oxford: Oxford University Press), 282–304.

Freeman, G. (1985), "National Styles and Policy Sectors: Explaining Structured Variation", *Journal of Public Policy* 5:467–96.

Freeman, H. E. and P. H. Rossi (1995), *Evaluation: A Systematic Analysis* (Newbury Park, CA: Sage).

Fukuyama, F. (2014), *State-building, Governance and World Order in the 21st Century* (Ithaca, NY: Cornell University Press).

Fukuyama, F. (2015), "Why is Democracy Performing So Poorly?", *Journal of Democracy* 26:11–20.

Galaz, V. and A. Duit (2008), "Governance and Complexity Theory: Emerging Issues in Governance Theory", *Governance* 21:311–25.

Galnoor, I. (1982), *Steering the Polity: Communication and Politics in Israel* (Beverly Hills, CA: Sage).

Gamble, A. (1994), *Britain in Decline* (4th edn) (London: Macmillan).

Gandhi, J. (2008), *Political Institutions Under Dictatorship* (Cambridge: Cambridge University Press).

Ganghof, S. (2003), "Promises and Pitfalls of Veto Player Analysis", *Swiss Political Science Review* 9:1–25.

Geddes, B. (1994), *Politician's Dilemma: Building State Capacity in Latin America* (Berkeley, CA: University of California Press).

Geen, R., S. Waters Boots and K. C. Tumlin (1999), *The Cost of Protecting Vulnerable Children: Understanding Federal, State, and Local Child Welfare Spending* (Washington, DC: The Urban Institute).

Gerbaudo, P. (2013) *Tweets and the Streets: Social Media and Contemporary Activism* (London: Pluto).

Geva-May, I. (2004), "Riding the Wave of Opportunity: Termination in Public Policy", *Journal of Public Administration Research and Theory* 14: 309–33.

Giddens, A. (1975), "Functionalism: Apres la lute", *Social Research* 43:325–66.

Gilley, B. (2009), *The Right to Rule: How States and Win and Lose Legitimacy* (New York: Columbia University Press).

Gingrich, J. R. (2011), *Making Markets in the Welfare State: The Politics of Varying Market Reforms* (Cambridge: Cambridge University Press).

Goldfinch, S. and P. 't Hart (2003), "Leadership and Institutional Reform: Engineering Macroeconomic Policy Change in Australia", *Governance:*

An International Journal of Policy, Administration, and Institutions 16: 235–70.

Goldsmith, M. (1992), "Local Government", *Urban Studies* 29:393–410.

Goodin, R. E. (2003), *Reflective Democracy* (Oxford: Oxford University Press).

Goodsell, C. T. (2000), *The Case for Bureaucracy* (4th edn) (Washington, DC: CQ Press).

Goodsell, C. T. (2011), *Mission Mystique: Belief Systems in Public Agencies* (Washington, DC: CQ Press).

Gormley, W. T. and D. L. Weimer (1999), *Organizational Report Cards* (Cambridge, MA: Harvard University Press).

Gough, I. (1979), *The Political Economy of the Welfare State* (Basingstoke: Macmillan).

Gray, V. and D. Lowery (2005), *The Population Ecology Model of Interest Representation: Lobbying Communities in the American States* (Ann Arbor, MI: University of Michigan Press).

Gregory, R. (2011), "Normativity and NPM: A Need for Some Theoretical Coherence", in T. Christensen and P. Laegreid (eds.), *The Ashgate Research Companion to New Public Management* (New York: Routledge), 375–90.

Gurr, T. R. and D. S. King (1987), *The State and the City* (Basingstoke: Macmillan; Chicago: The University of Chicago Press).

Gustafsson, G. (1987), *Decentralisering av politisk makt* [Decentralization of Political Power] (Stockholm: Carlssons).

Hacker, J. S., M. A. Levin and M. Shapiro (2004), "Reform Without Change, Change Without Reform: The Politics of US Health Policy Reform in Comparative Perspective", in M. A Levin and M. Shapiro (eds.), *Transatlantic Policymaking in an Age of Austerity: Diversity and Drift* (Washington, DC: Georgetown University Press), 13–63.

Haldén, P. (2011), *Stability without Statehood: Lessons from Europe's History Before the Sovereign State* (Basingstoke: Palgrave).

Hall, P. (2011), *Managementbyråkrati* (Malmö: Liber).

Hall, P. A. (1986), *Governing the Economy: The Politics of State Intervention in Britain and France* (Oxford: Oxford University Press).

Hall, P. A. (1989), *The Political Power of Economic Ideas: Keynesianism Across Nations* (Princeton, NJ: Princeton University Press).

Halligan, J. A. (1997), "New Public Sector Models: Reform in Australia and New Zealand", in J.-E. Lane (ed.), *Public Sector Reform: Rationale, Trends and Problems* (London: Sage), 17–47.

Hanusch, H. (1983), *Anatomy of Government Deficiencies* (Berlin: Springer).

Hardin, R. (1989), "Why a Constitution?", in B. Grofman and D. Whitman (eds.), *The Federalist Papers and the New Institutionalism* (New York: Agathon Press), 100–120.

Harding, A. (1998), "Public-Private Partnerships in the UK", in J. Pierre (ed.), *Partnerships in Urban Governance: European and American Experience* (Basingstoke: Macmillan), 71–92.

't Hart, P. (1980), *Groupthink in Government: A Study of Small Groups and Policy Failure* (Lisse: Swets and Zeitlinger).

't Hart, P., E. Stern and B. Sundelius (1997), *Beyond Groupthink: Political Group Dynamics and Foreign Policymaking* (Ann Arbor, MI: University of Michigan Press).

Haskins, R. and G. Margolis (2015), *Show Me the Evidence: Obama's Fight for Rigor and Results in Social Policy* (Washington, DC: The Brookings Institution).

Hatry, H. (2013), "Sorting the Relationships Among Performance Measurement, Program Evaluation and Performance Management", *New Directions for Evaluation* 137:19–32.

Hay, C. and B. Rosamond (2002), "Globalization, European Integration and the Discursive Construction of Economic Imperatives", *Journal of European Public Policy* 9:147–67.

Hayes, M. (2013), "Incrementalism", in E. Araral, S. Fritzen, M. Howlett, M. Ramesh and X. Wu (eds.), *Routledge Handbook of Public Policy* (London: Routledge), 287–98.

Hayes-Renshaw, F. and H. Wallace (2006), *The Council of Ministers* (Basingstoke: Palgrave Macmillan).

Hazareesingh, S. (1994), *Political Traditions in Modern France* (Oxford: Oxford University Press).

Head, B. W. (2008), "Wicked Problems in Public Policy", *Public Policy* 3: 101–18.

Heclo, H. (1974), *Modern Social Politics in Britain and Sweden* (New Haven, CT: Yale University Press).

Heclo, H. and A. Wildavsky (1974), *The Private Government of Public Money* (Berkeley, CA: University of California Press).

Hedström, P. and R. Swedborg (1998), *Social Mechanisms: An Analytical Approach to Social Theory* (Cambridge: Cambridge University Press).

Heisler, M. O. (1974), "The European Policy Model", in M. O. Heisler (ed.), *Politics in Western Europe* (New York: Longman).

Helleiner, E. and A. Pickel (2004), *Economic Nationalism in a Globalizing World* (Cambridge: Cambridge University Press).

Helm, D. (2010), "Government Failure, Rent-Seeking and Capture: The Design of Climate Change Policy", *Oxford Review of Economic Policy* 25:182–96.

Helmke, G. and S. Levitsky (2004), "Informal Institutions and Comparative Politics: A Research Agenda", *Perspectives on Politics* 2:725–40.

Helms, L. (2012), "Democratic Political Leadership in the New Media Age: A Farewell to Excellence", *British Journal of Politics and International Relations* 14:651–70.

Héritier, A. and D. Lehmkuhl (2008), "The Shadow of Hierarchy and New Modes of Governance", *Journal of Public Policy* 28:1–17.

Héritier, A. and M. Rhodes (2008), *New Modes of Governance in Europe* (Basingstoke: Macmillan).

Héritier, A. and M. Rhodes (eds.) (2011), *New Modes of Governance in Europe: Governing in the Shadow of Hierarchy* (Basingstoke: Palgrave).

Hertting, N. (2007), "Mechanisms of Governance Network Formation: A Contextual Rational Choice Perspective", in E. Sørensen and J. Torfing (eds.), *Theories of Democratic Network Governance* (Basingstoke: Palgrave), 43–60.

Hill, D. M. (1974), *Democratic Theory and Local Government* (London: Allen and Unwin).

Hill, H. C. (2003), "Understanding Implementation: Street-Level Bureaucrats' Resources for Reform", *Journal of Public Administration Research and Theory* 13:265–82.

Hill, M. J. and P. L. Hupe (2015), *Implementing Public Policy* (3rd edn) (London: Sage).

Hindmoor, A. and B. Taylor (2015), *Rational Choice* (2nd edn) (London: Palgrave).

Hirst, P. and G. Thompson (1999), *Globalization in Question: The International Economy and the Possibilities of Governance* (Oxford: Polity Press).

Hjern, B. and D. O. Porter (1981), "Implementation Structures: A New Unit of Organizational Analysis", *Organization Studies* 2:211–27.

Hogwood, B. W. and B. G. Peters (1983), *Policy Dynamics* (Brighton: Wheatsheaf).

Holliday, I. (2000), "Is the British State Hollowing Out?", *The Political Quarterly* 71:167–76.

Hood, C. (1976a), *The Tools of Government* (Chatham, NJ: Chatham House).

Hood, C. (1976b), *The Limits of Administration* (New York: John Wiley).

Hood, C. (1991), "A Public Management for All Seasons?" *Public Administration* 69:3–19.

Hood, C. (2011), *The Blame Game: Spin, Bureaucracy and Self-Preservation in Government* (Princeton, NJ: Princeton University Press).

Hood, C., O. James, B. G. Peters and C. Scott (eds.) (2004), *Controlling Modern Government: Variety, Commonality and Change* (Cheltenham: Edward Elgar).

Hood, C. and H. Margetts (2007), *Tools of Government in a Digital Age* (Basingstoke: Macmillan).

Hooghe, L. and G. Marks (2003), "Unraveling the State, but How? Types of multilevel Governance", *American Political Science Review* 97:233–43.

Hoppe, R. (2010), *The Governance of Problems: Puzzling, Powering and Participation* (Bristol: Policy Press).

Horn, M. J. (1995), *The Political Economy of Public Administration: Institutional Choice in the Public Sector* (Cambridge: Cambridge University Press).

Hough, J. F. (1965), *The Soviet Prefects: Local Party Organs in Industrial Decision-Making* (Durham, NC: Duke University Press).

Houngnikpo, M. (2011), *Guarding the Guardians: Civil-Military Relations in Africa* (Aldershot: Ashgate).

Howlett, M. and R. Lejano (2013), "Tales from the Crypt: The Rise and Fall (and Rebirth?) of Policy Design", *Administration & Society* 45: 356–80.

Howlett, M., M. Ramesh and A. Perl (2009), *Studying Public Policy: Policy Cycles and Policy Subsystems* (Don Mills, ON: Oxford University Press).

Howlett, M., M. Ramesh and X. Wu (2015), "Understanding the Persistence of Policy Failures: The Role of Politics, Governance and Uncertainty", *Public Policy and Administration* 30:209–20.

Howlett, M. and J. Rayner (2007), "Design Principles for Policy Mixes: Cohesion and Coherence in 'New Governance Arrangements'", *Policy and Society* 26:1–18.

Huber, J. D. and C. R. Shipan (2002), *Deliberate Discretion: The Institutional Foundations of Bureaucratic Autonomy* (Cambridge: Cambridge University Press).

Hueglin, T. O. and A. Fenna (2015), *Comparative Federalism: A Systematic Inquiry* (2nd edn) (Toronto: University of Toronto Press).

Huntington, S. P. (1968), *Political Order in Changing Societies* (New Haven, CT: Yale University Press).

Huntington, S. P., M. Crozier and J. Watanuki (1975), *The Crisis of Democracy: Report on the Governability of Democracies to the Trilateral Commission* (New York: New York University Press).

Hupe, P. and M. J. Hill (2006), "The Three Actions of Governance: Re-framing the Policy Process Beyond the Stages Model", in B. G. Peters and J. Pierre (eds.), *Handbook of Public Policy* (London: Sage), 13–30.

Hustedt, T. and H. Houlberg Salomonsen (2014), "Ensuring Political Responsiveness: Politicization Mechanisms in Ministerial Bureaucracies", *International Review of Administrative Sciences* doi: 10.1177/0020852314533449.

Inglehart, R. and C. Welzel (2003), *Modernization, Cultural Change, and Democracy: The Human Development Sequence* (Cambridge: Cambridge University Press).

Jacobs, A. J. (2004), "Federations of Municipalities: A Practical Alternative to Local Government Consolidations in Japan?", *Governance: An International Journal of Policy, Administration, and Institutions* 17: 247–74.

Jacobs, A. M. (2011), *Governing for the Long Term: Democracy and the Politics of Investment* (Cambridge: Cambridge University Press).

Jacobsson, B. and G. Sundström (2006), *Från Hemvävd till invävd: Europeiseringen av svensk förvaltning och politik* [Frome Homegrown to Embedded: The Europeanization of Swedish Administration and Politics] (Malmö: Liber).

Jacobsson, B., J. Pierre and G. Sundström (2015), *Governing the Embedded State: The Organizational Dimension of Governance* (Oxford: Oxford University Press).

James, M. O. (2002), *Congressional Oversight* (Hauppauge, NY: Nova Publishers).

Jänicke, M. (1990), *State Failure: The Impotence of Politics in Industrial Society* (University Park, PA: Pennsylvania State University Press).

Jayasuriya, K. (2006), *Law, Capitalism and Power in Asia: The Rule of Law and Legal Institutions* (London: Routledge).

Jenkins, B. and A. Gray (1985), *Administrative Politics in British Government* (Brighton: Wheatsheaf).

Jensen, L. (2003), "Aiming for Centrality: the Politico-Administrative Strategies of the Danish Ministry of Finance", in J. Wanna, L. Jensen and J. de Vries (eds.), *Controlling Public Expenditure: The Changing Roles of Central Budget Agencies–Better Guardians* (Cheltenham: Edward Elgar), 166–92.

Jessop, B. (2000) "Governance Failure", in G. Stoker (ed.), *The New Politics of British Local Governance* (Basingstoke: Palgrave), 11–32.

Jessop, B. (2002), "Governance and Meta-Governance: On Reflexivity, Requisite Variety, and Requisite Irony" (online version. Department of Sociology, University of Lancaster).

John, P. (2001), *Local Governance in Western Europe* (London: Sage).

John, J. D. (2010), "The Concept, Causes and Consequences of Failed States: A Critical Review of Literature and Agenda for Research with Specific Reference to Sub-Saharan Africa", *European Journal of Development Research* 22:1–30.

Johnson, C. A. (1982), *MITI and the Japanese Miracle* (Stanford: Stanford University Press).

Jones, C. O. (1984), *An Introduction to the Study of Public Policy* (3rd edn) (Monterey: Brooks/Cole).

Jones, B. D. (2001), *Politics and the Architecture of Choice: Bounded Rationality and Governance* (Chicago: University of Chicago Press).

Jones, B. D. (2002), "Bounded Rationality and Public Policy: Herbert A. Simon and the Decisional Foundation of Collective Choice", *Policy Sciences* 35:269–84.

Katz, R. S. and P. Mair (2009), "The Cartel Party Thesis: A Restatement", *Perspectives on Politics* 7:753–66.

Katzenstein, P. J. (1984), *Corporatism and Change* (Ithaca, NY: Cornell University Press).

Katzenstein, P. J. (1985), *Small States in World Markets: Industrial Policy in Europe* (Ithaca, NY: Cornell University Press).

Katzenstein, P. J. (1987), *Policy and Politics in West Germany: The Growth of a Semi-Sovereign State* (Philadelphia, PA: Temple University Press).

Kaufmann, D. (2005), "Myths and Realities of Governance and Corruption" (Washington, DC: The World Bank).

Kaufmann, F. X., G. Majone and V. Ostrom (eds.) (1988), *Guidance, Control and Evaluation in the Public Sector* (Chicago: Aldine-de Gruyter).

Keane, J. (2009), *Life and Death of Democracy* (New York: W. W. Norton).

Keating, M. (1991), *Comparative Urban Politics* (Cheltenham: Edward Elgar).

Kekkonen, S. and T. Raunio (2011), "Towards Stronger Political Steering: Program Management Reform in the Finnish Government", in C. Dahlström, B. G. Peters and J. Pierre (eds.), *Steering from the Centre: Strengthening Political Control in Western Democracies* (Toronto: University of Toronto Press), 241–62.

Keman, H. (2002), *Comparative Democratic Politics: A Guide to Contemporary Research and Theory* (London: Sage).

Keohane, R. O. and J. S. Nye (2000), "Introduction", in J. S. Nye and J. D. Donahue (eds.), *Governance in a Globalizing World* (Washington, DC: Brookings Institution), 1–44.

Kerwin, C. (2011), *Rulemaking: How Governments Write Law and Make Policy* (Washington, DC: Sage).

Kettl, D. F. (2002), *The Transformation of Governance: Public Administration for the Twenty-First Century America* (Baltimore, MD: Johns Hopkins University Press).

Kickert, W. J. M. (1995), "Steering at a Distance: A New Paradigm of Public Governance in Dutch Higher Education", *Governance* 8:135–57.

Kickert, W. J. M. (2012), "State Responses to the Fiscal Crisis in Britain, Germany and the Netherlands", *Public Management Review* 14:293–309.

Kickert, W. J. M., E. Klijn and J. F. M. Koppenjan (1997), *Managing Complex Networks* (London: Sage).

Kickert, W. J. M. and T. Randma-Liiv (2015), "The Politics of Fiscal Consolidation: A Comparative Analysis", *International Review of Administrative Sciences* 81:274–97.

Kim, M. (2012), "Economic Globalization, Democracy, and Social Protection: Institutional Divergence of Welfare Capitalism in East Asia", in Z. Zhu (ed.), *New Dynamics in East Asian Politics: Security, Political Economy, and Society* (New York: Continuum International Publishing), 125–47.

King, A. (1976), "Ideas, Institutions and Policies of Government: A Comparative Analysis. Parts 1 and II", *British Journal of Political Science* 3:291–313.

Kingdon, J. W. (2003), *Agendas, Alternatives, and Public Policies* (2nd edn) (New York: Longman).

Kjaer, A. M. (2004), *Governance* (Cambridge: Polity Press).

Klijn, E. and C. Skelcher (2007), "Democracy and Governance Networks: Compatible or Not?", *Public Administration* 85:587–608.

Knill, C. (1999), "Explaining Cross-National Variance in Administrative Reform: Autonomous versus Instrumental Bureaucracies", *Journal of Public Policy* 19:113–39.

Knill, C. (2004), "Modes of Governance and Their Evaluation", *Praxis* 8: 352–71.

Kohler-Koch, B. and B. Rittberger (2006), "Review Article: The 'Governance Turn' in EU Studies", *Journal of Common Market Studies Annual Review* 44:27–49.

Kooiman, J. (1993), "Social-Political Governance: Introduction", in J. Kooiman (ed.), *Modern Governance: New Government-Society Interactions* (London: Sage), 1–8.

Kooiman, J. (2003), *Governing as Governance* (London: Sage).

Kooiman, J., M. Bavnick, R. Chunpagdee, R. Mahon and R. Pullin (2008), "Interactive Governance and Governability", *Journal of Transdisciplinary Environmental Studies* 7:1–11.

Koppenjan, J. (2008), "Creating a Playing Field for Assessing the Effectiveness of Network Collaboration by Performance Measures", *Public Management Review* 10:699–714.

Koppenjan, J. and E.-H. Klijn (2004), *Managing Uncertainties in Networks: A Network Approach to Problem-Solving and Decision Making* (London: Routledge).

Kopstein, J. and S. Steinmo (eds.) (2008), *Growing Apart? America and Europe in the Twenty-First Century* (Cambridge: Cambridge University Press).

Kratz, M. S. (2015), *Institutions and Ideas: Philip Selznick's Legacy in Organizational Studies* (Bingley: Emerald).

Kriekhaus, J. (2002), "Reconceptualizing the Developmental State: Public Savings and Economic Growth", *World Development* 30:1697–712.

Kumlin, S. (2004), *The Personal and the Political: How Personal Welfare State Experiences Affect Political Trust and Ideology* (Basingstoke: Palgrave).

Kvavik, R. B. (1976), *Interest Groups in Norwegian Politics* (Oslo: Universitetsforlaget).

Laegreid, P. and K. Verhoest (eds.) (2010), *Governance of Public Sector Organizations: Proliferation, Autonomy and Performance* (Basingstoke: Palgrave).

Lane, J.-E. (1983), "The Concept of Implementation", *Statsvetenskaplig Tidskrift* 86:17–40.

Lane, J.-E. (2000), *New Public Management* (London: Routledge).

Lane, R. (1994), 'Structural-Functionalism Reconsidered: A Proposed Research Model', *Comparative Politics* 26:461–77.

Lascoumbes, P. and P. Le Gales (2007), "Understanding Public Policy Through Its Instruments–From the Nature of Instruments to the Sociology of Public Policy Instrumentation", *Governance: An International Journal of Policy, Administration, and Institutions* 20:1–21.

Lasswell, H. D. (1936), *Politics: Who Gets What How and Why* (New York: Harper and Row).

Laycock, D. H. (2002), *The New Right and Democracy in Canada: Understanding Reform and the Canadian Alliance* (New York: Oxford University Press).

Leftwich, A. (1994), "Governance, the State, and the Politics of Development", *Development and Change* 25:363–85.

Le Galès, P. and C. Lequesne (eds.) (1998), *Regions in Europe* (London: Routledge).

Lewis-Beck, M. (2008), *The American Voter Revisited* (Ann Arbor, MI: University of Michigan Press).

Light, P. C. (1997), *The Tides of Reform: Making Government Work, 1945–1995* (New Haven, CT: Yale University Press).

Light, P. C. (2002), *Government's Greatest Achievements: From Civil Rights to Homeland Defense* (Washington, DC: The Brookings Institution).

Lijphart, A. (1984), *Democracies: Patterns of Majoritarian and Consensus Government in Twenty-One Countries* (New Haven, CT: Yale University Press).

Lijphart, A. (1999), *Patterns of Democracy: Government Forms and Performance in Thirty-Six Countries* (New Haven, CT: Yale University Press).

Lindblom, C. (1979), "Still Muddling, Not Yet Through", *Public Administration Review* 39:517–26.

Linder, S. H. and B. G. Peters (1984), "From Social Theory to Policy Design", *Journal of Public Policy* 4:237–59.

Linn, R. L., E. L. Baker and D. W. Betebenner (2002), "Accountability Systems: Implications of Requirement of the No Child Left Behind Act of 2001", *Educational Researcher* 31:3–16.

Lipsky, M. (1980), *Street-Level Bureaucracy: Dilemmas of the Individual in Public Services* (New York: Russel Sage Foundation).

Lodge, M., L. Stirton and K. Moloney (2015), "Whitehall in the Caribbean? The Legacy of Colonial Administration for Post-Colonial Democratic Development", *Commonwealth & Comparative Politics* 53:8–28.

Lodge, M. and K. Weigrich (2015), "Crowdsourcing and Regulatory Review: A New Way of Challenging Red Tape in British Government", *Regulation & Governance* 9:30–46.

Lowi, T. J. (1979), *The End of Liberalism: The Second Republic of the United States* (New York: W. W. Norton).

Lund, C. (2011), *Twilight Institutions: Public Authority and Local Politics in Africa* (Oxford: Blackwells).

Lundqvist, L. J. (1980), *The Hare and the Tortoise: Clean Air Policies in the United States and Sweden* (Ann Arbor, MI: University of Michigan Press).

Macdonald, R. A. (2008), "The Swiss Army Knife of Governance", in P. Eliadis, M. Hill and M. Howlett (eds.), *Designing Government from Instruments to Governance* (Montreal: McGill/Queens University Press), 203–41.

Madrick, J. (2009), *The Case for Big Government* (Princeton, NJ: Princeton University Press).

Mahoney, J. (2004), "Comparative-Historical Methodology", *Annual Review of Sociology* 30:81–101.

Maier, C. S. (1987), "Introduction", in C. S. Maier (ed.), *Changing Boundaries of the Political* (Cambridge, MA: Cambridge University Press), 1–26.

Mair, P. (1997), *Party System Change: Approaches and Interpretations* (Oxford: Clarendon Press).

Mair, P. and I. van Biezen (2001), "Party Membership in Twenty European Democracies, 1980–2000", *Party Politics* 7:5–21.

Majone, G. (2002), "Delegation of Powers in a Mixed Polity", *European Law Journal* 8:319–39.

Mann, T. E. and N. J. Ornstein (2012), *It's Even Worse Than It Looks: How the American Constitutional System Collided with the New Politics of Extremism* (New York: Basic Books).

Maor, M. (2012), "Policy Overreaction", *Journal of Public Policy* 32:231–59.

March, J. G. and J. P. Olsen (1989), *Rediscovering Institutions: The Organizational Basis of Politics* (New York: Free Press).

March, J. G. and J. P. Olsen (1995), *Democratic Governance* (New York: Free Press).

Marin, B. and R. Mayntz (1991), *Policy Networks: Empirical Evidence and Theoretical Considerations* (Frankfurt: Campus Verlag).

Markoff, J. and V. Montecinos (1993), "The Ubiquitous Rise of Economists", *Journal of Public Policy* 13:37–68.

Markusen, A. R. (2003), "The Case Against Privatizing National Security", *Governance* 16:471–501.

Marsh, D. (2008), "Understanding British Government: Analysing Competing Models", *British Journal of Politics and International Affairs* 10:251–68.

Marston, G. and R. Watts (2003), "Tampering with the Evidence: A Critical Appraisal of Evidence-Based Policy-Making", *The Drawing Board: An Australian Review of Public Affairs* 3:143–63.

May, J. D. (1973), "Opinion Structure of Political Parties: The Special Law of Curvlinear Disparity", *Political Studies* 21:135–51.

McConnell, A. (2010), *Understanding Policy Success: Rethinking Public Policy* (Basingstoke: Macmillan).

McFarland, A. S. (2007), "Neopluralism", *Annual Review of Political Science* 10:45–66.

McLeod, T. H. (1963), "Glassco Commission Report", *Canadian Public Administration* 6:386–406.

Meguid, B. M. (2010), *Party Competition Between Unequals* (Cambridge: Cambridge University Press).

Merton, R. K. (1957), *Social Theory and Social Structure* (New York: The Free Press).

Meyer, M. K. and S. Vorsanger (2003), "Street Level Bureaucracy", in B. G. Peters and J. Pierre (eds.), *Handbook of Public Administration* (London: Sage), 245–56.

Meynaud, J. (1964) *La technocratie: Mythe ou réalité?* (Paris: Payot).

Meynaud, J. (1968), *Technocratie, mythe ou realité* (Paris: A. Colin).

Migdal, J. S. (1988), *Strong Societies and Weak States: State-Society Relations and State Capabilities in the Third World* (Princeton, NJ: Princeton University Press).

Migdal, J. S. (2001), *State in Society: Studying how States and Societies Transform and Constitute One Another* (Cambridge: Cambridge University Press).

Mills, C. W. (1959), *The Sociological Imagination* (Oxford: Oxford University Press).

Milward, H. B. and K. C. Provan (2000), "Governing the Hollow State", *Journal of Public Administration Research and Practice* 10:359–80.

Molina, O. and M. Rhodes (2002), "Corporatism: The Past, Present and Future of a Concept", *Annual Review of Political Science* 5:305–31.

Mommsen, W. J. (1989), *The Political and Social Theory of Max Weber* (Chicago: University of Chicago Press).

Montero, A. P. (2005), *Brazilian Politics: Reforming a Democratic State in a Changing World* (Cambridge: Cambridge University Press).

Mooney, L. A., D. Knox and C. Schacht (2011), *Understanding Social Problems* (Belmont, CA: Wadsworth).

Mörth, U. (ed.) (2004), *Soft Law in Governance and Regulation: An Interdisciplinary Analysis* (Cheltenham: Edward Elgar).

Mucciaroni, G. (2013), "The Garbage Can Model and the Study of the Policy-Making Process", in E. Araral, S. Fritzen, M. Howlett, M. Ramesh and X. Wu (eds.), *Routledge Handbook of Public Policy* (London: Routledge), 320–28.

Mueller, D. (1979), *Public Choice* (Cambridge: Cambridge University Press).

Muramatsu, M. (1997), *Local Power in the Japanese State* (Berkeley, CA: University of California Press).

Musgrave, R. and P. Musgrave (1989), *Public Finance in Theory and Practice* (5th edn) (New York: McGraw-Hill).

Nelson, B. (1984), *Making an Issue of Child Abuse: Political Agenda-Setting for Social Problems* (Chicago: University of Chicago Press).

Nettl, J. P. (1968), "The State as a Conceptual Variable", *World Politics* 20: 559–92.

Niemann, C. (2013), *Villkorat förtroende* (PhD dissertation. Stockholm: Department of Political Science, Stockholm University).

Niskanen, W. (1971), *Bureaucracy and Representative Government* (Chicago: Aldine/Atherton).

Norris, P. (2011), *Democratic Deficit: Critical Citizens Revisited* (Cambridge: Cambridge University Press).

Nye, J. S., P. D. Zelikow and D. C. King (eds.) (1997), *Why People Don't Trust Government* (Cambridge, MA: Harvard University Press).

O'Donnell, G. A. (2001), "Democracy, Law and Comparative Politics", *Studies in Comparative International Development* 36:7–36.

Offe, C. (1984), *Contradictions of the Welfare State* (Cambridge, MA: MIT Press).

Offe, C. (2009), "Governance: An Empty Signifier?", *Constellations* 16: 550–62.

Okimoto, D. I. (1988), *Between MITI and the Market* (Stanford: Stanford University Press).

Oliver, C. (1991), "Strategic Responses to Institutional Processes", *The Academy of Management Review* 16:145–79.

Olson, M. (1984), *The Rise and Decline of Nations: Economic Growth, Stagflation, and Social Rigidities* (New Haven: Yale University Press).

Olsen, J. P. (1983), *Organized Democracy: Political Institutions in the Welfare State* (Bergen: Universitetsforlaget).

Olsen, J. P. (2008), "The Ups and Downs of Bureaucratic Organization", *Annual Review of Political Science* 11:13–37.

Ongaro, E. (2010), *Public Management Reform and Modernization: Trajectories of Administrative Change in Italy, France, Greece, Portugal and Spain* (Cheltenham: Edward Elgar).

Osborne, D. and T. Gaebler (1992), *Reinventing Government* (Reading, MA: Addison-Wesley).

Ostrom, E. (1990), *Governing the Commons: The Evolution of Institutions for Collective Action* (Cambridge: Cambridge University Press).

O'Toole, L. J. (2012), "Interorganizational Relations and Policy Implementation", in B. G. Peters and J. Pierre (eds.), *Handbook of Public Administration* (2nd edn) (London: Sage), 292–304.

Page, E. C. (2001), *Governing by Numbers: Delegated Legislation and Everyday Policy Making* (Oxford: Hart Publishing).

Page, E. C. (2010), "Accountability as a Bureaucratic Minefield: Lessons from a Comparative Study", *West European Politics* 33:1010–29.

Page, E. C. (2012), *Policy without Politicians: Bureaucratic Influence in Comparative Perspective* (Oxford: Oxford University Press).

Page, E. C. and V. Wright (eds.) (2006), *From the Active to the Enabling State: The Changing Role of Top Officials in European Nations* (Basingstoke: Palgrave).

Painter, M. and B. G. Peters (eds.) (2010), *Tradition and Public Administration* (Basingstoke: Palgrave).

Painter, M. and J. Pierre (eds.) (2005), *Challenges to State Policy Capacity: Global Trends and Comparative Perspectives* (Basingstoke: Palgrave).

Parkinson, J. (2003), "Legitimacy Problems in Deliberative Democracy", *Political Studies* 51:180–98.

Parsons, T. (1975), *Structure and Process in Modern Societies*, rev. ed. (Glencoe, IL: Free Press).

Parsons, T. (1977), *Social Systems and the Evolution of Action Theory* (New York: The Free Press).

Persson, A. (2008), *The Institutional Sources of Statehood* (PhD dissertation. Gothenburg: Department of Political Science, University of Gothenburg).

Peters, B. G. (1987), "Politicians and Bureaucrats in the Politics of Policy Making", in J. E. Lane (ed.), *Bureaucracy and Public Choice* (London: Sage), 256–82.

Peters, B. G. (2001a), *The Future of Governing: Four Emerging Models* (2nd edn) (Lawrence, KS: University of Kansas Press).

Peters, B. G. (2001b), "The Politics of Policy Instruments", in L. M. Salamon (ed.), *Handbook of Policy Instruments* (New York: Oxford University Press).

Peters, B. G. (2009), *The Politics of Bureaucracy* (6th edn) (London: Routledge).

Peters, B. G. (2012a), "Information and Governing: Cybernetic Models of Governance", in D. Levi-Faur (ed.), *Oxford Handbook of Governance* (Oxford: Oxford University Press), 113–29.

Peters, B. G. (2012b), "On Leading Horses to Water: Developing the Information Capacity of Governments", *Administrative Culture* 13:10–19.

Peters, B. G. (2012c), "The Fiscal Crisis of Governance: The Case of the United States", paper presented at the IRSPM Conference, Rome, Italy.

Peters, B. G. (2013) "On Leading Horses to Water: Developing the Information Capacity of Government", *Administrative Culture* 13: 10–19.

Peters, B. G. (2014), "State Failure, Governance Failure and Policy Failure; Exploring the Linkages", paper presented at Conference on Policy Failure, Lee Kwan Yew School of Public Policy, National University of Singapore.

Peters, B. G. (2015), *Pursuing Horizontal Management: The Politics of Policy Coordination* (Lawrence, KS: University Press of Kansas).

Peters, B. G. and J. Hoornbeek (2005), "The Problem of Policy Problems", in P. Eliadis, M. Hill and M. Howlett (eds.), *Designing Government: From Instruments to Governance* (Montreal: McGill/Queens University Press), 77–105.

Peters, B. G. and J. Pierre (1998), "Governance without Government: Rethinking Public Administration", *Journal of Public Administration Research and Theory* 8:223–42.

Peters, B. G. and J. Pierre (2001), "Developments in Intergovernmental Relationships: Towards multilevel Governance", *Policy and Politics* 29: 131–6.

Peters, B. G. and J. Pierre (2004), "multilevel Governance and Democracy: A Faustian Bargain?", in Ian Bache and

Matthew Flinders (eds.), *multilevel Governance* (Oxford: Oxford University Press, 2004), 79–92.

Peters, B. G., J. Pierre and T. Randma-Liiv (2011), "Global Financial Crisis, Public Administration and Governance: Do New Problems Require New Solutions?", *Public Organization Review* 11:13–27.

Piattoni, S. (2003), *Clientelism, Interests and Democratic Representation: The European Experience in Historical and Comparative Perspective* (Cambridge: Cambridge University Press).

Piattoni, S. (2010), *The Theory of multilevel Governance: Conceptual, Theoretical and Empirical Challenges* (Cambridge: Cambridge University Press).

Piazza, J. A. (2008), "Incubators of Terror: Do Failed and Failing States Promote Transnational Terrorism?", *International Studies Quarterly* 52: 469–88.

Pierce, N. R. (1993), *Citistates* (Washington, DC: Seven Locks Press).

Pierre, J. (ed.) (2000), *Debating Governance: Authority, Democracy, and Steering* (Oxford: Oxford University Press).

Pierre, J. (2009), "Reinventing Governance, Reinventing Democracy?", *Policy and Politics* 37:591–609.

Pierre, J. (2011a), *The Politics of Urban Governance* (Basingstoke: Palgrave).

Pierre, J. (2011b), "Stealth Economy?: Economic Theory and the Politics of Administrative Reform", *Administration and Society* 43:672–92.

Pierre, J. (2013), *Globalization and Governance* (Cheltenham: Edward Elgar).

Pierre, J. and B. G. Peters (2000), *Governance, Politics and the State* (Basingstoke: Palgrave).

Pierre, J. and B. G. Peters (2005), *Governing Complex Societies: Trajectories and Scenarios* (Basingstoke: Palgrave).

Pierre, J. and M. Painter (2010), "Why Legality Cannot Be Contracted Out: Exploring the Limits of New Public Management", in M. Ramesh, E. Araral Jr. and X. Wu (eds.), *Reasserting the Public in Public Services: New Public Management Reforms* (London: Routledge), 49–62.

Pierre, J., A. Röiseland, B. G. Peters and A. Gustavsen (2015), "Comparing Local Politicians' and Bureaucrats' Assessments of Democratic Participation: The Cases of Norway and Sweden", *International Review of Administrative Sciences*, doi:10.1177/0020852315598214.

Pierre, J. and G. Stoker (2000), "Towards multilevel Governance", in P. Dunleavy, A. Gamble, I. Holliday and G. Peele (eds.), *Developments in British Politics* (6th edn) (Basingstoke: Macmillan), 29–46.

Pierson, P. (1994), *Dismantling the Welfare State? Reagan, Thatcher and the Politics of Retrenchment* (Cambridge: Cambridge University Press).

Pierson, P. (1995), "Fragmented Welfare States: Federal Institutions and the Development of Social Policy", *Governance: An International Journal of Policy, Administration, and Institutions* 8:449–78.

Poguntke, T. and P. Webb (eds.) (2007), *The Presidentialization of Politics: A Comparative Study of Modern Democracies* (Oxford: Oxford University Press).

Pollack, M. A. and E. Haffner-Burton (2000), "Mainstreaming Gender in the European Union", *Journal of European Public Policy* 7:432–56.

Pollitt, C. (1988), *Manipulating the Machine: Changing the Pattern of Ministerial Departments, 1960–83* (London: George Allen & Unwin).

Pollitt, C. and G. Bouckaert (2011), *Public Management Reform: A Comparative Analysis* (2nd edn) (Oxford: Oxford University Press).

Pollitt, C. and C. Talbot (eds.) (2003), *Unbundled Government: A Critical Analysis of the Global Trend to Agencies, Quangos and Contractualization* (London: Routledge).

Porter, M. E. (1990), *The Competitive Advantage of Nations* (New York: Free Press).

Posner, P. L. (2007), *The Politics of Unfunded Mandates: Whither Federalism?* (Washington, DC: Georgetown University Press).

Pressman, J. L. and A. Wildavsky (1974), *Implementation* (Berkeley, CA: University of California Press).

Przeworski, A. (2003), *States and Markets: A Primer in Political Economy* (Cambridge: Cambridge University Press).

Putnam, R. D. (2002), *Democracies in Flux: The Evolution of Social Capital in Contemporary Society* (Oxford: Oxford University Press).

Pülzl, H. and O. Treib (2006), "Implementing Public Policy", in F. Fisher, G. J. Miller and M. S. Sidney (eds.), *Handbook of Public Policy Analysis* (Boca Raton, FL: CRC Press), 89–108.

Radian, A. (1980), *Resource Mobilization in Poor Countries: Implementing Tax Policies* (New Brunswick, NJ: Transaction Publishers).

Radin, B. A. (2006), *Challenges to the Performance Movement: Accountability, Complexity and Democratic Values* (Washington, DC: Georgetown University Press).

Rhodes, R. A. W. (1986), *The National World of Local Government* (London: Allen & Unwin).

Rhodes, R. A. W. (1994), "The Hollowing Out of the State: The Changing Nature of the Public Service in Britain", *The Political Quarterly* 65: 138–51.

Rhodes, R. A. W. (1996), "The New Governance: Governing Without Government", *Political Studies* 44:652–67.

Rhodes, R. A. W. (1997), *Understanding Governance: Policy Networks, Governance, Reflexivity and Accountability* (Buckingham: Open University Press).

Richardson, J. J. (1982), *Policy Styles in Western Europe* (London: Allen and Unwin).

Riggs, F. W. (1964), *Administration in Developing Countries: The Theory of the Prismatic Society* (Boston: Houghton-Mifflin).

Riker, W. H. (1962), *A Theory of Political Coalitions* (New Haven, CT: Yale University Press).

Röiseland, A., J. Pierre, B. G. Peters and A. Gustavsen (2015), "Comparing local politicians' and bureaucrats' assessments of democratic participation: The cases of Norway and Sweden", *International Review of Administrative Sciences*.

Rokkan, S. (1966), "Norway: Corporate Pluralism", in R. A. Dahl (ed.), *Political Oppositions in Western Democracies* (New Haven, CT: Yale University Press).

Rosanvallon, P. (2004), *Le modèle politique française: la société civile coontre la jacobinisme de 1789 à nos jours* (Paris: Seuil).

Rose, R. (1975), *The Problem of Party Government* (London: Macmillan).

Rose, R. (1976) *Managing Presidential Objectives* (New York: Free Press).

Rose, R. (1979), "Ungovernability: Is there Fire Behind the Smoke?", *Political Studies* 27:351–70.

Rose, R. (1993), *Lesson-Drawing in Public Policy: A Guide to Learning Across Time and Space* (Chatham, NJ: Chatham House).

Rosenau, J. (1992), "Governance, Order and Change in World Politics", in J. Rosenau and E.-O. Czempiel (eds.), *Governance without Government: Order and Change in World Politics* (Cambridge: Cambridge University Press), 1–30.

Rotberg, R. I. (ed.) (2003), *When States Fail: Causes and Consequences* (Princeton, NJ: Princeton University Press).

Rothstein, B. (1988), "State and Capital and Sweden: The Importance of Corporatist Arrangements", *Scandinavian Political Studies* 11:235–60.

Rothstein, B. (1998), *The Social Democratic State: The Swedish Model and the Bureaucratic Problem of Social Reforms* (Pittsburgh, PA: University of Pittsburgh Press).

Rothstein, B. (2012), "Good Governance", in D. Levi-Faur (ed.), *Oxford Handbook of Governance* (Oxford: Oxford University Press), 143–54.

Rothstein, B. (2014), "Guilty as Charged: Human Well-Being and the Unsung Relevance of Political Science", in G. Stoker, B. G. Peters and J. Pierre (eds.), *The Relevance of Political Science* (Basingstoke: Palgrave), 84–103.

Rothstein, B. and J. Teorell (2012), "Defining and Measuring Quality of Government", in S. Holmberg and B. Rothstein (eds.), *Good Government: Relevance of Political Science* (Cheltenham: Edward Elgar), 13–39.

Ruggie, J. G. (2008), *Protect, Respect and Remedy: A Framework for Business and Human Rights* (New York: United Nations)

Sabatier, P. A. and H. C. Jenkins-Smith (eds.) (1993), *Policy Change and Learning: An Advocacy Coalition Framework* (Boulder, CO: Westview Press).

Salamon, L. (1981), "The Question of Goals", in P. Szanton (ed.), *Federal Reorganization* (Chatham, NJ: Chatham House).

Salamon, L. M. (2001), "Introduction", in L. M. Salamon (ed.), *Handbook of Policy Instruments* (New York: Oxford University Press).

Sanderson, I. (2002), "Evaluation, Policy Learning and Evidence-Based Policy", *Public Administration* 80:1–22.

Sartori, G. (1991), "Comparing and Miscomparing", *Journal of Theoretical Politics* 3:243–57.

Savoie, D. J. (1994), *Thatcher, Reagan, Mulroney: In Search of a New Bureaucracy* (Pittsburgh, PA: Pittsburgh University Press).

Savoie, D. J. (2008), *Court Government and the Collapse of Accountability in Canada and the United Kingdom* (Toronto: University of Toronto Press).

Savoie, D. J. (2010), *Power: Where Is It?* (Montreal and Kingston: McGill-Queen's University Press).

Scharpf, F. W. (1988), "The Joint-Decision Trap: Lessons from German Federalism and European Integration", *Public Administration* 68: 239–78.

Scharpf, F. W. (1994), "Games Real Actors Could Play: Positive and Negative Coordination in Embedded Negotiations", *Journal of Theoretical Politics* 6:27–53.

Scharpf, F. W. (1997), *Games Real Actors Play: Actor-Centered Institutionalism in Policy Research* (Boulder, CO: Westview Press).

Scharpf, F. W. (2009), "Legitimacy in the Multilevel European Union", *European Political Science Review* 1:173–204.

Schattschneider, E. E. (1960), *The Semi-Sovereign People* (Hinsdale, IL: Dryden Press).

Schlozman, K. L., S. Verba and H. E. Brady (2012), *Unheavenly Chorus: Unequal Political Voice and the Broken Promise of American Democracy* (Princeton, NJ: Princeton University Press).

Schmidt, V. (1999), "Convergent Pressures, Divergent Responses: France, Great Britain and Germany between Globalization and Europeanization", in D. A. Smith, D. J. Solinger and S. C. Topik (eds.),

States and Sovereignty in the Global Economy (London: Routledge), 172–92.

Schmitter, P. C. (1974), "Still the Century of Corporatism?", *Review of Politics* 36:85–131.

Schmitter, P. C. (1989), "Corporatism is Dead! Long Live Corporatism!", *Government and Opposition* 24:54–73.

Schneider, G. (1991), *Time, Planning and Policymaking: An Evaluation of a Complex Relationship* (Bern: Peter Lang).

Scholte, J. A. (2004), "Civil Society and Democratically Accountable Local Governance", *Government and Opposition* 39:211–33.

Schön, D. A. (1983), *The Reflective Practitioner: How Professionals Think in Action* (New York: Basic Books).

Schulman, P. R. (1980), *Large-Scale Policymaking* (New York: Elsevier-North Holland).

Self, P. (1975), *Econocrats and the Policy Process* (Basingstoke: Macmillan).

Shah, A. (2007), *Performance Accountability and Combating Corruption* (Washington, DC: The World Bank).

Sieber, S. (1981), *Fatal Remedies* (New York: Plenum).

Simon, H. A. (1947), *Administrative Behavior* (2nd edn) (New York: Macmillan).

Skelcher, C., N. Mathur and M. Smith (2004), "The Public Governance of Collaborative Spaces: Discourse, Design and Democracy", *Public Administration* 83:573–96.

Skelcher, C. and H. Sullivan (2008), "Theory-Driven Approaches to Analysing Collaborative Performance", *Public Management Review* 10: 751–71.

Smith, L. (2010), "Egypt after Mubarak", *The Middle East Quarterly* 17:79–83.

Smoke, P. (2003), "Decentralization in Africa: Goals, Dimensions, Myths and Challenges", *Public Administration and Development* 23:7–16.

Sørensen, G. (2004), *The Transformation of the State: Beyond the Myth of Retreat* (Basingstoke: Palgrave).

Sørensen, E. and J. Torfing (2003), "Network Politics, Political Capital and Democracy", *International Journal of Public Administration* 26:609–34.

Sørensen, E. and J. Torfing (2005), "The Democratic Anchorage of Governance Networks", *Scandinavian Political Studies* 28:195–218.

Sørensen, E. and J. Torfing (2007), "Theoretical Approaches to Metagovernance", in E. Sørensen and J. Torfing (eds.), *Theories of Democratic Network Governance* (Basingstoke: Macmillan).

Sørensen, E. and J. Torfing (2013), "Collaborative Innovation: A Viable Alternative to Market Competition and Organizational Entrepreneurship", *Public Administration* 73:821–39.

Sotiropolous, D. (2004), "Southern European Public Bureaucracies in Comparative Perspective", *West European Politics* 27:405–22.

Speer, A. (1981), *Inside the Third Reich* (New York: Collier Books).

Spoon, J.-J. (2011), *Political Survival of Small Parties in Europe* (Ann Arbor, MI: University of Michigan Press).

Stiglitz, J. E. (2003), *Globalization and Its Discontents* (New York: W. W. Norton).

Stiglitz, J. (2012), *The Price of Inequality* (New York: W. W. Norton).

Stoker, G. (1998), "Governance as Theory: Five Propositions", *International Social Science Journal* 155:17–28.

Stolfi, F. (2013), *Budget Reform in the Mediterranean: The Political Determinants of State Modernization* (Basingstoke: Macmillan).

Strange, S. (1996), *The Retreat of the State: The Diffusion of Power in the World Economy* (Cambridge: Cambridge University Press).

Streeck, W. and P. C. Schmitter (eds.) (1986), *Private Interest Government: Beyond Market and State* (London: Sage).

Streeck, W. and K. A. Thelen (2005), *Beyond Continuity: Institutional Change in Advanced Industrial Economies* (Oxford: Oxford University Press).

Suleiman, E. (2003), *Dismantling Democratic States* (Princeton, NJ: Princeton University Press).

Sullivan, H. and C. Skelcher (2002), *Working Across Boundaries: Collaboration in Public Services* (Basingstoke: Palgrave).

Sundström, G. (2003), *Stat på villovägar: Resultatstyrningens framväxt ur ett historiskt-institutionellt perspektiv* (Stockholm: University of Stockholm, Department of Political Science).

Swank, D. (2002), *Global Capital, Political Institutions, and Policy Change in Developed Welfare States* (Cambridge: Cambridge University Press).

Szanton, P. L. (1981), *Federal Reorganization: What Have We Learned?* (Chatham, NJ: Chatham House).

Tarschys, D. (2003), "Goal Congestion: Multi-purpose Governance in the European Union", in E. O. Eriksen, J. E. Fossum and A. J. Menendez (eds.), *The Chartering of Europe* (Baden-Baden: Nomos), 178–99.

Thomas, C. I. P. (2014), *In Food We Trust: The Politics of Purity in American Food Regulation* (Lincoln: University of Abraska Press).

Tilly, C. (1986), *The Contentious French* (Cambridge, MA: Harvard University Press).

Torfing, J. (2007), "Introduction: Democratic Network Governance", in M. Marcussen and J. Torfing (eds.), *Democratic Network Governance in Europe* (Basingstoke: Palgrave), 1–25.

Torfing, J. and E. Sørensen (eds.) (2007), *Theories of Democratic Network Governance* (Basingstoke: Palgrave).

Torfing, J. and P. Triantafillou (2015), *Enhancing Innovation by Improving Public Governance* (Oxford: Oxford University Press).

Torfing, J., B. G. Peters, J. Pierre and E. Sørensen (2012), *Interactive Governance: Advancing the Paradigm* (Oxford: Oxford University Press).

Trondal, J. and B. Guy Peters (2003), "The Rise of European Administrative Space: Lessons Learned", *Journal of European Public Policy* 20:295–307.

Tsebelis, G. (1990), *Nested Games: Rational Choice in Comparative Politics* (Berkeley, CA: University of California Press).

Tsebelis, G. and G. Garrett (2001), "The Institutional Foundations of Intergovernmentalism and Supranationalism in the European Union", *International Organization* 55:357–90.

Urban, M. E. (1982), *The Ideology of Administration: Soviet and American Examples* (Albany, NY: State University of New York Press).

van der Heiden, N. (2010), *Urban Foreign Policy and Domestic Dilemmas* (Colchester: ECPR Press).

van Waarden, F. (1995), "The Persistence of National Policy Styles: A Study of Their Institutional Foundations", in B. Unger and F. van Waarden (eds.), *Convergence or Diversity?: Internationalization and Economic Policy Responses* (Aldershot: Avebury), 333–72.

Vedung, E. (2006), "Evaluation Research", in B. G. Peters and J. Pierre (eds.), *Handbook of Public Policy* (London: Sage), 397–416.

Verhoest, K., B. G. Peters, G. Bouckaert and B. Verschuere (2004), "The Study of Organizational Autonomy: A Conceptual Review", *Public Administration and Development* 24:101–18.

Vibert, F. (2007), *The Rise of the Unelected: Democracy and the New Separation of Powers* (Cambridge: Cambridge University Press).

Wampler, B. (2007), *Participatory Budgeting in Brazil: Contestation, Cooperation and Accountability* (University Park, PA: Pennsylvania State University Press).

Weaver, R. K. (1986), "The Politics of Blame Avoidance", *Journal of Public Policy* 6:371–98.

Weaver, R. K. and B. A. Rockman (eds.) (1993), *Do Institutions Matter?: Government Capabilities in the United States and Abroad* (Washington, DC: The Brookings Institution).

Weible, C. M., P. A. Sabatier and K. McQueen (2009), "Themes and Variations: Taking Stock of the Advocacy Coalition Framework", *Policy Studies Journal* 37:121–40.

Weiler, J. M. H. (2012), "In the Face of Crisis: Input Legitimacy, Output Legitimacy and the Political Messianism of European Integration", *Journal of European Integration* 34:825–41.

Weimer, D. L. and A. R. Vining (2011), *Policy Analysis* (5th edn) (Boston: Longman).

Weiss, L. (1998), *The Myth of the Powerless State* (Cambridge: Cambridge University Press).

West, W. F. (2011), *Program Budgeting and the Performance Movement* (Washington, DC: Georgetown University Press).

White, G. (1994), "Civil Society, Democratization and Development (1): Clearing the Analytic Ground", *Democratization* 1:375–90.

Wiarda, H. (2000), *Corporatism: The Other "Ism"* (Boulder, CO: Westview Press).

Wildavsky, A. (1978), "A Budget for All Seasons? Why the Traditional Budget Lasts", *Public Administration Review* 38:501–9.

Wilson, J. Q. (1980), *The Politics of Regulation* (New York; Basic Books).

Winter, S. (2012), "The Implementation Perspective", in B. G. Peters and J. Pierre (eds.), *Handbook of Public Administration* (2nd edn) (London: Sage), 265–78.

Wolf, C. (1987), "Market and Nonmarket Failures: Comparison and Assessment", *Journal of Public Policy* 7:43–70.

Wollmann, H. (2010), "Comparing Two Logics of Interlocal Cooperation: The Cases of France and Germany", *Urban Affairs Review* 46:263–92.

Wright, D. S. (1974), "Intergovernmental Relations: An Analytical Overview", *The Annals of the American Academy of Political and Social Science* 416:1–17.

Zeitz, P. (1999), *The Art and Craft of Problem-Solving* (New York: John Wiley).

Ziblatt, D. (2006), *Structuring the State: The Formation of Italy and Germany and the Puzzle of Federalism* (Princeton, NJ: Princeton University Press).

Zittoun, P. (2014), *Le fabrique politique des politiques publiques* (Paris: Presses de Sciences Po).

Index